PALGRAVE'S GOLDEN TREASURY
OF SONGS AND LYRICS

BOOK FOURTH

MACMILLAN AND CO., Limited
LONDON · BOMBAY · CALCUTTA · MADRAS
MELBOURNE

THE MACMILLAN COMPANY
NEW YORK · BOSTON · CHICAGO
DALLAS · SAN FRANCISCO

THE MACMILLAN CO. OF CANADA, Ltd.
TORONTO

Palgrave's Golden Treasury of Songs and Lyrics

Book Fourth

Edited with Notes

By
J. H. Fowler, M.A.
Assistant Master at Clifton College

MACMILLAN AND CO., LIMITED
ST. MARTIN'S STREET, LONDON
1922

PRINTED IN GREAT BRITAIN

EDITOR'S PREFACE.

To the annotator of a school or college edition of the poets the fear must often present itself that he may unconsciously be guilty of drawing away the attention of his readers from the text to his notes. In such a case he must feel that, if it should ever be his fortune to penetrate to the Elysian fields, he will receive but a chilling welcome from the "bards of Passion and of Mirth" there reposing "in soft ease." Not for him an invitation to join their company, "Pledging with contented smack The Mermaid in the Zodiac"! Forecasting, then, the reception of that day, he must ask himself from time to time what extenuating plea he is prepared to urge.

This at least. That he did in his Preface solemnly warn the student that the text is the one thing of importance, and that the value of the notes is wholly subsidiary; that he urged him to read the poems first, and the notes (if at all) afterwards, and the poems again many times—*Nocturna versate manu, versate diurna*; and, finally, that he tried, even in writing notes, to bear in mind the principle that the poets are the best interpreters of themselves and of each other. Writing always in this spirit, he ventures to hope that he may sometimes help others to see beauties which they might

possibly have overlooked. He is conscious in his own
case of the debt he owes to Mr. Aubrey de Vere and
to three critics no longer living, Mr. J. A. Symonds,
Mr. Frederick Myers, and Mr. F. T. Palgrave himself,
for illuminative comment. His greatest ambition is to
hand on the torch which these have passed to him.

The Editor has to thank Mr. R. H. Inglis Palgrave,
acting in the absence from England of Mr. Frank
Palgrave, for permission to annotate this volume. It
is a permission that he values very highly. And,
whilst it would be presumptuous on his part to praise
The Golden Treasury, he may permit himself to quote
the words which a critic of acknowledged distinction,
Mr. Quiller-Couch, has used in the preface to his recent
Oxford Book of English Verse: "Few of my contemporaries can erase—or would wish to erase—the dye
their minds took from the late Mr. Palgrave's *Golden
Treasury*; and he who has returned to it again and
again with an affection born of companionship on many
journeys must remember not only what the *Golden
Treasury* includes, but the moment when this or that
poem appealed to him, and even how it lies on the
page." Mr. Inglis Palgrave has added to his kindness
by reading the notes and making suggestions; and the
Editor is indebted, not for the first time, to his friend
and colleague, Mr. S. T. Irwin, for a similar favour.

J. H. FOWLER.

CLIFTON COLLEGE,
   March, 1901.

MR. PALGRAVE'S
PREFACE TO THE GOLDEN TREASURY.

THIS little Collection differs, it is believed, from others in the attempt made to include in it all the best original Lyrical pieces and Songs in our language (save a very few regretfully omitted on account of length), by writers not living,—and none beside the best. Many familiar verses will hence be met with; many also which should be familiar:—the Editor will regard as his fittest readers those who love Poetry so well that he can offer them nothing not already known and valued.

The Editor is acquainted with no strict and exhaustive definition of Lyrical Poetry; but he has found the task of practical decision increase in clearness and in facility as he advanced with the work, whilst keeping in view a few simple principles. Lyrical has been here held essentially to imply that each Poem shall turn on some single thought, feeling, or situation. In accordance with this, narrative, descriptive, and didactic poems,—unless accompanied by rapidity of movement, brevity, and the colouring of human passion,—have been excluded. Humorous poetry, except in the very unfrequent instances where a truly poetical tone pervades the whole, with what is strictly personal, occasional, and religious, has been considered foreign to the idea of the book. Blank verse and the ten-syllable couplet, with all pieces markedly dramatic, have been rejected as alien from what is commonly understood by Song, and rarely conforming to Lyrical conditions in treatment. But it is not anticipated, nor is it possible, that all readers shall think the line accurately drawn. Some poems, as Gray's Elegy, the Allegro and Penseroso, Wordsworth's Ruth or Campbell's Lord Ullin, might be claimed with perhaps equal justice for a narrative or descriptive selection: whilst with reference especially to Ballads and Sonnets, the Editor can only state that he has taken his utmost pains to decide without caprice or partiality.

This also is all he can plead in regard to a point even more liable to question;—what degree of merit should give rank among the Best. That a poem shall be worthy of the writer's genius,—that it shall reach a perfection commensurate with its aim,—that we should require finish in proportion to brevity,—that passion, colour, and originality cannot atone for serious imperfections in clearness, unity or truth,—that a few good lines do not make a good poem—that popular estimate is serviceable as a guidepost more than as a compass,—above all, that excellence should be looked for rather in the whole than in the parts,—such and other such canons have been always steadily regarded. He may however add that the pieces chosen, and a far larger number rejected, have been carefully and repeatedly considered; and that he has been aided throughout by two friends of independent and exercised judgment, besides the distinguished person [1] addressed in the Dedication. It is hoped that by this procedure the volume has been freed from that one-sidedness which must beset individual decisions;—but for the final choice the Editor is alone responsible.

[1] Alfred Tennyson, Poet Laureate.

Chalmers' vast collection, with the whole works of all accessible poets not contained in it, and the best Anthologies of different periods, have been twice systematically read through; and it is hence improbable that any omissions which may be regretted are due to oversight. The poems are printed entire, except in a very few instances where a stanza or passage has been omitted. These omissions have been risked only when the piece could be thus brought to a closer lyrical unity; and, as essentially opposed to this unity, extracts, obviously such, are excluded. In regard to the text, the purpose of the book has appeared to justify the choice of the most poetical version, wherever more than one exists; and much labour has been given to present each poem, in disposition, spelling, and punctuation, to the greatest advantage.

In the arrangement, the most poetically-effective order has been attempted. The English mind has passed through phases of thought and cultivation so various and so opposed during these three centuries of Poetry, that a rapid passage between old and new, like rapid alteration of the eye's focus in looking at the landscape, will always be wearisome and hurtful to the sense of Beauty. The poems have been therefore distributed into Books corresponding, I. to the ninety years closing about 1616, II thence to 1700, III. to 1800, IV. to the half century just ended. Or, looking at the Poets who more or less give each portion its distinctive character, they might be called the Books of Shakespeare, Milton, Gray, and Wordsworth. The volume, in this respect, so far as the limitations of its range allow, accurately reflects the natural growth and evolution of our Poetry. A rigidly chronological sequence, however, rather fits a collection aiming at instruction than at pleasure, and the wisdom which comes through pleasure :—within each book the pieces have therefore been arranged in gradations of feeling or subject. And it is hoped that the contents of this Anthology will thus be found to present a certain unity as "episodes," in the noble language of Shelley, "to that great Poem which all poets, like the co-operating thoughts of one great mind, have built up since the beginning of the world."

As he closes his long survey, the Editor trusts he may add without egotism, that he has found the vague general verdict of popular Fame more just than those have thought, who, with too severe a criticism, would confine judgments on Poetry to "the selected few of many generations." Not many appear to have gained reputation without some gift or performance that, in due degree, deserved it : and if no verses by certain writers who show less strength than sweetness, or more thought than mastery of expression, are printed in this volume, it should not be imagined that they have been excluded without much hesitation and regret,—far less that they have been slighted. Throughout this vast and pathetic array of Singers now silent, few have been honoured with the name Poet, and have not possessed a skill in words, a sympathy with beauty, a tenderness of feeling, or seriousness in reflection, which render their works, although never perhaps attaining that loftier and finer excellence here required,—better worth reading than much of what fills the scanty hours that most men spare for self-improvement, or for pleasure in any of its more elevated and permanent forms.—And if this be true of

even mediocre poetry, for how much more are we
indebted to the best! Like the fabled fountain of the
Azores, but with a more various power, the magic of this
Art can confer on each period of life its appropriate
blessing: on early years Experience, on maturity Calm,
on age Youthfulness. Poetry gives treasures "more
golden than gold," leading us in higher and healthier
ways than those of the world, and interpreting to us the
lessons of Nature. But she speaks best for herself. Her
true accents, if the plan has been executed with success,
may be heard throughout the following pages:—wherever the Poets of England are honoured, wherever the
dominant language of the world is spoken, it is hoped
that they will find fit audience.

1861.

CONTENTS.

CONTENTS

THE GOLDEN TREASURY

BOOK FOURTH

I.

TO THE MUSES.

Whether on Ida's shady brow,
  Or in the chambers of the East,
The chambers of the sun, that now
  From ancient melody have ceased;

Whether in Heaven ye wander fair,   5
  Or the green corners of the earth,
Or the blue regions of the air,
  Where the melodious winds have birth;

Whether on crystal rocks ye rove
  Beneath the bosom of the sea,   10
Wandering in many a coral grove,—
  Fair Nine, forsaking Poetry;

How have you left the ancient love
  That bards of old enjoy'd in you!
The languid strings do scarcely move,   15
  The sound is forced, the notes are few.

                    W. Blake.

II.

ODE ON THE POETS.

Bards of Passion and of Mirth
Ye have left your souls on earth!
Have ye souls in heaven too,
Double-lived in regions new?

—Yes, and those of heaven commune 5
With the spheres of sun and moon ;
With the noise of fountains wond'rous,
And the parle of voices thund'rous ;
With the whisper of heaven's trees
And one another, in soft ease 10
Seated on Elysian lawns
Browsed by none but Dian's fawns ;
Underneath large blue-bells tented,
Where the daisies are rose-scented,
And the rose herself has got 15
Perfume which on earth is not ;
Where the nightingale doth sing
Not a senseless, trancéd thing,
But divine melodious truth ;
Philosophic numbers smooth ; 20
Tales and golden histories
Of heaven and its mysteries.

Thus ye live on high, and then
On the earth ye live again ;
And the souls ye left behind you 25
Teach us, here, the way to find you,
Where your other souls are joying,
Never slumber'd, never cloying.
Here, your earth-born souls still speak
To mortals, of their little week ; 30
Of their sorrows and delights ;
Of their passions and their spites ;
Of their glory and their shame ;
What doth strengthen and what maim :—
Thus ye teach us, every day, 35
Wisdom, though fled far away.

Bards of Passion and of Mirth
Ye have left your souls on earth !
Ye have souls in heaven too,
Double-lived in regions new ! 40

J. Keats.

CCX.

III.
ON FIRST LOOKING INTO CHAPMAN'S HOMER.

Much have I travell'd in the realms of gold
And many goodly states and kingdoms seen ;

Round many western islands have I been *Among wes...*
Which bards in fealty to Apollo hold. *fealth*

Oft of one wide expanse had I been told 5
Wise (synonym That deep-brow'd Homer ruled as his demesne : *terroto...*
f Keats) Yet did I never breathe its pure serene
Till I heard Chapman speak out loud and bold :

—Then felt I like some watcher of the skies *astrono...*
When a new planet swims into his ken ; 10
mistake. Ought Or like stout Cortez, when with eagle eyes
to be Vasco Balboa
He stared at the Pacific—and all his men
Look'd at each other with a wild surmise—
Silent, upon a peak in Darien.

J. Keats.

IV. CCXI.

LOVE.

All thoughts, all passions, all delights,
Whatever stirs this mortal frame,
All are but ministers of Love,
    And feed his sacred flame.

Oft in my waking dreams do I 5
Live o'er again that happy hour,
When midway on the mount I lay,
    Beside the ruin'd tower.

The moonshine stealing o'er the scene
Had blended with the lights of eve ; 10
And she was there, my hope, my joy,
    My own dear Genevieve !

She lean'd against the arméd man,
The statue of the arméd knight ;
She stood and listen'd to my lay, 15
    Amid the lingering light.

Few sorrows hath she of her own,
My hope ! my joy ! my Genevieve !
She loves me best, whene'er I sing
    The songs that make her grieve. 20

*Deep-brow'd as one of compound words peculiar
to Keats*

I play'd a soft and doleful air,
I sang an old and moving story—
An old rude song, that suited well
    That ruin wild and hoary.

She listen'd with a flitting blush,   25
With downcast eyes and modest grace;
For well she knew, I could not choose
    But gaze upon her face.

I told her of the Knight that wore
Upon his shield a burning brand;   30
And that for ten long years he woo'd
    The Lady of the Land.

I told her how he pined: and ah!
The deep, the low, the pleading tone
With which I sang another's love   35
    Interpreted my own.

She listen'd with a flitting blush,
With downcast eyes, and modest grace;
And she forgave me, that I gazed
    Too fondly on her face!   40

But when I told the cruel scorn
That crazed that bold and lovely Knight,
And that he cross'd the mountain-woods,
    Nor rested day nor night;

That sometimes from the savage den,   45
And sometimes from the darksome shade,
And sometimes starting up at once
    In green and sunny glade,—

There came and look'd him in the face
An angel beautiful and bright;   50
And that he knew it was a Fiend,
    This miserable Knight!

And that unknowing what he did,
He leap'd amid a murderous band,
And saved from outrage worse than death   55
    The Lady of the Land;—

And how she wept, and clasp'd his knees;
And how she tended him in vain—

And ever strove to expiate
   The scorn that crazed his brain;—   60

And that she nursed him in a cave,
And how his madness went away,
When on the yellow forest-leaves
   A dying man he lay;—

His dying words—but when I reach'd   65
That tenderest strain of all the ditty,
My faltering voice and pausing harp
   Disturb'd her soul with pity!

All impulses of soul and sense
Had thrill'd my guileless Genevieve;   70
The music and the doleful tale,
   The rich and balmy eve;

And hopes, and fears that kindle hope,
An undistinguishable throng,
And gentle wishes long subdued,   75
   Subdued and cherish'd long!

She wept with pity and delight,
She blush'd with love, and virgin shame;
And like the murmur of a dream,
   I heard her breathe my name.   80

Her bosom heaved—she stepp'd aside,
As conscious of my look she stept—
Then suddenly, with timorous eye
   She fled to me and wept.

She half inclosed me with her arms,   85
She press'd me with a meek embrace;
And bending back her head, look'd up,
   And gazed upon my face.

'Twas partly love, and partly fear,
And partly 'twas a bashful art
That I might rather feel, than see,   90
   The swelling of her heart.

I calm'd her fears, and she was calm,
And told her love with virgin pride;
And so I won my Genevieve,
   My bright and beauteous Bride.   95

                  S. T. Coleridge.

V.   ALL FOR LOVE.   CCXII.

O talk not to me of a name great in story ;
The days of our youth are the days of our glory ;
And the myrtle and ivy of sweet two-and-twenty
Are worth all your laurels, though ever so plenty.

What are garlands and crowns to the brow that is wrinkled!
'Tis but as a dead flower with May-dew besprinkled :   6
Then away with all such from the head that is hoary—
What care I for the wreaths that can only give glory?

Oh Fame !—if I e'er took delight in thy praises,
'Twas less for the sake of thy high-sounding phrases,   10
Than to see the bright eyes of the dear one discover
She thought that I was not unworthy to love her.

There chiefly I sought thee, there only I found thee ;
Her glance was the best of the rays that surround thee ;
When it sparkled o'er aught that was bright in my story,
I knew it was love, and I felt it was glory.   16
                                        Lord Byron.

VI.   THE OUTLAW.   CCXIII.

O Brignall banks are wild and fair,
    And Greta woods are green,
And you may gather garlands there
    Would grace a summer-queen.
And as I rode by Dalton-Hall   5
    Beneath the turrets high,
A Maiden on the castle-wall
    Was singing merrily :
'O Brignall banks are fresh and fair,
    And Greta woods are green ;   10
I'd rather rove with Edmund there
    Than reign our English queen.'

'If, Maiden, thou wouldst wend with me,
    To leave both tower and town,
Thou first must guess what life lead we   15
    That dwell by dale and down.
And if thou canst that riddle read,
    As read full well you may,
Then to the greenwood shalt thou speed
    As blithe as Queen of May.'   20

Yet sung she, 'Brignall banks are fair,
  And Greta woods are green ;
I'd rather rove with Edmund there
  Than reign our English queen.

'I read you, by your bugle-horn   25
  And by your palfrey good,
I read you for a ranger sworn
  To keep the king's greenwood.'
'A Ranger, lady, winds his horn,
  And 'tis at peep of light ;   30
His blast is heard at merry morn,
  And mine at dead of night.'
Yet sung she, 'Brignall banks are fair,
  And Greta woods are gay ;
I would I were with Edmund there   35
  To reign his Queen of May !

'With burnish'd brand and musketoon
  So gallantly you come,
I read you for a bold Dragoon
  That lists the tuck of drum.'   40
'I list no more the tuck of drum,
  No more the trumpet hear ;
But when the beetle sounds his hum
  My comrades take the spear.
And O ! though Brignall banks be fair   45
  And Greta woods be gay,
Yet mickle must the maiden dare
  Would reign my Queen of May !

'Maiden ! a nameless life I lead,
  A nameless death I'll die ;   50
The fiend whose lantern lights the mead
  Were better mate than I !
And when I'm with my comrades met
  Beneath the greenwood bough,—
What once we were we all forget,   55
  Nor think what we are now.'

Chorus.

'Yet Brignall banks are fresh and fair,
  And Greta woods are green,
And you may gather garlands there
  Would grace a summer-queen.'   60

Sir W. Scott.

VII.

There be none of Beauty's daughters
  With a magic like Thee ;
And like music on the waters
  Is thy sweet voice to me :
When, as if its sound were causing   5
The charmed ocean's pausing,
The waves lie still and gleaming,
And the lull'd winds seem dreaming :

And the midnight moon is weaving
  Her bright chain o'er the deep,   10
Whose breast is gently heaving
  As an infant's asleep :
So the spirit bows before thee
To listen and adore thee ;
With a full but soft emotion,   15
Like the swell of Summer's ocean.
              Lord Byron.

VIII.

THE INDIAN SERENADE.

I arise from dreams of Thee
In the first sweet sleep of night,
When the winds are breathing low
And the stars are shining bright :
I arise from dreams of thee,   5
And a spirit in my feet
Hath led me—who knows how ?
To thy chamber-window, Sweet !

The wandering airs they faint
On the dark, the silent stream—   10
The champak odours fail
Like sweet thoughts in a dream ;
The nightingale's complaint
It dies upon her heart,
As I must die on thine   15
O belovéd as thou art !

Oh lift me from the grass !
I die, I faint, I fail !
Let thy love in kisses rain
On my lips and eyelids pale.   20

My cheek is cold and white, alas !
My heart beats loud and fast ;
Oh ! press it close to thine again
Where it will break at last.

P. B. Shelley.

IX

CCXVI.

She walks in beauty, like the night
Of cloudless climes and starry skies,
And all that's best of dark and bright
Meet in her aspect and her eyes ;
Thus mellow'd to that tender light 5
Which heaven to gaudy day denies.

One shade the more, one ray the less,
Had half impair'd the nameless grace
Which waves in every raven tress
Or softly lightens o'er her face, 10
Where thoughts serenely sweet express
How pure, how dear their dwelling-place.

And on that cheek and o'er that brow
So soft, so calm, yet eloquent,
The smiles that win, the tints that glow 15
But tell of days in goodness spent,—
A mind at peace with all below,
A heart whose love is innocent.

Lord Byron.

X.

CCXVII.

She was a Phantom of delight
When first she gleam'd upon my sight ;
A lovely Apparition, sent
To be a moment's ornament ;
Her eyes as stars of twilight fair ; 5
Like Twilight's, too, her dusky hair ;
But all things else about her drawn
From May-time and the cheerful dawn ;
A dancing shape, an image gay,
To haunt, to startle, and waylay. 10

I saw her upon nearer view,
A spirit, yet a Woman too !
Her household motions light and free,
And steps of virgin-liberty ;

A countenance in which did meet   15
Sweet records, promises as sweet ;
A creature not too bright or good
For human nature's daily food,
For transient sorrows, simple wiles,
Praise, blame, love, kisses, tears, and smiles.   20

And now I see with eye serene
The very pulse of the machine ;
A being breathing thoughtful breath,
A traveller between life and death :
The reason firm, the temperate will,   25
Endurance, foresight, strength, and skill ;
A perfect Woman, nobly plann'd
To warn, to comfort, and command ;
And yet a Spirit still, and bright
With something of an angel-light.   30

                                    W. Wordsworth.

                                            CCXVIII.
XI.

She is not fair to outward view
    As many maidens be ;
Her loveliness I never knew
    Until she smiled on me.
O then I saw her eye was bright,   5
A well of love, a spring of light.

But now her looks are coy and cold,
    To mine they ne'er reply,
And yet I cease not to behold
    The love-light in her eye :   10
Her very frowns are fairer far
Than smiles of other maidens are.

                                    H. Coleridge.

                                            CCXIX.
XII.

I fear thy kisses, gentle maiden ;
Thou needest not fear mine ;
My spirit is too deeply laden
Ever to burthen thine.

I fear thy mien, thy tones, thy motion ;   5
Thou needest not fear mine ;
Innocent is the heart's devotion
With which I worship thine.

                                    P. B. Shelley.

XIII.

She dwelt among the untrodden ways
  Beside the springs of Dove ;
A maid whom there were none to praise,
  And very few to love.

A violet by a mossy stone   5
  Half-hidden from the eye !
—Fair as a star, when only one
  Is shining in the sky.

She lived unknown, and few could know
  When Lucy ceased to be ;   10
But she is in her grave, and, oh,
  The difference to me !

              W. Wordsworth.

XIV.

I travell'd among unknown men
  In lands beyond the sea ;
Nor, England ! did I know till then
  What love I bore to thee.

'Tis past, that melancholy dream !   5
  Nor will I quit thy shore
A second time ; for still I seem
  To love thee more and more.

Among thy mountains did I feel
  The joy of my desire ;   10
And she I cherish'd turn'd her wheel
  Beside an English fire.

Thy mornings show'd, thy nights conceal'd
  The bowers where Lucy play'd ;
And thine too is the last green field   15
  That Lucy's eyes survey'd.

              W. Wordsworth.

XV.

THE EDUCATION OF NATURE.

Three years she grew in sun and shower ;
Then Nature said, 'A lovelier flower
On earth was never sown :

This Child I to myself will take;
She shall be mine, and I will make   5
A lady of my own.

'Myself will to my darling be
Both law and impulse: and with me
The girl, in rock and plain,
In earth and heaven, in glade and bower,   10
Shall feel an overseeing power
To kindle or restrain.

'She shall be sportive as the fawn
That wild with glee across the lawn
Or up the mountain springs;   15
And her's shall be the breathing balm,
And her's the silence and the calm
Of mute insensate things.

'The floating clouds their state shall lend
To her; for her the willow bend;   20
Nor shall she fail to see
Ev'n in the motions of the storm
Grace that shall mould the maiden's form
By silent sympathy.

'The stars of midnight shall be dear   25
To her; and she shall lean her ear
In many a secret place
Where rivulets dance their wayward round,
And beauty born of murmuring sound
Shall pass into her face.   30

'And vital feelings of delight
Shall rear her form to stately height,
Her virgin bosom swell;
Such thoughts to Lucy I will give
While she and I together live   35
Here in this happy dell.'

Thus Nature spake—The work was done—
How soon my Lucy's race was run!
She died, and left to me
This heath, this calm and quiet scene;   40
The memory of what has been,
And never more will be.

                                   W. Wordsworth.

XVI.

A slumber did my spirit seal;
  I had no human fears:
She seem'd a thing that could not feel
  The touch of earthly years.

No motion has she now, no force;   5
  She neither hears nor sees;
Roll'd round in earth's diurnal course
  With rocks, and stones, and trees.

W. Wordsworth.

XVII.

A LOST LOVE.

I meet thy pensive, moonlight face;
  Thy thrilling voice I hear;
And former hours and scenes retrace,
  Too fleeting, and too dear!

Then sighs and tears flow fast and free,   5
  Though none is nigh to share;
And life has nought beside for me
  So sweet as this despair.

There are crush'd hearts that will not break;
  And mine, methinks, is one;   10
Or thus I should not weep and wake,
  And thou to slumber gone.

I little thought it thus could be
  In days more sad and fair—
That earth could have a place for me,   15
  And thou no longer there.

Yet death cannot our hearts divide,
  Or make thee less my own:
'Twere sweeter sleeping at thy side
  Than watching here alone.   20

Yet never, never can we part,
  While Memory holds her reign:
Thine, thine is still this wither'd heart,
  Till we shall meet again.

H. F. Lyte.

XVIII.
LORD ULLIN'S DAUGHTER.

A Chieftain to the Highlands bound
Cries 'Boatman, do not tarry!
And I'll give thee a silver pound
To row us o'er the ferry!'

'Now who be ye, would cross Lochgyle,   5
This dark and stormy water?'
'O I'm the chief of Ulva's isle,
And this, Lord Ullin's daughter.

'And fast before her father's men   10
Three days we've fled together,
For should he find us in the glen,
My blood would stain the heather.

'His horsemen hard behind us ride—
Should they our steps discover,   15
Then who will cheer my bonnie bride,
When they have slain her lover?'

Out spoke the hardy Highland wight,
'I'll go, my chief, I'm ready:
It is not for your silver bright,   20
But for your winsome lady:—

'And by my word! the bonny bird
In danger shall not tarry;
So though the waves are raging white
I'll row you o'er the ferry.'   25

By this the storm grew loud apace,
The water-wraith was shrieking;
And in the scowl of Heaven each face
Grew dark as they were speaking.

But still as wilder blew the wind,   30
And as the night grew drearer,
Adown the glen rode arméd men,
Their trampling sounded nearer.

'O haste thee, haste!' the lady cries,
'Though tempests round us gather;   35
I'll meet the raging of the skies,
But not an angry father.'

The boat has left a stormy land,
A stormy sea before her,—
When, oh! too strong for human hand
The tempest gather'd o'er her.   40

And still they row'd amidst the roar
Of waters fast prevailing:
Lord Ullin reach'd that fatal shore,—
His wrath was changed to wailing.

For, sore dismay'd, through storm and shade   45
His child he did discover :—
One lovely hand she stretched for aid,
And one was round her lover.

'Come back! come back!' he cried in grief,
'Across this stormy water :   50
And I'll forgive your Highland chief,
My daughter!—Oh, my daughter!'

'Twas vain : the loud waves lash'd the shore,
Return or aid preventing :
The waters wild went o'er his child,   55
And he was left lamenting.

                                        T. Campbell.

XIX.

LUCY GRAY.

Oft I had heard of Lucy Gray :
And when I cross'd the wild,
I chanced to see at break of day
The solitary child.

No mate, no comrade Lucy knew ;   5
She dwelt on a wide moor,
The sweetest thing that ever grew
Beside a human door !

You yet may spy the fawn at play,
The hare upon the green ;   10
But the sweet face of Lucy Gray
Will never more be seen.

'To-night will be a stormy night—
You to the town must go;
And take a lantern, Child, to light   15
Your mother through the snow.'

'That, Father! will I gladly do:
'Tis scarcely afternoon—
The minster-clock has just struck two,
And yonder is the moon!'   20

At this the father raised his hook,
And snapp'd a faggot-band;
He plied his work;—and Lucy took
The lantern in her hand.

Not blither is the mountain roe: 25
With many a wanton stroke
Her feet disperse the powdery snow,
That rises up like smoke.

The storm came on before its time:
She wander'd up and down;   30
And many a hill did Lucy climb:
But never reach'd the town.

The wretched parents all that night
Went shouting far and wide;
But there was neither sound nor sight   35
To serve them for a guide.

At day-break on a hill they stood
That overlook'd the moor;
And thence they saw the bridge of wood
A furlong from their door.   40

They wept—and, turning homeward, cried
'In heaven we all shall meet!'
—When in the snow the mother spied
The print of Lucy's feet.

Then downwards from the steep hill's edge   45
They track'd the footmarks small;
And through the broken hawthorn hedge,
And by the long stone-wall:

And then an open field they cross'd:
The marks were still the same;   50
They track'd them on, nor ever lost;
And to the bridge they came:

They follow'd from the snowy bank
Those footmarks, one by one,
Into the middle of the plank;   55
And further there were none!

—Yet some maintain that to this day
She is a living child;
That you may see sweet Lucy Gray
Upon the lonesome wild.   60

O'er rough and smooth she trips along,
And never looks behind;
And sings a solitary song
That whistles in the wind.

W. Wordsworth.

XX.

CCXXVII.

JOCK OF HAZELDEAN.

Dramatic

Not contemporary

People

middle ages

Dames + Knight

Imaginary.

'Why weep ye by the tide, ladie?
Why weep ye by the tide?
I'll wed ye to my youngest son,
And ye sall be his bride:
And ye sall be his bride, ladie,   5
Sae comely to be seen'—
But aye she loot the tears down fa'
For Jock of Hazeldean.

'Now let this wilfu' grief be done,
And dry that cheek so pale;   10
Young Frank is chief of Errington
And lord of Langley-dale;
His step is first in peaceful ha',
His sword in battle keen'—
But aye she loot the tears down fa'   15
For Jock of Hazeldean.

'A chain of gold ye sall not lack,
Nor braid to bind your hair,
Nor mettled hound, nor managed hawk,
Nor palfrey fresh and fair;   20
And you the foremost o' them a'
Shall ride our forest-queen'—
But aye she loot the tears down fa'
For Jock of Hazeldean.

G.T. IV.   B

The kirk was deck'd at morning-tide,   25
  The tapers glimmer'd fair ;
The priest and bridegroom wait the bride,
  And dame and knight are there :
They sought her baith by bower and ha' ;
  The ladie was not seen !   30
She's o'er the Border, and awa'
  Wi' Jock of Hazeldean.

Sir W. Scott.

XXI.   CCXXVIII.

LOVE'S PHILOSOPHY.

The fountains mingle with the river
And the rivers with the ocean,
The winds of heaven mix for ever
With a sweet emotion ;
Nothing in the world is single,   5
All things by a law divine
In one another's being mingle—
Why not I with thine ?

See the mountains kiss high heaven,
And the waves clasp one another ;   10
No sister-flower would be forgiven
If it disdain'd its brother :
And the sunlight clasps the earth,
And the moonbeams kiss the sea—
What are all these kissings worth,   15
If thou kiss not me ?

P. B. Shelley.

XXII.   CCXXIX.

ECHOES.

How sweet the answer Echo makes
To Music at night
When, roused by lute or horn, she wakes,
And far away o'er lawns and lakes
Goes answering light !   5

Yet love hath echoes truer far
And far more sweet

Than e'er, beneath the moonlight's star,
Of horn or lute or soft guitar
The songs repeat. 10

'Tis when the sigh,—in youth sincere
And only then,
The sigh that's breathed for one to hear—
Is by that one, that only Dear
Breathed back again. 15

T. Moore.

XXIII.

CCXXX.

A SERENADE.

Ah! County Guy, the hour is nigh,
 The sun has left the lea,
The orange-flower perfumes the bower,
 The breeze is on the sea.
The lark, his lay who thrill'd all day, 5
 Sits hush'd his partner nigh;
Breeze, bird, and flower confess the hour,
 But where is County Guy?

The village maid steals through the shade
 Her shepherd's suit to hear; 10
To Beauty shy, by lattice high
 Sings high-born Cavalier.
The star of Love, all stars above,
 Now reigns o'er earth and sky,
And high and low the influence know— 15
 But where is County Guy?

Sir W. Scott.

XXIV.

CCXXXI

TO THE EVENING STAR.

Gem of the crimson-colour'd Even,
Companion of retiring day,
Why at the closing gates of heaven,
Beloved Star, dost thou delay?

So fair thy pensile beauty burns 5
When soft the tear of twilight flows;
So due thy plighted love returns
To chambers brighter than the rose;

To Peace, to Pleasure, and to Love
So kind a star thou seem'st to be,　　　　　10
Sure some enamour'd orb above
Descends and burns to meet with thee.

Thine is the breathing, blushing hour
When all unheavenly passions fly,
Chased by the soul-subduing power　　　　15
Of Love's delicious witchery.

O! sacred to the fall of day,
Queen of propitious stars, appear,
And early rise, and long delay,
When Caroline herself is here!　　　　　20

Shine on her chosen green resort
Whose trees the sunward summit crown,
And wanton flowers, that well may court
An angel's feet to tread them down:—

Shine on her sweetly scented road,　　　25
Thou star of evening's purple dome,
That lead'st the nightingale abroad,
And guid'st the pilgrim to his home.

Shine where my charmer's sweeter breath
Embalms the soft exhaling dew,　　　　30
Where dying winds a sigh bequeath
To kiss the cheek of rosy hue:—

Where, winnow'd by the gentle air,
Her silken tresses darkly flow
And fall upon her brow so fair,　　　　35
Like shadows on the mountain snow.

Thus, ever thus, at day's decline
In converse sweet to wander far—
O bring with thee my Caroline,
And thou shalt be my Ruling Star!　　　40

　　　　　　　　　　　　　　　T. Campbell.

XXV.　　　　　TO THE NIGHT.　　　CCXXXII.

Swiftly walk over the western wave,
　　　　Spirit of Night!
Out of the misty Eastern cave
Where, all the long and lone daylight,

Thou wovest dreams of joy and fear   5
Which make thee terrible and dear,—
      Swift be thy flight !

Wrap thy form in a mantle gray
      Star-inwrought ;
Blind with thine hair the eyes of Day,   10
Kiss her until she be wearied out :
Then wander o'er city and sea and land,
Touching all with thine opiate wand—
      Come, long-sought !

When I arose and saw the dawn,   15
      I sigh'd for thee ;
When light rode high, and the dew was gone,
And noon lay heavy on flower and tree,
And the weary Day turn'd to his rest
Lingering like an unloved guest,   20
      I sigh'd for thee.

Thy brother Death came, and cried
      Wouldst thou me ?
Thy sweet child Sleep, the filmy-eyed,
Murmur'd like a noon-tide bee   25
Shall I nestle near thy side ?
Wouldst thou me ?—And I replied
      No, not thee !

Death will come when thou art dead,
      Soon, too soon—   30
Sleep will come when thou art fled ;
Of neither would I ask the boon
I ask of thee, belovéd Night—
Swift be thine approaching flight,
      Come soon, soon !   35

                P. B. Shelley.

XXVI.

TO A DISTANT FRIEND.

Why art thou silent ? Is thy love a plant
Of such weak fibre that the treacherous air
Of absence withers what was once so fair ?
Is there no debt to pay, no boon to grant ?

Yet have my thoughts for thee been vigilant,   5
Bound to thy service with unceasing care—
The mind's least generous wish a mendicant
For nought but what thy happiness could spare.

Speak !—though this soft warm heart, once free to hold
A thousand tender pleasures, thine and mine,   10
Be left more desolate, more dreary cold

Than a forsaken bird's-nest fill'd with snow
'Mid its own bush of leafless eglantine—
Speak, that my torturing doubts their end may know !
W. Wordsworth.

XXVII.   CCXXXIV.

When we two parted
In silence and tears,
Half broken-hearted,
To sever for years,
Pale grew thy cheek and cold,   5
Colder thy kiss ;
Truly that hour foretold
Sorrow to this !

The dew of the morning
Sunk chill on my brow ;   10
It felt like the warning
Of what I feel now.
Thy vows are all broken,
And light is thy fame :
I hear thy name spoken   15
And share in its shame.

They name thee before me,
A knell to mine ear ;
A shudder comes o'er me—
Why wert thou so dear ?   20
They know not I knew thee
Who knew thee too well :
Long, long shall I rue thee,
Too deeply to tell.

In secret we met :   25
In silence I grieve
That thy heart could forget,
Thy spirit deceive.

If I should meet thee
After long years,   30
How should I greet thee?—
With silence and tears.

Lord Byron.

XXVIII.

CCXXXV.

HAPPY INSENSIBILITY.

it says it is
better not
to remember

In a drear-nighted December,   *compound*
Too happy, happy tree,
Thy branches ne'er remember
Their green felicity: *happiness by greenness arou*
The north cannot undo them   5
With a sleety whistle through them,   *Keats*
Nor frozen thawings glue them
From budding at the prime.

In a drear-nighted December,
Too happy, happy brook,
Thy bubblings ne'er remember   10
Apollo's summer look;
But with a sweet forgetting
They stay their crystal fretting,   *ruffled*
Never, never petting
About the frozen time.   15

I wish there
was someone
who could not be   Ah! would 'twere so with many
sad by remember   A gentle girl and boy!
no one in   But were there ever any
has ever forgotten Writhed not at passéd joy?   20
To know the change and feel it,
When there is none to heal it,
Nor numbéd sense to steal it—
Was never said in rhyme.

J. Keats.

XXIX.

CCXXXVI.

Where shall the lover rest
    Whom the fates sever
From his true maiden's breast
    Parted for ever?
Where, through groves deep and high   5
    Sounds the far billow,

Where early violets die
  Under the willow.
      Eleu loro
  Soft shall be his pillow.   10

There through the summer day
  Cool streams are laving:
There, while the tempests sway,
  Scarce are boughs waving;
There thy rest shalt thou take,   15
  Parted for ever,
Never again to wake
  Never, O never!
      Eleu loro
  Never, O never!   20

Where shall the traitor rest,
  He, the deceiver,
Who could win maiden's breast,
  Ruin, and leave her?
In the lost battle,   25
  Borne down by the flying,
Where mingles war's rattle
  With groans of the dying;
      Eleu loro
  There shall he be lying.   30

Her wing shall the eagle flap
  O'er the falsehearted;
His warm blood the wolf shall lap
  Ere life be parted:
Shame and dishonour sit   35
  By his grave ever;
Blessing shall hallow it
  Never, O never!
      Eleu loro
  Never, O never!   40
                              Sir W. Scott.

                                          CCXXXVII
XXX.
        LA BELLE DAME SANS MERCI.

'O what can ail thee, knight-at-arms,
  Alone and palely loitering?
The sedge has wither'd from the lake,
  And no birds sing.

'O what can ail thee, knight-at-arms !   5
   So haggard and so woe-begone?
The squirrel's granary is full,
   And the harvest's done.

'I see a lily on thy brow
   With anguish moist and fever-dew,   10
And on thy cheeks a fading rose
   Fast withereth too.'

answer

'I met a lady in the meads,
   Full beautiful—a faery's child,
Her hair was long, her foot was light,   15
   And her eyes were wild.

'I made a garland for her head,
   And bracelets too, and fragrant zone ;   *girdle*
She look'd at me as she did love,
   And made sweet moan.   20

'I set her on my pacing steed
   And nothing else saw all day long,
For sidelong would she bend, and sing
   A faery's song.

'She found me roots of relish sweet,   25
   And honey wild and manna-dew,
And sure in language strange she said
   "I love thee true."

'She took me to her elfin grot,
   And there she wept and sigh'd full sore ;   30
And there I shut her wild wild eyes
   With kisses four.

'And there she lulléd me asleep,
   And there I dream'd—Ah ! woe betide !
The latest dream I ever dream'd   *Just before dawn* **35**
   On the cold hill's side.   *when vitality is low*

'I saw pale kings and princes too,
   Pale warriors, death-pale were they all :
They cried—"La belle Dame sans Merci
   Hath thee in thrall !"   40

'I saw their starved lips in the gloam
  With horrid warning gapéd wide,
And I awoke and found me here
  On the cold hill's side.

'And this is why I sojourn here   45
  Alone and palely loitering,
Though the sedge is wither'd from the lake,
  And no birds sing.'

                                        J. Keats.

XXXI.   CCXXXVIII.

                    THE ROVER.

        A weary lot is thine, fair maid,
          A weary lot is thine!
Symbolical   To pull the thorn thy brow to braid,
          And press the rue for wine.   sorrow + repentance
        A lightsome eye, a soldier's mien,   5
          A feather of the blue,
        A doublet of the Lincoln green—
          No more of me you knew
                    My Love!
        No more of me you knew.   10

        'This morn is merry June, I trow,
          The rose is budding fain;
        But she shall bloom in winter snow
          Ere we two meet again.'
        He turn'd his charger as he spake   15
          Upon the river shore,
        He gave the bridle-reins a shake,
          Said 'Adieu for evermore
                    My Love!
        And adieu for evermore.'   20

                                        Sir W. Scott.

XXXII.   CCXXXIX.

                THE FLIGHT OF LOVE.

        When the lamp is shatter'd
        The light in the dust lies dead—
        When the cloud is scatter'd,
        The rainbow's glory is shed.

When the lute is broken,   5
Sweet tones are remember'd not;
When the lips have spoken,
Loved accents are soon forgot.

As music and splendour
Survive not the lamp and the lute,   10
The heart's echoes render
No song when the spirit is mute—
No song but sad dirges,
Like the wind through a ruin'd cell,
Or the mournful surges   15
That ring the dead seaman's knell.

When hearts have once mingled,
Love first leaves the well-built nest;
The weak one is singled
To endure what it once possesst.   20
O Love! who bewailest
The frailty of all things here,
Why choose you the frailest
For your cradle, your home, and your bier?

Its passions will rock thee   25
As the storms rock the ravens on high;
Bright reason will mock thee
Like the sun from a wintry sky.
From thy nest every rafter
Will rot, and thine eagle home   30
Leave thee naked to laughter,
When leaves fall and cold winds come.

                                P. B. Shelley.

XXXIII.
                                          CCXL.
THE MAID OF NEIDPATH.

O lovers' eyes are sharp to see,
  And lovers' ears in hearing;
And love, in life's extremity,
  Can lend an hour of cheering.
Disease had been in Mary's bower   5
  And slow decay from mourning,
Though now she sits on Neidpath's tower
  To watch her Love's returning.

All sunk and dim her eyes so bright,
  Her form decay'd by pining,   10
Till through her wasted hand, at night,
  You saw the taper shining.
By fits a sultry hectic hue
  Across her cheek was flying;
By fits so ashy pale she grew   15
  Her maidens thought her dying.

Yet keenest powers to see and hear
  Seem'd in her frame residing;
Before the watch-dog prick'd his ear
  She heard her lover's riding;   20
Ere scarce a distant form was kenn'd
  She knew and waved to greet him,
And o'er the battlement did bend
  As on the wing to meet him.

He came—he pass'd—an heedless gaze   25
  As o'er some stranger glancing;
Her welcome, spoke in faltering phrase,
  Lost in his courser's prancing—
The castle-arch, whose hollow tone
  Returns each whisper spoken,   30
Could scarcely catch the feeble moan
  Which told her heart was broken.

                            Sir W. Scott.

XXXIV.   CCXLI.

Earl March look'd on his dying child,
  And, smit with grief to view her—
The youth, he cried, whom I exiled
  Shall be restored to woo her.

She's at the window many an hour   5
  His coming to discover:
And he look'd up to Ellen's bower
  And she look'd on her lover—

But ah! so pale, he knew her not,
  Though her smile on him was dwelling— 10
And am I then forgot—forgot?
  It broke the heart of Ellen.

In vain he weeps, in vain he sighs,
　　Her cheek is cold as ashes ;
Nor love's own kiss shall wake those eyes   15
　　To lift their silken lashes.

T. Campbell.

XXXV.

CCXLII.

Bright Star ! would I were steadfast as thou art— *The poet*
Not in lone splendour hung aloft the night,   *he were unch*
And watching, with eternal lids apart,
Like Nature's patient sleepless Eremite,

The moving waters at their priestlike task   5
Of pure ablution round earth's human shores,
Or gazing on the new soft fallen mask
Of snow upon the mountains and the moors :—

No—yet still steadfast, still unchangeable,
Pillow'd upon my fair Love's ripening breast   10
To feel for ever its soft fall and swell,
Awake for ever in a sweet unrest ;

Still, still to hear her tender-taken breath,
And so live ever,—or else swoon to death.

J. Keats.

XXXVI.   THE TERROR OF DEATH.   CCXLIII.

When I have fears that I may cease to be
Before my pen has glean'd my teeming brain, *put down*
Before high-piléd books, in charact'ry *symbols*
Hold like rich garners the full-ripen'd grain ;

When I behold, upon the night's starr'd face,   5
Huge cloudy symbols of a high romance, *whole mystery of*
And think that I may never live to trace
Their shadows, with the magic hand of chance ;

And when I feel, fair Creature of an hour !
That I shall never look upon thee more,   10
Never have relish in the faery power *lifts you out of you*
Of unreflecting love—then on the shore

Of the wide world I stand alone, and think
Til! Love and Fame to nothingness do sink.

Keats.

Shakespearean form of sonnet
full of   comparisons

XXXVII.   CCXLIV

DESIDERIA.

Surprized by joy—impatient as the wind—
I turn'd to share the transport—Oh! with whom
But Thee—deep buried in the silent tomb,
That spot which no vicissitude can find?

Love, faithful love recall'd thee to my mind—   5
But how could I forget thee? Through what power
Even for the least division of an hour
Have I been so beguiled as to be blind

To my most grievous loss?—That thought's return
Was the worst pang that sorrow ever bore   10
Save one, one only, when I stood forlorn,

Knowing my heart's best treasure was no more;
That neither present time, nor years unborn
Could to my sight that heavenly face restore.
                                    W. Wordsworth.

XXXVIII.   CCXLV.

At the mid hour of night, when stars are weeping, I fly
To the lone vale we loved, when life shone warm in thine
          eye;
And I think oft, if spirits can steal from the regions of air
To revisit past scenes of delight, thou wilt come to me there
And tell me our love is remember'd, even in the sky!   5

Then I sing the wild song it once was rapture to hear
When our voices, commingling, breathed like one on the
          ear;
And as Echo far off through the vale my sad orison rolls,
I think, oh my Love! 'tis thy voice, from the Kingdom
          of Souls
Faintly answering still the notes that once were so dear. 10
                                    T. Moore.

XXXIX.

ELEGY ON THYRZA.

And thou art dead, as young and fair
　　As aught of mortal birth;
And forms so soft and charms so rare
　　Too soon return'd to Earth!
Though Earth received them in her bed,   **5**
And o'er the spot the crowd may tread
　　In carelessness or mirth,
There is an eye which could not brook
A moment on that grave to look.

I will not ask where thou liest low   **10**
　　Nor gaze upon the spot;
There flowers or weeds at will may grow
　　So I behold them not:
It is enough for me to prove
That what I loved, and long must love,   **15**
　　Like common earth can rot;
To me there needs no stone to tell
'Tis Nothing that I loved so well.

Yet did I love thee to the last,
　　As fervently as thou
Who didst not change through all the past   **20**
　　And canst not alter now.
The love where Death has set his seal
Nor age can chill, nor rival steal,
　　Nor falsehood disavow:　 **25**
And, what were worse, thou canst not see
Or wrong, or change, or fault in me.

The better days of life were ours;
　　The worst can be but mine:
The sun that cheers, the storm that lours,   **30**
　　Shall never more be thine.
The silence of that dreamless sleep
I envy now too much to weep;
　　Nor need I to repine
That all those charms have pass'd away   **35**
I might have watch'd through long decay.

The flower in ripen'd bloom unmatch'd
  Must fall the earliest prey;
Though by no hand untimely snatch'd,
  The leaves must drop away.   40
And yet it were a greater grief
To watch it withering, leaf by leaf,
  Than see it pluck'd today;
Since earthly eye but ill can bear
To trace the change to foul from fair.   45

I know not if I could have borne
  To see thy beauties fade;
The night that follow'd such a morn
  Had worn a deeper shade: 50
Thy day without a cloud hath past,
And thou wert lovely to the last,
  Extinguish'd, not decay'd;
As stars that shoot along the sky
Shine brightest as they fall from high.

                                                 55
As once I wept, if I could weep,
  My tears might well be shed
To think I was not near, to keep
  One vigil o'er thy bed:
To gaze, how fondly! on thy face,   60
To fold thee in a faint embrace,
  Uphold thy drooping head;
And show that love, however vain,
Nor thou nor I can feel again.

Yet how much less it were to gain,   65
  Though thou hast left me free,
The loveliest things that still remain
  Than thus remember thee!
The all of thine that cannot die
Through dark and dread Eternity   70
  Returns again to me,
And more thy buried love endears
Than aught except its living years.   *Lord Byron.*

                                          CCXLVII.

XL.
        One word is too often profaned
          For me to profane it,
        One feeling too falsely disdain'd
          For thee to disdain it.

One hope is too like despair
    For prudence to smother,
And pity from thee more dear
    Than that from another.

I can give not what men call love;
    But wilt thou accept not
The worship the heart lifts above
    And the Heavens reject not:
The desire of the moth for the star,
    Of the night for the morrow,
The devotion to something afar
    From the sphere of our sorrow?

                                        P. B. Shelley.

XLI.   CCXLVIII.

GATHERING SONG OF DONALD THE BLACK.

Pibroch of Donuil Dhu
    Pibroch of Donuil
Wake thy wild voice anew,
    Summon Clan Conuil.
Come away, come away,
    Hark to the summons!
Come in your war-array,
    Gentles and commons.

Come from deep glen, and
    From mountain so rocky;
The war-pipe and pennon
    Are at Inverlocky.
Come every hill-plaid, and
    True heart that wears one,
Come every steel blade, and
    Strong hand that bears one.

Leave untended the herd,
    The flock without shelter;
Leave the corpse uninterr'd,
    The bride at the altar;
Leave the deer, leave the steer,
    Leave nets and barges:
Come with your fighting gear,
    Broadswords and targes.

Come as the winds come, when   25
    Forests are rended,
Come as the waves come, when
    Navies are stranded :
Faster come, faster come,
    Faster and faster,   30
Chief, vassal, page and groom,
    Tenant and master.

Fast they come, fast they come ;
    See how they gather !
Wide waves the eagle plume   35
    Blended with heather.
Cast your plaids, draw your blades,
    Forward each man set !
Pibroch of Donuil Dhu
    Knell for the onset !   40

                            Sir W. Scott.

XLII.   CCXLIX.

A wet sheet and a flowing sea,
    A wind that follows fast
And fills the white and rustling sail
    And bends the gallant mast ;
And bends the gallant mast, my boys,   5
    While like the eagle free
Away the good ship flies, and leaves
    Old England on the lee.

O for a soft and gentle wind !
    I heard a fair one cry ;   10
But give to me the snoring breeze
    And white waves heaving high ;
And white waves heaving high, my lads,
    The good ship tight and free—
The world of waters is our home,   15
    And merry men are we.

There's tempest in yon hornéd moon,
    And lightning in yon cloud ;
But hark the music, mariners !
    The wind is piping loud ;   20
The wind is piping loud, my boys,
    The lightning flashes free—
While the hollow oak our palace is,
    Our heritage the sea.   *A. Cunningham.*

XLIII.

Ye Mariners of England
That guard our native seas !
Whose flag has braved, a thousand years,
The battle and the breeze !
Your glorious standard launch again   5
To match another foe :
And sweep through the deep,
While the stormy winds do blow ;
While the battle rages loud and long
And the stormy winds do blow.   10

The spirits of your fathers
Shall start from every wave—
For the deck it was their field of fame,
And Ocean was their grave :
Where Blake and mighty Nelson fell   15
Your manly hearts shall glow,
As ye sweep through the deep,
While the stormy winds do blow ;
While the battle rages loud and long
And the stormy winds do blow.   20

Britannia needs no bulwarks,
No towers along the steep ;
Her march is o'er the mountain-waves,
Her home is on the deep.
With thunders from her native oak   25
She quells the floods below—
As they roar on the shore,
When the stormy winds do blow ;
When the battle rages loud and long,
And the stormy winds do blow.   30

The meteor flag of England
Shall yet terrific burn ;
Till danger's troubled night depart
And the star of peace return.
Then, then, ye ocean-warriors !   35
Our song and feast shall flow
To the fame of your name,
When the storm has ceased to blow ;
When the fiery fight is heard no more,
And the storm has ceased to blow.   40

                                    T. Campbell.

XLIV.   BATTLE OF THE BALTIC.   CCLI.

Of Nelson and the North
Sing the glorious day's renown,
When to battle fierce came forth
All the might of Denmark's crown,
And her arms along the deep proudly shone ;   5
By each gun the lighted brand
In a bold determined hand,
And the Prince of all the land
Led them on.

Like leviathans afloat   10
Lay their bulwarks on the brine ;
While the sign of battle flew
On the lofty British line :
It was ten of April morn by the chime :
As they drifted on their path   15
There was silence deep as death ;
And the boldest held his breath
For a time.

But the might of England flush'd
To anticipate the scene ;   20
And her van the fleeter rush'd
O'er the deadly space between.
'Hearts of oak !' our captains cried, when each gun
From its adamantine lips
Spread a death-shade round the ships,   25
Like the hurricane eclipse
Of the sun.

Again ! again ! again !
And the havoc did not slack,
Till a feeble cheer the Dane   30
To our cheering sent us back ;—
Their shots along the deep slowly boom :—
Then ceased—and all is wail,
As they strike the shatter'd sail ;
Or in conflagration pale   35
Light the gloom.

Out spoke the victor then
As he hail'd them o'er the wave,
'Ye are brothers ! ye are men !
And we conquer but to save :   40

So peace instead of death let us bring:
But yield, proud foe, thy fleet
With the crews, at England's feet,
And make submission meet
To our King.'   45

Then Denmark bless'd our chief
That he gave her wounds repose;
And the sounds of joy and grief
From her people wildly rose,
As death withdrew his shades from the day: 50
While the sun look'd smiling bright
O'er a wide and woeful sight,
Where the fires of funeral light
Died away.

Now joy, old England, raise!   55
For the tidings of thy might,
By the festal cities' blaze,
Whilst the wine-cup shines in light;
And yet amidst that joy and uproar,
Let us think of them that sleep   60
Full many a fathom deep
By thy wild and stormy steep,
Elsinore!

Brave hearts! to Britain's pride
Once so faithful and so true,   65
On the deck of fame that died,
With the gallant good Riou:
Soft sigh the winds of Heaven o'er their grave!
While the billow mournful rolls
And the mermaid's song condoles   70
Singing glory to the souls
Of the brave!

T. Campbell.

XLV.   CCLII.

ODE TO DUTY.

Stern Daughter of the Voice of God!
O Duty! if that name thou love
Who art a light to guide, a rod
To check the erring, and reprove;

Thou who art victory and law   5
When empty terrors overawe ;
From vain temptations dost set free,
And calm'st the weary strife of frail humanity !

There are who ask not if thine eye
Be on them ; who, in love and truth   10
Where no misgiving is, rely
Upon the genial sense of youth :
Glad hearts ! without reproach or blot,
Who do thy work, and know it not :
Oh ! if through confidence misplaced   15
They fail, thy saving arms, dread Power ! around them
    cast.

Serene will be our days and bright
And happy will our nature be
When love is an unerring light,
And joy its own security.   20
And they a blissful course may hold
Ev'n now, who, not unwisely bold,
Live in the spirit of this creed ;
Yet seek thy firm support, according to their need.

I, loving freedom, and untried,   25
No sport of every random gust,
Yet being to myself a guide,
Too blindly have reposed my trust :
And oft, when in my heart was heard
Thy timely mandate, I deferr'd   30
The task, in smoother walks to stray ;
But thee I now would serve more strictly, if I may.

Through no disturbance of my soul
Or strong compunction in me wrought,
I supplicate for thy controul,   35
But in the quietness of thought :
Me this uncharter'd freedom tires ;
I feel the weight of chance-desires :
My hopes no more must change their name ;
I long for a repose that ever is the same.   40

Stern Lawgiver ! yet thou dost wear
The Godhead's most benignant grace ;
Nor know we anything so fair
As is the smile upon thy face :

Flowers laugh before thee on their beds,   45
And fragrance in thy footing treads ;
Thou dost preserve the Stars from wrong ;
And the most ancient Heavens, through Thee, are fresh
    and strong.

To humbler functions, awful Power !
I call thee : I myself commend   50
Unto thy guidance from this hour ;
Oh let my weakness have an end !
Give unto me, made lowly wise,
The spirit of self-sacrifice ;
The confidence of reason give ;   55
And in the light of truth thy Bondman let me live.

                             W. Wordsworth.

XLVI.   CCLIII.
ON THE CASTLE OF CHILLON.

Eternal Spirit of the chainless Mind !
Brightest in dungeons, Liberty ! thou art,
For there thy habitation is the heart—
The heart which love of Thee alone can bind ;

And when thy sons to fetters are consign'd,   5
To fetters, and the damp vault's dayless gloom,
Their country conquers with their martyrdom,
And Freedom's fame finds wings on every wind.

Chillon ! thy prison is a holy place
And thy sad floor an altar, for 'twas trod,   10
Until his very steps have left a trace

Worn as if thy cold pavement were a sod,
By Bonnivard ! May none those marks efface !
For they appeal from tyranny to God.

                                  Lord Byron.

XLVII.   CCLIV.
ENGLAND AND SWITZERLAND, 1802.

Two Voices are there ; one is of the Sea,
One of the Mountains ; each a mighty voice :
In both from age to age thou didst rejoice,
They were thy chosen music, Liberty !

There came a tyrant, and with holy glee   5
Thou fought'st against him,—but hast vainly striven :
Thou from Thy Alpine holds at length art driven,
Where not a torrent murmurs heard by thee.

—Of one deep bliss thine ear hath been bereft ;
Then cleave, O cleave to that which still is left—   10
For, high-soul'd Maid, what sorrow would it be

That Mountain floods should thunder as before,
And Ocean bellow from his rocky shore,
And neither awful Voice be heard by Thee !

W. Wordsworth.

XLVIII.   CCLV.

ON THE EXTINCTION OF THE VENETIAN REPUBLIC.

Once did She hold the gorgeous East in fee
And was the safeguard of the West ; the worth
Of Venice did not fall below her birth,
Venice, the eldest child of Liberty.

She was a maiden city, bright and free ;   5
No guile seduced, no force could violate ;
And when she took unto herself a mate,
She must espouse the everlasting Sea.

And what if she had seen those glories fade,
Those titles vanish, and that strength decay,—   10
Yet shall some tribute of regret be paid

When her long life hath reach'd its final day :
Men are we, and must grieve when even the shade
Of that which once was great is pass'd away.

W. Wordsworth.

XLIX.   LONDON, 1802.   CCLVI

O Friend ! I know not which way I must look
For comfort, being, as I am, opprest
To think that now our life is only drest
For shew ; mean handy-work of craftsman, cook,

Or groom!—We must run glittering like a brook   5
In the open sunshine, or we are unblest ;
The wealthiest man among us is the best :
No grandeur now in nature or in book

Delights us. Rapine, avarice, expense,
This is idolatry ; and these we adore :   10
Plain living and high thinking are no more :

The homely beauty of the good old cause
Is gone ; our peace, our fearful innocence,
And pure religion breathing household laws.

W. Wordsworth.

L.   CCLVII.

THE SAME.

Milton ! thou shouldst be living at this hour :
England hath need of thee : she is a fen
Of stagnant waters : altar, sword, and pen,
Fireside, the heroic wealth of hall and bower,

Have forfeited their ancient English dower   5
Of inward happiness. We are selfish men :
Oh ! raise us up, return to us again ;
And give us manners, virtue, freedom, power.

Thy soul was like a Star, and dwelt apart :
Thou hadst a voice whose sound was like the sea, 10
Pure as the naked heavens, majestic, free ;

So didst thou travel on life's common way
In cheerful godliness ; and yet thy heart
The lowliest duties on herself did lay.

W. Wordsworth.

LI.   CCLVIII.

When I have borne in memory what has tamed
Great nations ; how ennobling thoughts depart
When men change swords for ledgers, and desert
The student's bower for gold,—some fears unnamed

I had, my Country !—am I to be blamed?   5
Now, when I think of thee, and what thou art,
Verily, in the bottom of my heart
  Of those unfilial fears I am ashamed.

For dearly must we prize thee ; we who find
In thee a bulwark for the cause of men ;   10
And I by my affection was beguiled :

What wonder if a Poet now and then,
Among the many movements of his mind,
Felt for thee as a lover or a child !

                       W. Wordsworth.

LII.   CCLIX.

HOHENLINDEN.

  On Linden, when the sun was low,
  All bloodless lay the untrodden snow ;
  And dark as winter was the flow
    Of Iser, rolling rapidly.

  But Linden saw another sight,   5
  When the drum beat at dead of night
  Commanding fires of death to light
    The darkness of her scenery.

  By torch and trumpet fast array'd
  Each horseman drew his battle-blade,   10
  And furious every charger neigh'd
    To join the dreadful revelry.

  Then shook the hills with thunder riven ;
  Then rush'd the steed, to battle driven :
  And louder than the bolts of Heaven   15
    Far flash'd the red artillery.

  But redder yet that light shall glow
  On Linden's hills of stainéd snow ;
  And bloodier yet the torrent flow
    Of Iser, rolling rapidly.   20

  'Tis morn ; but scarce yon level sun
  Can pierce the war-clouds, rolling dun,
  Where furious Frank and fiery Hun
    Shout in their sulphurous canopy.

The combat deepens. On, ye Brave   25
Who rush to glory, or the grave!
Wave, Munich! all thy banners wave,
    And charge with all thy chivalry!

Few, few shall part, where many meet!
The snow shall be their winding-sheet,   30
And every turf beneath their feet
    Shall be a soldier's sepulchre.

                T. Campbell.

LIII.   AFTER BLENHEIM.   **CCLX.**

It was a summer evening,
  Old Kaspar's work was done,
And he before his cottage door
  Was sitting in the sun;
And by him sported on the green   5
His little grandchild Wilhelmine.

She saw her brother Peterkin
  Roll something large and round
Which he beside the rivulet
  In playing there had found;   10
He came to ask what he had found
That was so large and smooth and round.

Old Kaspar took it from the boy
  Who stood expectant by;
And then the old man shook his head,   15
  And with a natural sigh
''Tis some poor fellow's skull,' said he,
'Who fell in the great victory.

'I find them in the garden,
  For there's many here about;   20
And often when I go to plough
  The ploughshare turns them out.
For many thousand men,' said he,
'Were slain in that great victory.'

'Now tell us what 'twas all about,'   25
  Young Peterkin he cries;
And little Wilhelmine looks up
  With wonder-waiting eyes;
'Now tell us all about the war,
And what they fought each other for.'   30

'It was the English,' Kaspar cried,
  'Who put the French to rout ;
But what they fought each other for
  I could not well make out.
But every body said,' quoth he,   35
  That 'twas a famous victory.

'My father lived at Blenheim then,
  Yon little stream hard by ;
They burnt his dwelling to the ground,
  And he was forced to fly :   40
So with his wife and child he fled,
  Nor had he where to rest his head.

'With fire and sword the country round
  Was wasted far and wide,
And many a childing mother then   45
  And newborn baby died :
But things like that, you know, must be
At every famous victory.

'They say it was a shocking sight
  After the field was won ;   50
For many thousand bodies here
  Lay rotting in the sun ;
But things like that, you know, must be
After a famous victory.

'Great praise the Duke of Marlbro' won   55
  And our good Prince Eugene ;'
'Why 'twas a very wicked thing !'
  Said little Wilhelmine ;
'Nay . . nay . . my little girl,' quoth he,
'It was a famous victory.   60

'And every body praised the Duke
  Who this great fight did win.'
'But what good came of it at last ?'
  Quoth little Peterkin : —
'Why that I cannot tell,' said he,   65
'But 'twas a famous victory.'

                                      R. Southey.

LIV.   CCLXI.

PRO PATRIA MORI.

When he who adores thee has left but the name
  Of his fault and his sorrows behind,
Oh! say wilt thou weep, when they darken the fame
  Of a life that for thee was resign'd!
Yes, weep, and however my foes may condemn,   5
  Thy tears shall efface their decree;
For, Heaven can witness, though guilty to them,
  I have been but too faithful to thee.

With thee were the dreams of my earliest love;
  Every thought of my reason was thine: 10
In my last humble prayer to the Spirit above
  Thy name shall be mingled with mine!
Oh! blest are the lovers and friends who shall live
  The days of thy glory to see;
But the next dearest blessing that Heaven can give   15
  Is the pride of thus dying for thee.

                                        T. Moore.

LV.   CCLXII

THE BURIAL OF SIR JOHN MOORE
AT CORUNNA.

Not a drum was heard, not a funeral note,
  As his corpse to the rampart we hurried;
Not a soldier discharged his farewell shot
  O'er the grave where our hero we buried.

We buried him darkly at dead of night,   5
  The sods with our bayonets turning;
By the struggling moonbeam's misty light
  And the lantern dimly burning.

No useless coffin enclosed his breast,
  Not in sheet or in shroud we wound him;   10
But he lay like a warrior taking his rest,
  With his martial cloak around him.

Few and short were the prayers we said,
  And we spoke not a word of sorrow;
But we steadfastly gazed on the face that was dead,
  And we bitterly thought of the morrow.   16

We thought, as we hollow'd his narrow bed
  And smoothed down his lonely pillow,
That the foe and the stranger would tread o'er his
    head,
  And we far away on the billow!   20

Lightly they'll talk of the spirit that's gone
  And o'er his cold ashes upbraid him,—
But little he'll reck, if they let him sleep on
  In the grave where a Briton has laid him.

But half of our heavy task was done   25
  When the clock struck the hour for retiring;
And we heard the distant and random gun
  That the foe was sullenly firing.

Slowly and sadly we laid him down,
  From the field of his fame fresh and gory;   30
We carved not a line, and we raised not a stone,
  But we left him alone with his glory.

Glory of John moore

                                  C. Wolfe.

LVI.

SIMON LEE THE OLD HUNTSMAN.

In the sweet shire of Cardigan,
Not far from pleasant Ivor Hall,
An old man dwells, a little man,—
'Tis said he once was tall.
Full five-and-thirty years he lived   5
A running huntsman merry;
And still the centre of his cheek
Is red as a ripe cherry.

No man like him the horn could sound,
And hill and valley rang with glee,   10
When Echo bandied, round and round,
The halloo of Simon Lee.
In those proud days he little cared
For husbandry or tillage;
To blither tasks did Simon rouse   15
The sleepers of the village.

He all the country could outrun,
Could leave both man and horse behind;

And often, ere the chase was done,
He reel'd and was stone-blind.   20
And still there's something in the world
At which his heart rejoices ;
For when the chiming hounds are out,
He dearly loves their voices.

But oh the heavy change !—bereft   25
Of health, strength, friends and kindred, see !
Old Simon to the world is left
In liveried poverty :—
His master's dead, and no one now
Dwells in the Hall of Ivor ;   30
Men, dogs, and horses, all are dead ;
He is the sole survivor.

And he is lean and he is sick,
His body, dwindled and awry,
Rests upon ankles swoln and thick ;   35
His legs are thin and dry.
One prop he has, and only one,—
His wife, an aged woman,
Lives with him, near the waterfall,
Upon the village common.   40

Beside their moss-grown hut of clay,
Not twenty paces from the door
A scrap of land they have, but they
Are poorest of the poor.
This scrap of land he from the heath   45
Enclosed when he was stronger ;
But what to them avails the land
Which he can till no longer ?

Oft, working by her husband's side,
Ruth does what Simon cannot do ;   50
For she, with scanty cause for pride,
Is stouter of the two.
And, though you with your utmost skill
From labour could not wean them,
'Tis little, very little, all   55
That they can do between them.

Few months of life has he in store
As he to you will tell,
For still, the more he works, the more
Do his weak ankles swell.   60
My gentle Reader, I perceive
How patiently you've waited,
And now I fear that you expect
Some tale will be related.

O Reader! had you in your mind   65
Such stores as silent thought can bring,
O gentle Reader! you would find
A tale in every thing.
What more I have to say is short,
And you must kindly take it: 70
It is no tale; but, should you think,
Perhaps a tale you'll make it.

One summer-day I chanced to see
This old Man doing all he could
To unearth the root of an old tree,   75
A stump of rotten wood.
The mattock totter'd in his hand;
So vain was his endeavour
That at the root of the old tree
He might have work'd for ever.   80

'You're overtask'd, good Simon Lee,
Give me your tool,' to him I said;
And at the word right gladly he
Received my proffer'd aid.
I struck, and with a single blow   85
The tangled root I sever'd,
At which the poor old man so long
And vainly had endeavour'd.

The tears into his eyes were brought,
And thanks and praises seem'd to run   90
So fast out of his heart, I thought
They never would have done.
—I've heard of hearts unkind, kind deeds
With coldness still returning;
Alas! the gratitude of men   95
Hath oftener left me mourning.

                              W. Wordsworth

THE OLD FAMILIAR FACES.

I have had playmates, I have had companions,
In my days of childhood, in my joyful school-days;
All, all are gone, the old familiar faces.

I have been laughing, I have been carousing
Drinking late, sitting late, with my bosom cronies; 5
All, all are gone, the old familiar faces.

I loved a Love once, fairest among women :
Closed are her doors on me, I must not see her—
All, all are gone, the old familiar faces.

I have a friend, a kinder friend has no man :   10
Like an ingrate, I left my friend abruptly;
Left him, to muse on the old familiar faces.

Ghost-like I paced round the haunts of my childhood,
Earth seem'd a desert I was bound to traverse,
Seeking to find the old familiar faces.   15

Friend of my bosom, thou more than a brother,
Why wert not thou born in my father's dwelling,
So might we talk of the old familiar faces,

How some they have died, and some they have left me,
And some are taken from me; all are departed; 20
All, all are gone, the old familiar faces.

                                             C. Lamb.

THE JOURNEY ONWARDS.

As slow our ship her foamy track
    Against the wind was cleaving,
Her trembling pennant still look'd back
    To that dear isle 'twas leaving.
So loth we part from all we love,   5
    From all the links that bind us;
So turn our hearts, as on we rove,
    To those we've left behind us!

When, round the bowl, of vanish'd years
  We talk with joyous seeming—   10
With smiles that might as well be tears,
  So faint, so sad their beaming ;
While memory brings us back again
  Each early tie that twined us,
Oh, sweet's the cup that circles then   15
  To those we've left behind us !

And when, in other climes, we meet
  Some isle or vale enchanting,
Where all looks flowery, wild, and sweet,
  And nought but love is wanting ;   20
We think how great had been our bliss
  If Heaven had but assign'd us
To live and die in scenes like this,
  With some we've left behind us !

As travellers oft look back at eve   25
  When eastward darkly going,
To gaze upon that light they leave
  Still faint behind them glowing,—
So, when the close of pleasure's day
  To gloom hath near consign'd us,   30
We turn to catch one fading ray
  Of joy that's left behind us.

                        T. Moore.

LIX.   CCLXVI.
YOUTH AND AGE.

There's not a joy the world can give like that it takes away
When the glow of early thought declines in feeling's dull
  decay ;
'Tis not on youth's smooth cheek the blush alone, which
  fades so fast,
But the tender bloom of heart is gone, ere youth itself
  be past.

Then the few whose spirits float above the wreck of
  happiness   5
Are driven o'er the shoals of guilt, or ocean of excess :
The magnet of their course is gone or only points in vain
The shore to which their shiver'd sail shall never stretch
  again.

Then the mortal coldness of the soul like death itself
  comes down ;
It cannot feel for others' woes, it dare not dream its
  own ;   10
That heavy chill has frozen o'er the fountain of our tears,
And though the eye may sparkle still, 'tis where the ice
  appears.

Though wit may flash from fluent lips, and mirth distract
  the breast,
Through midnight hours that yield no more their former
  hope of rest ;
'Tis but as ivy-leaves around the ruin'd turret wreathe, 15
All green and wildly fresh without, but worn and gray
  beneath.

Oh could I feel as I have felt, or be what I have been,
Or weep as I could once have wept o'er many a vanish'd
  scene,—
As springs in deserts found seem sweet, all brackish
  though they be,
So midst the wither'd waste of life those tears would flow
  to me !   20

Lord Byron.

LX.   CCLXVII.

A LESSON.

There is a Flower, the lesser Celandine,
That shrinks like many more from cold and rain,
And the first moment that the sun may shine,
Bright as the sun himself, 'tis out again !

When hailstones have been falling, swarm on swarm, 5
Or blasts the green field and the trees distrest,
Oft have I seen it muffled up from harm
In close self-shelter, like a thing at rest.

But lately, one rough day, this Flower I past,
And recognized it, though an alter'd form,   10
Now standing forth an offering to the blast,
And buffeted at will by rain and storm.

I stopp'd and said, with inly-mutter'd voice,
'It doth not love the shower, nor seek the cold;
This neither is its courage nor its choice,   15
But its necessity in being old.

'The sunshine may not cheer it, nor the dew;
It cannot help itself in its decay;
Stiff in its members, wither'd, changed of hue,'—
And, in my spleen, I smiled that it was gray.   20

To be a prodigal's favourite—then, worse truth,
A miser's pensioner—behold our lot!
O Man! that from thy fair and shining youth
Age might but take the things Youth needed not!
                                        W. Wordsworth.

LXI.   CCLXVIII.
                PAST AND PRESENT.

          I remember, I remember
          The house where I was born,
          The little window where the sun
          Came peeping in at morn;
          He never came a wink too soon   5
          Nor brought too long a day;
          But now, I often wish the night
          Had borne my breath away.

          I remember, I remember
          The roses, red and white,   10
          The violets, and the lily-cups—
          Those flowers made of light!
          The lilacs where the robin built,
          And where my brother set
          The laburnum on his birth-day,—   15
          The tree is living yet!

          I remember, I remember
          Where I was used to swing,
          And thought the air must rush as fresh
          To swallows on the wing;   20
          My spirit flew in feathers then
          That is so heavy now,
          And summer pools could hardly cool
          The fever on my brow.

I remember, I remember   25
The fir trees dark and high ;
I used to think their slender tops
Were close against the sky :
It was a childish ignorance,
But now 'tis little joy   30
To know I'm farther off from Heaven
Than when I was a boy.

T. Hood.

LXII   CCLXIX.

THE LIGHT OF OTHER DAYS.

Commonplace
so that most people
like it

Oft in the stilly night
    Ere slumber's chain has bound me,
Fond Memory brings the light
    Of other days around me :
        The smiles, the tears   5
        Of boyhood's years,
    The words of love then spoken ;
        The eyes that shone,
        Now dimm'd and gone,
    The cheerful hearts now broken !   10
Thus in the stilly night
    Ere slumber's chain has bound me,
Sad Memory brings the light
    Of other days around me.

When I remember all   15
    The friends so link'd together
I've seen around me fall
    Like leaves in wintry weather,
        I feel like one
        Who treads alone   20
    Some banquet-hall deserted,
        Whose lights are fled
        Whose garlands dead,
    And all but he departed !
Thus in the stilly night   25
    Ere slumber's chain has bound me,
Sad Memory brings the light
    Of other days around me.

T. Moore.

LXIII. CCLXX.

STANZAS WRITTEN IN DEJECTION NEAR NAPLES.

The sun is warm, the sky is clear,
The waves are dancing fast and bright,
Blue isles and snowy mountains wear
The purple noon's transparent might:
The breath of the moist earth is light   5
Around its unexpanded buds;
Like many a voice of one delight—
The winds', the birds', the ocean-floods'—
The city's voice itself is soft like Solitude's.

I see the deep's untrampled floor   10
With green and purple sea-weeds strown;
I see the waves upon the shore
Like light dissolved in star-showers thrown:
I sit upon the sands alone;
The lightning of the noon-tide ocean   15
Is flashing round me, and a tone
Arises from its measured motion—
How sweet! did any heart now share in my emotion.

Alas! I have nor hope nor health,
Nor peace within nor calm around,   20
Nor that content, surpassing wealth,
The sage in meditation found,
And walk'd with inward glory crown'd—
Nor fame, nor power, nor love, nor leisure;
Others I see whom these surround—   25
Smiling they live, and call life pleasure;
To me that cup has been dealt in another measure.

Yet now despair itself is mild
Even as the winds and waters are;
I could lie down like a tired child,   30
And weep away the life of care
Which I have borne, and yet must bear,—
Till death like sleep might steal on me,
And I might feel in the warm air
My cheek grow cold, and hear the sea   35
Breathe o'er my dying brain its last monotony.

P. B. Shelley.

LXIV.   THE SCHOLAR.   CCLXXI

My days among the Dead are past;
Around me I behold,
Where'er these casual eyes are cast,
The mighty minds of old:
My never-failing friends are they,   5
With whom I converse day by day.

With them I take delight in weal
And seek relief in woe;
And while I understand and feel
How much to them I owe,   10
My cheeks have often been bedew'd
With tears of thoughtful gratitude.

My thoughts are with the Dead; with them
I live in long-past years,
Their virtues love, their faults condemn,   15
Partake their hopes and fears,
And from their lessons seek and find
Instruction with an humble mind.

My hopes are with the Dead; anon
My place with them will be,   20
And I with them shall travel on
Through all futurity;
Yet leaving here a name, I trust,
That will not perish in the dust.

                              R. Southey.

LXV,   THE MERMAID TAVERN.   CCLXXII.

Souls of Poets dead and gone,
What Elysium have ye known,
Happy field or mossy cavern,   *Ben Johnson*
Choicer than the Mermaid Tavern?   *Shakespeare*
Have ye tippled drink more fine   5
Than mine host's Canary wine?
Or are fruits of Paradise
Sweeter than those dainty pies
Of venison? O generous food!
Drest as though bold Robin Hood   10
Would, with his Maid Marian,
Sup and bowse from horn and can.   *drink Pony*

I have heard that on a day
Mine host's sign-board flew away
Nobody knew whither, till   15
An astrologer's old quill
To a sheepskin gave the story,   *parchments.*
Said he saw you in your glory,   *all you poets*
Underneath a new-old sign
Sipping beverage divine,   20
And pledging with contented smack
The Mermaid in the Zodiac.

Souls of Poets dead and gone,
What Elysium have ye known,
Happy field or mossy cavern,   25
Choicer than the Mermaid Tavern ?

                                    J. Keats.

LXVL   CCLXXIII.

THE PRIDE OF YOUTH.

personal.

Proud Maisie is in the wood,
    Walking so early ;
Sweet Robin sits on the bush,
    Singing so rarely.

'Tell me, thou bonny bird,   5
    When shall I marry me ?'
—' When six braw gentlemen
    Kirkward shall carry ye.'

'Who makes the bridal bed,
    Birdie, say truly ?'   10
—' The gray-headed sexton
    That delves the grave duly.

'The glowworm o'er grave and stone
    Shall light thee steady ;
The owl from the steeple sing   15
    Welcome, proud lady.'
                                    Sir W. Scott.

THE BRIDGE OF SIGHS

One more Unfortunate
Weary of breath
Rashly importunate,
Gone to her death !
Take her up tenderly,   5
Lift her with care ;
Fashion'd so slenderly,
Young, and so fair !

Look at her garments
Clinging like cerements ;   10
Whilst the wave constantly
Drips from her clothing ;
Take her up instantly,
Loving, not loathing.

Touch her not scornfully ;   15
Think of her mournfully,
Gently and humanly ;
Not of the stains of her—
All that remains of her
Now is pure womanly.   20

Make no deep scrutiny
Into her mutiny
Rash and undoubtful :
Past all dishonour,
Death has left on her   25
Only the beautiful.

Still, for all slips of hers,
One of Eve's family—
Wipe those poor lips of hers
Oozing so clammily.   30

Loop up her tresses
Escaped from the comb,
Her fair auburn tresses ;
Whilst wonderment guesses
Where was her home ?   35

Who was her father ?
Who was her mother ?
Had she a sister ?
Had she a brother ?
Or was there a dearer one   40
Still, and a nearer one
Yet than all other ?

Alas ! for the rarity
Of Christian charity
Under the sun !   45
Oh ! it was pitiful !
Near a whole city full,
Home she had none.

Sisterly, brotherly,
Fatherly, motherly   50
Feelings had changed :
Love, by harsh evidence,
Thrown from its eminence ;
Even God's providence
Seeming estranged.   55

Where the lamps quiver
So far in the river,
With many a light
From window and casement,
From garret to basement,   60
She stood, with amazement,
Houseless by night.

The bleak wind of March
Made her tremble and shiver
But not the dark arch,   65
Or the black flowing river ;
Mad from life's history,
Glad to death's mystery
Swift to be hurl'd—
Any where, any where   70
Out of the world !

In she plunged boldly,
No matter how coldly
The rough river ran,—
Over the brink of it,   75

Picture it—think of it,
Dissolute Man!
Lave in it, drink of it,
Then, if you can!

Take her up tenderly,   80
Lift her with care;
Fashion'd so slenderly,
Young, and so fair!

Ere her limbs frigidly
Stiffen too rigidly,   85
Decently, kindly,
Smooth and compose them,
And her eyes, close them,
Staring so blindly!

Dreadfully staring   90
Thro' muddy impurity,
As when with the daring
Last look of despairing
Fix'd on futurity.

Perishing gloomily,   95
Spurr'd by contumely,
Cold inhumanity,
Burning insanity,
Into her rest.
—Cross her hands humbly   100
As if praying dumbly,
Over her breast!

Owning her weakness,
Her evil behaviour,
And leaving, with meekness,   105
Her sins to her Saviour.

T. Hood.

LXVIII.   CCLXXV.

ELEGY.

Oh snatch'd away in beauty's bloom!
On thee shall press no ponderous tomb;
But on thy turf shall roses rear
Their leaves, the earliest of the year,
And the wild cypress wave in tender gloom: 5

And oft by yon blue gushing stream
Shall Sorrow lean her drooping head,
And feed deep thought with many a dream,
And lingering pause and lightly tread;
Fond wretch! as if her step disturb'd the dead!   10

Away! we know that tears are vain,
That Death nor heeds nor hears distress:
Will this unteach us to complain?
Or make one mourner weep the less?
And thou, who tell'st me to forget,   15
Thy looks are wan, thine eyes are wet.

Lord Byron.

LXIX.   CCLXXVI.

HESTER.

When maidens such as Hester die
Their place ye may not well supply,
Though ye among a thousand try
    With vain endeavour.
A month or more hath she been dead,   5
Yet cannot I by force be led
To think upon the wormy bed
    And her together.

A springy motion in her gait,
A rising step, did indicate   10
Of pride and joy no common rate
    That flush'd her spirit:
I know not by what name beside
I shall it call: if 'twas not pride,
It was a joy to that allied   15
    She did inherit.

Her parents held the Quaker rule,
Which doth the human feeling cool;
But she was train'd in Nature's school,
    Nature had blest her.   20
A waking eye, a prying mind,
A heart that stirs, is hard to bind;
A hawk's keen sight ye cannot blind,
    Ye could not Hester.

My sprightly neighbour! gone before 25
To that unknown and silent shore,
Shall we not meet, as heretofore
    Some summer morning—
When from thy cheerful eyes a ray
Hath struck a bliss upon the day, 30
A bliss that would not go away,
    A sweet fore-warning?

C. Lamb.

LXX.   CCLXXVII.

TO MARY.

If I had thought thou couldst have died,
    I might not weep for thee;
But I forgot, when by thy side,
    That thou couldst mortal be:
It never through my mind had past 5
    The time would e'er be o'er,
And I on thee should look my last,
    And thou shouldst smile no more!

And still upon that face I look,
    And think 'twill smile again; 10
And still the thought I will not brook
    That I must look in vain!
But when I speak—thou dost not say
    What thou ne'er left'st unsaid;
And now I feel, as well I may, 15
    Sweet Mary! thou art dead!

If thou wouldst stay, e'en as thou art,
    All cold and all serene—
I still might press thy silent heart,
    And where thy smiles have been. 20
While e'en thy chill, bleak corse I have,
    Thou seemest still mine own;
But there I lay thee in thy grave—
    And I am now alone!

I do not think, where'er thou art, 25
    Thou hast forgotten me;
And I, perhaps, may soothe this heart,
    In thinking too of thee:

Yet there was round thee such a dawn
   Of light ne'er seen before,   30
As fancy never could have drawn,
   And never can restore!

C. Wolfe.

LXXI.   CCLXXVIII.

CORONACH.

He is gone on the mountain,
   He is lost to the forest,
Like a summer-dried fountain,
   When our need was the sorest.
The font reappearing   5
   From the raindrops shall borrow,
But to us comes no cheering,
   To Duncan no morrow!

The hand of the reaper
   Takes the ears that are hoary,   10
But the voice of the weeper
   Wails manhood in glory.
The autumn winds rushing
   Waft the leaves that are searest,
But our flower was in flushing   15
   When blighting was nearest.

Fleet foot on the correi,
   Sage counsel in cumber,
Red hand in the foray,
   How sound is thy slumber!   20
Like the dew on the mountain,
   Like the foam on the river,
Like the bubble on the fountain,
   Thou art gone; and for ever!

Sir W. Scott.

LXXII.   CCLXXIX.
THE DEATH BED.

We watch'd her breathing thro' the night,
   Her breathing soft and low,
As in her breast the wave of life
   Kept heaving to and fro.

So silently we seem'd to speak,   5
    So slowly moved about,
As we had lent her half our powers
    To eke her living out.

Our very hopes belied our fears,
    Our fears our hopes belied—   10
We thought her dying when she slept,
    And sleeping when she died.

For when the morn came dim and sad
    And chill with early showers,
Her quiet eyelids closed—she had   15
    Another morn than ours.

                                        T. Hood.

LXXIII   CCLXXX.

AGNES.

I saw her in childhood—
    A bright, gentle thing,
Like the dawn of the morn,
    Or the dews of the spring:
The daisies and hare-bells   5
    Her playmates all day;
Herself as light-hearted
    And artless as they.

I saw her again—
    A fair girl of eighteen,   10
Fresh glittering with graces
    Of mind and of mien.
Her speech was all music;
    Like moonlight she shone;
The envy of many,   15
    The glory of one.

Years, years fleeted over—
    I stood at her foot:
The bud had grown blossom,
    The blossom was fruit.   20
A dignified mother,
    Her infant she bore;
And look'd, I thought, fairer
    Than ever before.

  I saw her once more—   **25**
   'Twas the day that she died;
  Heaven's light was around her,
   And God at her side;
  No wants to distress her,
   No fears to appal—   **30**
  O then, I felt, then
   She was fairest of all !

            H. F. Lyte.

LXXIV.   CCLXXXI.

     ROSABELLE.

[margin: strel calls to Listen]

 O listen, listen, ladies gay !
  No haughty feat of arms I tell ;
 Soft is the note, and sad the lay
  That mourns the lovely Rosabelle.

 'Moor, moor the barge, ye gallant crew ! **5**
  And, gentle ladye, deign to stay !
 Rest thee in Castle Ravensheuch,
  Nor tempt the stormy firth to-day.

 'The blackening wave is edged with white ;
  To inch and rock the sea-mews fly ; **10**
 The fishers have heard the Water-Sprite,
  Whose screams forebode that wreck is nigh.

 'Last night the gifted Seer did view
  A wet shroud swathed round ladye gay ;
 Then stay thee, Fair, in Ravensheuch ; **15**
  Why cross the gloomy firth to-day ?'

[margin: Lady]

 'Tis not because Lord Lindesay's heir
  To-night at Roslin leads the ball,
 But that my ladye-mother there
  Sits lonely in her castle-hall. **20**

 'Tis not because the ring they ride,
  And Lindesay at the ring rides well,
 But that my sire the wine will chide
  If 'tis not fill'd by Rosabelle.'

 —O'er Roslin all that dreary night **25**
  A wondrous blaze was seen to gleam ;
 'Twas broader than the watch-fire's light,
  And redder than the bright moonbeam.

It glared on Roslin's castled rock,
    It ruddied all the copse-wood glen;   30
'Twas seen from Dryden's groves of oak,
    And seen from cavern'd Hawthornden.

Seem'd all on fire that chapel proud
    Where Roslin's chiefs uncoffin'd lie,
Each Baron, for a sable shroud,   35
    Sheathed in his iron panoply.

Seem'd all on fire within, around—
    Deep sacristy and altar's pale;
Shone every pillar foliage-bound,
    And glimmer'd all the dead men's mail.   40

Blazed battlement and pinnet high,
    Blazed every rose-carved buttress fair—
So still they blaze, when fate is nigh
    The lordly line of high Saint Clair.

There are twenty of Roslin's barons bold—   45
    Lie buried within that proud chapelle;
Each one the holy vault doth hold—
    But the sea holds lovely Rosabelle.

And each Saint Clair was buried there,
    With candle, with book, and with knell;   50
But the sea-caves rung, and the wild winds sung
    The dirge of lovely Rosabelle.

             Sir W. Scott.

LXXV.   CCLXXXII.

ON AN INFANT DYING AS SOON AS BORN.

I saw where in the shroud did lurk
A curious frame of Nature's work;
A flow'ret crushéd in the bud,
A nameless piece of Babyhood,
Was in her cradle-coffin lying;   5
Extinct, with scarce the sense of dying:
So soon to exchange the imprisoning womb
For darker closets of the tomb!
She did but ope an eye, and put
A clear beam forth, then straight up shut   10
For the long dark: ne'er more to see
Through glasses of mortality.

E

Riddle of destiny, who can show
What thy short visit meant, or know
What thy errand here below?   15
Shall we say, that Nature blind
Check'd her hand, and changed her mind
Just when she had exactly wrought
A finish'd pattern without fault?
Could she flag, or could she tire,   20
Or lack'd she the Promethean fire
(With her nine moons' long workings sicken'd)
That should thy little limbs have quicken'd?
Limbs so firm, they seem'd to assure
Life of health, and days mature: 25
Woman's self in miniature!
Limbs so fair, they might supply
(Themselves now but cold imagery)
The sculptor to make Beauty by.
Or did the stern-eyed Fate descry   30
That babe or mother, one must die;
So in mercy left the stock
And cut the branch; to save the shock
Of young years widow'd, and the pain
When Single State comes back again   35
To the lone man who, reft of wife,
Thenceforward drags a maiméd life?
The economy of Heaven is dark,
And wisest clerks have miss'd the mark
Why human buds, like this, should fall,   40
More brief than fly ephemeral
That has his day; while shrivell'd crones
Stiffen with age to stocks and stones;
And crabbéd use the conscience sears
In sinners of an hundred years.   45
—Mother's prattle, mother's kiss,
Baby fond, thou ne'er wilt miss:
Rites, which custom does impose,
Silver bells, and baby clothes;
Coral redder than those lips   50
Which pale death did late eclipse;
Music framed for infants' glee,
Whistle never tuned for thee;
Though thou want'st not, thou shalt have them,
Loving hearts were they which gave them.   55
Let not one be missing; nurse,

See them laid upon the hearse
Of infant slain by doom perverse.
Why should kings and nobles have
Pictured trophies to their grave,   60
And we, churls, to thee deny
Thy pretty toys with thee to lie—
A more harmless vanity?

C. Lamb.

LXXVI.   CCLXXXIII.

IN MEMORIAM.

A child's a plaything for an hour;
　Its pretty tricks we try
For that or for a longer space,—
　Then tire, and lay it by.

But I knew one that to itself   5
　All seasons could control;
That would have mock'd the sense of pain
　Out of a grievéd soul.

Thou straggler into loving arms,
　Young climber up of knees,   10
When I forget thy thousand ways
　Then life and all shall cease!

M. Lamb.

LXXVII.   CCLXXXIV.

THE AFFLICTION OF MARGARET.

Where art thou, my beloved Son,
Where art thou, worse to me than dead?
Oh find me, prosperous or undone!
Or if the grave be now thy bed,
Why am I ignorant of the same   5
That I may rest; and neither blame
Nor sorrow may attend thy name?

Seven years, alas! to have received
No tidings of an only child—
To have despair'd, have hoped, believed,   10
And been for evermore beguiled,—
Sometimes with thoughts of very bliss!
I catch at them, and then I miss;
Was ever darkness like to this?

He was among the prime in worth,   15
An object beauteous to behold;
Well born, well bred; I sent him forth
Ingenuous, innocent, and bold:
If things ensued that wanted grace
As hath been said, they were not base;   20
And never blush was on my face.

Ah! little doth the young-one dream,
When full of play and childish cares,
What power is in his wildest scream
Heard by his mother unawares!   25
He knows it not, he cannot guess;
Years to a mother bring distress;
But do not make her love the less.

Neglect me! no, I suffer'd long
From that ill thought; and being blind   30
Said 'Pride shall help me in my wrong:
Kind mother have I been, as kind
As ever breathed:' and that is true;
I've wet my path with tears like dew,
Weeping for him when no one knew.   35

My Son, if thou be humbled, poor,
Hopeless of honour and of gain,
Oh! do not dread thy mother's door;
Think not of me with grief and pain:
I now can see with better eyes;   40
And worldly grandeur I despise
And fortune with her gifts and lies.

Alas! the fowls of heaven have wings,
And blasts of heaven will aid their flight;
They mount—how short a voyage brings   45
The wanderers back to their delight!
Chains tie us down by land and sea;
And wishes, vain as mine, may be
All that is left to comfort thee.

Perhaps some dungeon hears thee groan   50
Maim'd, mangled by inhuman men;
Or thou upon a desert thrown
Inheritest the lion's den;
Or hast been summon'd to the deep
Thou, thou, and all thy mates, to keep   55
An incommunicable sleep.

I look for ghosts : but none will force
Their way to me ; 'tis falsely said
That there was ever intercourse
Between the living and the dead ;   60
For surely then I should have sight
Of him I wait for day and night
With love and longings infinite.

My apprehensions come in crowds ;
I dread the rustling of the grass ;   65
The very shadows of the clouds
Have power to shake me as they pass :
I question things, and do not find
One that will answer to my mind ;
And all the world appears unkind.   70

Beyond participation lie
My troubles, and beyond relief :
If any chance to heave a sigh,
They pity me, and not my grief.
Then come to me, my Son, or send   75
Some tidings that my woes may end !
I have no other earthly friend.

W. Wordsworth.

LXXVIII.   CCLXXXV.
HUNTING SONG.

Waken, lords and ladies gay,
On the mountain dawns the day ;
All the jolly chase is here
With hawk and horse and hunting-spear ;
Hounds are in their couples yelling,   5
Hawks are whistling, horns are knelling,
Merrily merrily mingle they,
'Waken, lords and ladies gay.'

Waken, lords and ladies gay,
The mist has left the mountain gray,   10
Springlets in the dawn are steaming,
Diamonds on the brake are gleaming ;
And foresters have busy been
To track the buck in thicket green ;
Now we come to chant our lay,   15
'Waken, lords and ladies gay.'

Waken, lords and ladies gay,
To the greenwood haste away;
We can show you where he lies,
Fleet of foot and tall of size;   20
We can show the marks he made
When 'gainst the oak his antlers fray'd;
You shall see him brought to bay;
'Waken, lords and ladies gay.'

Louder, louder chant the lay   25
Waken, lords and ladies gay!
Tell them youth and mirth and glee
Run a course as well as we;
Time, stern huntsman! who can baulk,
Stanch as hound and fleet as hawk;   30
Think of this, and rise with day,
Gentle lords and ladies gay!

Sir W. Scott.

LXXIX.   CCLXXXVI.

TO THE SKYLARK.

Ethereal minstrel! pilgrim of the sky!
Dost thou despise the earth where cares abound?
Or while the wings aspire, are heart and eye
Both with thy nest upon the dewy ground?
Thy nest which thou canst drop into at will,   5
Those quivering wings composed, that music still!

To the last point of vision, and beyond,
Mount, daring warbler!—that love-prompted strain
—'Twixt thee and thine a never-failing bond—
Thrills not the less the bosom of the plain: 10
Yet might'st thou seem, proud privilege! to sing
All independent of the leafy Spring.

Leave to the nightingale her shady wood;
A privacy of glorious light is thine,
Whence thou dost pour upon the world a flood   15
Of harmony, with instinct more divine;
Type of the wise, who soar, but never roam—
True to the kindred points of Heaven and Home.

W. Wordsworth.

LXXX.   CCLXXXVII.

TO A SKYLARK.

Hail to thee, blithe Spirit !
   Bird thou never wert,
That from heaven, or near it
   Pourest thy full heart
In profuse strains of unpremeditated art.   5

Higher still and higher
   From the earth thou springest,
Like a cloud of fire,
   The blue deep thou wingest,
And singing still dost soar, and soaring ever singest.   10

In the golden lightning
   Of the sunken sun
O'er which clouds are brightening,
   Thou dost float and run,
Like an unbodied joy whose race is just begun.   15

The pale purple even
   Melts around thy flight ;   *like dissolved*
Like a star of heaven
   In the broad daylight
Thou art unseen, but yet I hear thy shrill delight :   20

Keen as are the arrows
   Of that silver sphere,
Whose intense lamp narrows
   In the white dawn clear
Until we hardly see, we feel that it is there.   25

All the earth and air
   With thy voice is loud,
As, when night is bare,
   From one lonely cloud
The moon rains out her beams, and heaven is overflow'd.

What thou art we know not ;   31
   What is most like thee ?
From rainbow clouds there flow not
   Drops so bright to see
As from thy presence showers a rain of melody ;—   35

Skylarke has no feeling of death if he had
he would not be able to sing so
merrily

Like a poet hidden
    In the light of thought,
Singing hymns unbidden,
    Till the world is wrought
To sympathy with hopes and fears it heeded not: 40

Like a high-born maiden
    In a palace tower,
Soothing her love-laden
    Soul in secret hour
With music sweet as love, which overflows her bower:

Like a glow-worm golden   46
    In a dell of dew,
Scattering unbeholden
    Its aerial hue
Among the flowers and grass, which screen it from the view:

Like a rose embower'd   51
    In its own green leaves,
By warm winds deflower'd,
    Till the scent it gives
Makes faint with too much sweet these heavy-wingéd thieves.

Sound of vernal showers   56
    On the twinkling grass,
Rain-awaken'd flowers,
    All that ever was
Joyous, and clear, and fresh, thy music doth surpass.   60

Teach us, sprite or bird,
    What sweet thoughts are thine:
I have never heard
    Praise of love or wine
That panted forth a flood of rapture so divine.   65

Chorus hymeneal
    Or triumphal chaunt,
Match'd with thine, would be all
    But an empty vaunt—
A thing wherein we feel there is some hidden want.   70

What objects are the fountains
    Of thy happy strain?
What fields, or waves, or mountains?
    What shapes of sky or plain?
What love of thine own kind? what ignorance of pain?

Ignorance of pain

With thy clear keen joyance 76
   Languor cannot be:
Shadow of annoyance
   Never came near thee:
Thou lovest; but ne'er knew love's sad satiety. 80

Waking or asleep
   Thou of death must deem
Things more true and deep
   Than we mortals dream,
Or how could thy notes flow in such a crystal stream?

We look before and after, 86
   And pine for what is not:
Our sincerest laughter
   With some pain is fraught;
Our sweetest songs are those that tell of saddest thought.

Yet if we could scorn 91
   Hate, and pride, and fear;
If we were things born
   Not to shed a tear,
I know not how thy joy we ever should come near. 95

Better than all measures
   Of delightful sound,
Better than all treasures
   That in books are found,
Thy skill to poet were, thou scorner of the ground! 100

Teach me half the gladness
   That thy brain must know,
Such harmonious madness
   From my lips would flow,
The world should listen then, as I am listening now! 105

               P. B. Shelley.

LXXXI.   CCLXXXVIII.
THE GREEN LINNET.

Beneath these fruit-tree boughs that shed
Their snow-white blossoms on my head,
With brightest sunshine round me spread
   Of Spring's unclouded weather,

In this sequester'd nook how sweet   5
To sit upon my orchard-seat!
And flowers and birds once more to greet,
My last year's friends together.

One have I mark'd, the happiest guest
In all this covert of the blest: 10
Hail to Thee, far above the rest
In joy of voice and pinion!
Thou, Linnet! in thy green array
Presiding Spirit here to-day
Dost lead the revels of the May;   15
And this is thy dominion.

While birds, and butterflies, and flowers,
Make all one band of paramours,
Thou, ranging up and down the bowers,
Art sole in thy employment;   20
A Life, a Presence like the air,
Scattering thy gladness without care,
Too blest with any one to pair;
Thyself thy own enjoyment.

Amid yon tuft of hazel trees   25
That twinkle to the gusty breeze,
Behold him perch'd in ecstasies
Yet seeming still to hover;
There! where the flutter of his wings
Upon his back and body flings   30
Shadows and sunny glimmerings,
That cover him all over.

My dazzled sight he oft deceives—
A brother of the dancing leaves;
Then flits, and from the cottage-eaves   35
Pours forth his song in gushes;
As if by that exulting strain
He mock'd and treated with disdain
The voiceless Form he chose to feign,
While fluttering in the bushes.   40

W. Wordsworth.

TO THE CUCKOO.

O blithe new-comer! I have heard,
I hear thee and rejoice:
O Cuckoo! shall I call thee Bird,
Or but a wandering Voice?

While I am lying on the grass   5
Thy twofold shout I hear;
From hill to hill it seems to pass,
At once far off and near.

Though babbling only to the vale
Of sunshine and of flowers,   10
Thou bringest unto me a tale
Of visionary hours.

Thrice welcome, darling of the Spring!
Even yet thou art to me
No bird, but an invisible thing,   15
A voice, a mystery;

The same whom in my school-boy days
I listen'd to; that Cry
Which made me look a thousand ways
In bush, and tree, and sky.   20

To seek thee did I often rove
Through woods and on the green;
And thou wert still a hope, a love;
Still long'd for, never seen!

And I can listen to thee yet;   25
Can lie upon the plain
And listen, till I do beget
That golden time again.

O blesséd Bird! the earth we pace
Again appears to be   30
An unsubstantial, faery place,
That is fit home for Thee!

W. Wordsworth.

LXXXIII.   ODE TO A NIGHTINGALE.   CCXC.

My heart aches, and a drowsy numbness pains
  My sense, as though of hemlock I had drunk,
Or emptied some dull opiate to the drains
  One minute past, and Lethe-wards had sunk:
'Tis not through envy of thy happy lot,   5
  But being too happy in thine happiness,—
    That thou, light-wingèd Dryad of the trees,
      In some melodious plot
Of beechen green, and shadows numberless,
  Singest of summer in full-throated ease.   10

O, for a draught of vintage! that hath been
  Cool'd a long age in the deep-delvèd earth,
Tasting of Flora and the country green,
  Dance, and Provençal song, and sunburnt mirth!
O for a beaker full of the warm South,   15
  Full of the true, the blushful Hippocrene,
    With beaded bubbles winking at the brim,
      And purple-stainèd mouth;
That I might drink, and leave the world unseen,
  And with thee fade away into the forest dim: 20

Fade far away, dissolve, and quite forget
  What thou among the leaves hast never known,
The weariness, the fever, and the fret
  Here, where men sit and hear each other groan;
Where palsy shakes a few, sad, last gray hairs,   25
  Where youth grows pale, and spectre-thin, and dies;
    Where but to think is to be full of sorrow
      And leaden-eyed despairs;
Where Beauty cannot keep her lustrous eyes,
  Or new Love pine at them beyond to-morrow.   30

Away! away! for I will fly to thee,
  Not charioted by Bacchus and his pards,
But on the viewless wings of Poesy,
  Though the dull brain perplexes and retards:
Already with thee! tender is the night,   35
  And haply the Queen-Moon is on her throne,
    Cluster'd around by all her starry Fays;
      But here there is no light,
Save what from heaven is with the breezes blown
  Through verdurous glooms and winding mossy ways.

I cannot see what flowers are at my feet,   41
  Nor what soft incense hangs upon the boughs,
But, in embalméd darkness, guess each sweet
  Wherewith the seasonable month endows
The grass, the thicket, and the fruit-tree wild;   45
  White hawthorn, and the pastoral eglantine;
    Fast fading violets cover'd up in leaves;
      And mid-May's eldest child,
The coming musk-rose, full of dewy wine,
  The murmurous haunt of flies on summer eves.   50

Darkling I listen; and for many a time
  I have been half in love with easeful Death,
Call'd him soft names in many a muséd rhyme,
  To take into the air my quiet breath;
Now more than ever seems it rich to die,   55
  To cease upon the midnight with no pain,
    While thou art pouring forth thy soul abroad
      In such an ecstasy!
Still wouldst thou sing, and I have ears in vain—
  To thy high requiem become a sod.   60

Thou wast not born for death, immortal Bird!
  No hungry generations tread thee down;
The voice I hear this passing night was heard
  In ancient days by emperor and clown:
Perhaps the self-same song that found a path   65
  Through the sad heart of Ruth, when, sick for home,
    She stood in tears amid the alien corn;
      The same that oft-times hath
Charm'd magic casements, opening on the foam
  Of perilous seas, in faery lands forlorn.   70

Forlorn! the very word is like a bell
  To toll me back from thee to my sole self!
Adieu! the fancy cannot cheat so well
  As she is famed to do, deceiving elf.
Adieu! adieu! thy plaintive anthem fades   75
  Past the near meadows, over the still stream,
  Up the hill-side; and now 'tis buried deep
    In the next valley-glades:
Was it a vision, or a waking dream?
  Fled is that music:—Do I wake or sleep?   80

                          J. Keats.

LXXXIV.   CCXCI.

UPON WESTMINSTER BRIDGE, SEPT. 3, 1802.

Earth has not anything to show more fair :
Dull would he be of soul who could pass by
A sight so touching in its majesty :
This City now doth like a garment wear

The beauty of the morning : silent, bare,   5
Ships, towers, domes, theatres, and temples lie
Open unto the fields, and to the sky,—
All bright and glittering in the smokeless air.

Never did sun more beautifully steep
In his first splendour valley, rock, or hill ;   10
Ne'er saw I, never felt, a calm so deep !

The river glideth at his own sweet will :
Dear God ! the very houses seem asleep ;
And all that mighty heart is lying still !

                              W. Wordsworth.

LXXXV.   CCXCII.

To one who has been long in city pent,
'Tis very sweet to look into the fair
And open face of heaven,—to breathe a prayer
Full in the smile of the blue firmament.

Who is more happy, when, with heart's content,   5
Fatigued he sinks into some pleasant lair
Of wavy grass, and reads a debonair
And gentle tale of love and languishment?

Returning home at evening, with an ear
Catching the notes of Philomel,—an eye   10
Watching the sailing cloudlet's bright career,

He mourns that day so soon has glided by :
E'en like the passage of an angel's tear
That falls through the clear ether silently.

                                    J. Keats.

LXXXVI.

CCXCIII.

OZYMANDIAS OF EGYPT.

I met a traveller from an antique land
Who said : Two vast and trunkless legs of stone
Stand in the desert. Near them on the sand,
Half sunk, a shatter'd visage lies, whose frown
And wrinkled lip and sneer of cold command   5
Tell that its sculptor well those passions read
Which yet survive, stamp'd on these lifeless things,
The hand that mock'd them and the heart that fed ;
And on the pedestal these words appear :
'My name is Ozymandias, king of kings :   10
Look on my works, ye Mighty, and despair !'
Nothing beside remains. Round the decay
Of that colossal wreck, boundless and bare,
The lone and level sands stretch far away.

P. B. Shelley.

LXXXVII.

CCXCIV.

COMPOSED AT NEIDPATH CASTLE, THE PROPERTY OF LORD QUEENSBERRY,
1803.

Degenerate Douglas ! oh, the unworthy lord !
Whom mere despite of heart could so far please
And love of havoc, (for with such disease
Fame taxes him,) that he could send forth word

To level with the dust a noble horde,   5
A brotherhood of venerable trees,
Leaving an ancient dome, and towers like these,
Beggar'd and outraged !—Many hearts deplored

The fate of those old trees ; and oft with pain
The traveller at this day will stop and gaze   10
On wrongs, which Nature scarcely seems to heed :

For shelter'd places, bosoms, nooks, and bays,
And the pure mountains, and the gentle Tweed,
And the green silent pastures, yet remain.

W. Wordsworth.

LXXXVIII.   CCXCV.

THE BEECH TREE'S PETITION.

O leave this barren spot to me!
Spare, woodman, spare the beechen tree!
Though bush or floweret never grow
My dark unwarming shade below;
Nor summer bud perfume the dew   5
Of rosy blush, or yellow hue;
Nor fruits of autumn, blossom-born,
My green and glossy leaves adorn;
Nor murmuring tribes from me derive
Th' ambrosial amber of the hive;   10
Yet leave this barren spot to me:
Spare, woodman, spare the beechen tree!

Thrice twenty summers I have seen
The sky grow bright, the forest green;
And many a wintry wind have stood   15
In bloomless, fruitless solitude,
Since childhood in my pleasant bower
First spent its sweet and sportive hour;
Since youthful lovers in my shade
Their vows of truth and rapture made,   20
And on my trunk's surviving frame
Carved many a long-forgotten name.
Oh! by the sighs of gentle sound,
First breathed upon this sacred ground;
By all that Love has whisper'd here,   25
Or Beauty heard with ravish'd ear;
As Love's own altar honour me:
Spare, woodman, spare the beechen tree!

T. Campbell.

LXXXIX.   CCXCVI.

ADMONITION TO A TRAVELLER.

Yes, there is holy pleasure in thine eye!
—The lovely Cottage in the guardian nook
Hath stirr'd thee deeply; with its own dear brook,
Its own small pasture, almost its own sky!

But covet not the abode; forbear to sigh 5
As many do, repining while they look;
Intruders—who would tear from Nature's book
This precious leaf with harsh impiety.

—Think what the home must be if it were thine,
Even thine, though few thy wants!—Roof, window, door,
The very flowers are sacred to the Poor, 11

The roses to the porch which they entwine:
Yea, all that now enchants thee, from the day
On which it should be touch'd, would melt away!

W. Wordsworth.

XC. CCXCVII.
TO THE HIGHLAND GIRL OF INVERSNEYDE.

Sweet Highland Girl, a very shower
Of beauty is thy earthly dower!
Twice seven consenting years have shed
Their utmost bounty on thy head:
And these gray rocks, that household lawn, 5
Those trees—a veil just half withdrawn,
This fall of water that doth make
A murmur near the silent lake,
This little bay, a quiet road
That holds in shelter thy abode; 10
In truth together ye do seem
Like something fashion'd in a dream;
Such forms as from their covert peep
When earthly cares are laid asleep!
But O fair Creature! in the light 15
Of common day, so heavenly bright,
I bless Thee, Vision as thou art,
I bless thee with a human heart:
God shield thee to thy latest years!
Thee neither know I nor thy peers: 20
And yet my eyes are fill'd with tears.

With earnest feeling I shall pray
For thee when I am far away;
For never saw I mien or face
In which more plainly I could trace 25
Benignity and home-bred sense
Ripening in perfect innocence.

Here scatter'd, like a random seed,
Remote from men, Thou dost not need
The embarrass'd look of shy distress,   30
And maidenly shamefacédness:
Thou wear'st upon thy forehead clear
The freedom of a Mountaineer:
A face with gladness overspread;
Soft smiles, by human kindness bred;   35
And seemliness complete, that sways
Thy courtesies, about thee plays;
With no restraint, but such as springs
From quick and eager visitings
Of thoughts that lie beyond the reach   40
Of thy few words of English speech:
A bondage sweetly brook'd, a strife
That gives thy gestures grace and life!
So have I, not unmoved in mind,
Seen birds of tempest-loving kind—   45
Thus beating up against the wind.

What hand but would a garland cull
For thee who art so beautiful?
O happy pleasure! here to dwell
Beside thee in some heathy dell;   50
Adopt your homely ways, and dress,
A shepherd, thou a shepherdess!
But I could frame a wish for thee
More like a grave reality:
Thou art to me but as a wave   55
Of the wild sea: and I would have
Some claim upon thee, if I could,
Though but of common neighbourhood.
What joy to hear thee, and to see!
Thy elder brother I would be,   60
Thy father—anything to thee.

Now thanks to Heaven! that of its grace
Hath led me to this lonely place:
Joy have I had; and going hence
I bear away my recompence.   65
In spots like these it is we prize
Our Memory, feel that she hath eyes:
Then why should I be loth to stir?
I feel this place was made for her;

To give new pleasure like the past, 70
Continued long as life shall last.
Nor am I loth, though pleased at heart,
Sweet Highland Girl! from thee to part;
For I, methinks, till I grow old
As fair before me shall behold 75
As I do now, the cabin small,
The lake, the bay, the waterfall;
And Thee, the Spirit of them all!

W. Wordsworth.

XCI.   CCXCVIII.

THE REAPER.

Behold her, single in the field,
Yon solitary Highland Lass!
Reaping and singing by herself;
Stop here, or gently pass!
Alone she cuts and binds the grain, 5
And sings a melancholy strain;
O listen! for the vale profound
Is overflowing with the sound.

No nightingale did ever chaunt
More welcome notes to weary bands 10
Of travellers in some shady haunt,
Among Arabian sands:
A voice so thrilling ne'er was heard
In spring-time from the cuckoo-bird,
Breaking the silence of the seas 15
Among the farthest Hebrides.

Will no one tell me what she sings?
Perhaps the plaintive numbers flow
For old, unhappy, far-off things,
And battles long ago: 20
Or is it some more humble lay,
Familiar matter of to-day?
Some natural sorrow, loss, or pain,
That has been, and may be again!

Whate'er the theme, the maiden sang 25
As if her song could have no ending;

I saw her singing at her work,
And o'er the sickle bending ;—
I listen'd, motionless and still ;
And, as I mounted up the hill,   30
The music in my heart I bore
Long after it was heard no more.

W. Wordsworth.

XCII.   THE REVERIE OF POOR SUSAN.   CCXCIX.

At the corner of Wood Street, when daylight appears,
Hangs a Thrush that sings loud, it has sung for three years :
Poor Susan has pass'd by the spot, and has heard
In the silence of morning the song of the bird.

'Tis a note of enchantment ; what ails her ? She sees   5
A mountain ascending, a vision of trees ;
Bright volumes of vapour through Lothbury glide,
And a river flows on through the vale of Cheapside.

Green pastures she views in the midst of the dale
Down which she so often has tripp'd with her pail ;   10
And a single small cottage, a nest like a dove's,
The one only dwelling on earth that she loves.

She looks, and her heart is in heaven : but they fade,
The mist and the river, the hill and the shade ;
The stream will not flow, and the hill will not rise,   15
And the colours have all pass'd away from her eyes !

W. Wordsworth.

XCIII.   TO A LADY, WITH A GUITAR.   CCC.

Ariel to Miranda :—Take
This slave of music, for the sake
Of him, who is the slave of thee ;
And teach it all the harmony
In which thou canst, and only thou,   5
Make the delighted spirit glow,
Till joy denies itself again
And, too intense, is turn'd to pain.
For by permission and command
Of thine own Prince Ferdinand,   10
Poor Ariel sends this silent token
Of more than ever can be spoken ;

Your guardian spirit, Ariel, who
From life to life must still pursue
Your happiness, for thus alone   15
Can Ariel ever find his own.
From Prospero's enchanted cell,
As the mighty verses tell,
To the throne of Naples he
Lit you o'er the trackless sea,   20
Flitting on, your prow before,
Like a living meteor.
When you die, the silent Moon
In her interlunar swoon
Is not sadder in her cell   25
Than deserted Ariel :—
When you live again on earth
Like an unseen Star of birth
Ariel guides you o'er the sea
Of life from your nativity :—   30
Many changes have been run
Since Ferdinand and you begun
Your course of love, and Ariel still
Has track'd your steps and served your will.
Now in humbler, happier lot,   35
This is all remember'd not ;
And now, alas ! the poor Sprite is
Imprison'd for some fault of his
In a body like a grave—
From you he only dares to crave,   40
For his service and his sorrow
A smile to day, a song to morrow.
The artist who this idol wrought
To echo all harmonious thought
Fell'd a tree, while on the steep   45
The woods were in their winter sleep,
Rock'd in that repose divine
On the wind-swept Apennine ;
And dreaming, some of Autumn past,
And some of Spring approaching fast,   50
And some of April buds and showers,
And some of songs in July bowers,
And all of love : And so this tree,—
Oh that such our death may be !—
Died in sleep, and felt no pain,   55
To live in happier form again :

From which, beneath heaven's fairest star
The artist wrought this loved Guitar;
And taught it justly to reply
To all who question skilfully　　　　　　60
In language gentle as thine own;
Whispering in enamour'd tone
Sweet oracles of woods and dells,
And summer winds in sylvan cells:
—For it had learnt all harmonies　　　　65
Of the plains and of the skies,
Of the forests and the mountains,
And the many-voicéd fountains;
The clearest echoes of the hills,
The softest notes of falling rills,　　　　70
The melodies of birds and bees,
The murmuring of summer seas,
And pattering rain, and breathing dew,
And airs of evening; and it knew
That seldom-heard mysterious sound　　　75
Which, driven on its diurnal round,
As it floats through boundless day,
Our world enkindles on its way:
—All this it knows, but will not tell
To those who cannot question well　　　80
The Spirit that inhabits it;
It talks according to the wit
Of its companions; and no more
Is heard than has been felt before
By those who tempt it to betray　　　　85
These secrets of an elder day.
But, sweetly as its answers will
Flatter hands of perfect skill,
It keeps its highest holiest tone
For our beloved Friend alone.　　　　　90

P. B. Shelley.

XCIV.　　　　THE DAFFODILS.　　　　CCCI.

I wander'd lonely as a cloud
That floats on high o'er vales and hills,
When all at once I saw a crowd,
A host of golden daffodils,
Beside the lake, beneath the trees,　　　5
Fluttering and dancing in the breeze.

Continuous as the stars that shine
And twinkle on the milky way,
They stretch'd in never-ending line
Along the margin of a bay :   10
Ten thousand saw I at a glance
Tossing their heads in sprightly dance.

The waves beside them danced, but they
Out-did the sparkling waves in glee :—
A Poet could not but be gay   15
In such a jocund company !
I gazed—and gazed—but little thought
What wealth the show to me had brought :

For oft, when on my couch I lie
In vacant or in pensive mood,   20
They flash upon that inward eye
Which is the bliss of solitude ;
And then my heart with pleasure fills,
And dances with the daffodils.

W. Wordsworth.

XCV.   CCCII.

TO THE DAISY.

With little here to do or see
Of things that in the great world be,
Sweet Daisy ! oft I talk to thee
    For thou art worthy,
Thou unassuming Common-place   5
Of Nature, with that homely face,
And yet with something of a grace
    Which Love makes for thee !

Oft on the dappled turf at ease
I sit and play with similes,   10
Loose types of things through all degrees,
    Thoughts of thy raising ;
And many a fond and idle name
I give to thee, for praise or blame
As is the humour of the game,   15
    While I am gazing.

A nun demure, of lowly port;
Or sprightly maiden, of Love's court,
In thy simplicity the sport
    Of all temptations;   20
A queen in crown of rubies drest;
A starveling in a scanty vest;
Are all, as seems to suit thee best,
    Thy appellations.

A little Cyclops, with one eye   25
Staring to threaten and defy,
That thought comes next—and instantly
    The freak is over,
The shape will vanish, and behold!
A silver shield with boss of gold   30
That spreads itself, some faery bold
    In fight to cover.

I see thee glittering from afar—
And then thou art a pretty star,
Not quite so fair as many are   35
    In heaven above thee!
Yet like a star, with glittering crest,
Self-poised in air thou seem'st to rest;
May peace come never to his nest
    Who shall reprove thee!   40

Sweet Flower! for by that name at last
When all my reveries are past
I call thee, and to that cleave fast,
    Sweet silent Creature!
That breath'st with me in sun and air,   45
Do thou, as thou art wont, repair
My heart with gladness, and a share
    Of thy meek nature!
                   W. Wordsworth.

XCVI.   CCCIII.

ODE TO AUTUMN.

Season of mists and mellow fruitfulness,
Close bosom-friend of the maturing sun;
Conspiring with him how to load and bless
With fruit the vines that round the thatch-eaves run;

To bend with apples the moss'd cottage-trees,   5
And fill all fruit with ripeness to the core ;
To swell the gourd, and plump the hazel shells
With a sweet kernel ; to set budding more,
And still more, later flowers for the bees,
Until they think warm days will never cease ;   10
For Summer has o'erbrimm'd their clammy cells.

Who hath not seen thee oft amid thy store ?
Sometimes whoever seeks abroad may find
Thee sitting careless on a granary floor,
Thy hair soft-lifted by the winnowing wind ;   15
Or on a half-reap'd furrow sound asleep,
Drowsed with the fume of poppies, while thy hook
Spares the next swath and all its twinéd flowers :
And sometimes like a gleaner thou dost keep
Steady thy laden head across a brook ;   20
Or by a cyder-press, with patient look,
Thou watchest the last oozings, hours by hours.

Where are the songs of Spring ? Ay, where are they ?
Think not of them, thou hast thy music too,—
While barréd clouds bloom the soft-dying day   25
And touch the stubble-plains with rosy hue ;
Then in a wailful choir the small gnats mourn
Among the river-sallows, borne aloft
Or sinking as the light wind lives or dies ;
And full-grown lambs loud bleat from hilly bourn ;   30
Hedge-crickets sing ; and now with treble soft
The red-breast whistles from a garden-croft ;
And gathering swallows twitter in the skies.

                                        J. Keats.

XCVII.   CCCIV.

ODE TO WINTER.

GERMANY, DECEMBER, 1800.

When first the fiery-mantled Sun
His heavenly race began to run,
Round the earth and ocean blue
His children four the Seasons flew.
    First, in green apparel dancing,   5
The young Spring smiled with angel-grace ;

Rosy Summer next advancing,
Rush'd into her sire's embrace—
Her bright-hair'd sire, who bade her keep
  For ever nearest to his smiles,   10
On Calpe's olive-shaded steep
  Or India's citron-cover'd isles :
More remote, and buxom-brown,
  The Queen of vintage bow'd before his throne ;
A rich pomegranate gemm'd her crown,   15
  A ripe sheaf bound her zone.

But howling Winter fled afar
To hills that prop the polar star ;
And loves on deer-borne car to ride
  With barren darkness by his side,   20
Round the shore where loud Lofoden
  Whirls to death the roaring whale,
Round the hall where Runic Odin
  Howls his war-song to the gale ;
Save when adown the ravaged globe   25
  He travels on his native storm,
Deflowering Nature's grassy robe
  And trampling on her faded form :—
Till light's returning Lord assume
  The shaft that drives him to his polar field, 30
Of power to pierce his raven plume
  And crystal-cover'd shield.

Oh, sire of storms ! whose savage ear
The Lapland drum delights to hear,
When Frenzy with her blood-shot eye
  Implores thy dreadful deity—   35
Archangel ! Power of desolation !
  Fast descending as thou art,
Say, hath mortal invocation
  Spells to touch thy stony heart ?   40
Then, sullen Winter ! hear my prayer,
And gently rule the ruin'd year ;
Nor chill the wanderer's bosom bare
Nor freeze the wretch's falling tear :
To shuddering Want's unmantled bed   45
  Thy horror-breathing agues cease to lend,
And gently on the orphan head
  Of Innocence descend.

But chiefly spare, O king of clouds!
The sailor on his airy shrouds,   50
When wrecks and beacons strew the steep,
And spectres walk along the deep.
Milder yet thy snowy breezes
  Pour on yonder tented shores,
Where the Rhine's broad billow freezes,   55
  Or the dark-brown Danube roars.
Oh, winds of winter! list ye there
  To many a deep and dying groan?
Or start, ye demons of the midnight air,
  At shrieks and thunders louder than your own?
Alas! ev'n your unhallow'd breath   61
  May spare the victim fallen low;
But Man will ask no truce to death,—
  No bounds to human woe.

                                   T. Campbell.

XCVIII.   CCCV.

YARROW UNVISITED.

1803.

From Stirling Castle we had seen
The mazy Forth unravell'd,
Had trod the banks of Clyde and Tay,
And with the Tweed had travell'd;
And when we came to Clovenford,   5
Then said my 'winsome Marrow,'
'Whate'er betide, we'll turn aside,
And see the Braes of Yarrow.'

'Let Yarrow folk, frae Selkirk town,
Who have been buying, selling,   10
Go back to Yarrow, 'tis their own,
Each maiden to her dwelling!
On Yarrow's banks let herons feed,
Hares couch, and rabbits burrow;
But we will downward with the Tweed,   15
Nor turn aside to Yarrow.

'There's Gala Water, Leader Haughs,
Both lying right before us;
And Dryburgh, where with chiming Tweed
The lintwhites sing in chorus;   20

There's pleasant Tiviot-dale, a land
Made blithe with plough and harrow :
Why throw away a needful day
To go in search of Yarrow ?

'What's Yarrow but a river bare   25
That glides the dark hills under ?
There are a thousand such elsewhere
As worthy of your wonder.'
—Strange words they seem'd of slight and scorn ;
My True-love sigh'd for sorrow,   30
And look'd me in the face, to think
I thus could speak of Yarrow !

'O green,' said I, 'are Yarrow's holms,
And sweet is Yarrow flowing !
Fair hangs the apple frae the rock,   35
But we will leave it growing.
O'er hilly path and open strath
We'll wander Scotland thorough ;
But, though so near, we will not turn
Into the dale of Yarrow.   40

'Let beeves and home-bred kine partake
The sweets of Burn-mill meadow ;
The swan on still Saint Mary's Lake
Float double, swan and shadow !
We will not see them ; will not go   45
To-day, nor yet to-morrow ;
Enough if in our hearts we know
There's such a place as Yarrow.

'Be Yarrow stream unseen, unknown !
It must, or we shall rue it :   50
We have a vision of our own,
Ah ! why should we undo it ?
The treasured dreams of times long past,
We'll keep them, winsome Marrow !
For when we're there, although 'tis fair, 55
'Twill be another Yarrow !

'If Care with freezing years should come
And wandering seem but folly,—
Should we be loth to stir from home,
And yet be melancholy ;   60

Should life be dull, and spirits low,
'Twill soothe us in our sorrow
That earth has something yet to show,
The bonny holms of Yarrow!'

W. Wordsworth.

XCIX.   YARROW VISITED.   CCCVI.

SEPTEMBER, 1814.

And is this—Yarrow ?—This the stream
Of which my fancy cherish'd
So faithfully, a waking dream,
An image that hath perish'd ?
O that some minstrel's harp were near   5
To utter notes of gladness
And chase this silence from the air,
That fills my heart with sadness !

Yet why ?—a silvery current flows
With uncontroll'd meanderings ;   10
Nor have these eyes by greener hills
Been soothed, in all my wanderings.
And, through her depths, Saint Mary's Lake
Is visibly delighted ;
For not a feature of those hills   15
Is in the mirror slighted.

A blue sky bends o'er Yarrow Vale,
Save where that pearly whiteness
Is round the rising sun diffused,
A tender hazy brightness ;   20
Mild dawn of promise ! that excludes
All profitless dejection ;
Though not unwilling here to admit
A pensive recollection.

Where was it that the famous Flower   25
Of Yarrow Vale lay bleeding ?
His bed perchance was yon smooth mound
On which the herd is feeding :
And haply from this crystal pool,
Now peaceful as the morning,   30
The Water-wraith ascended thrice,
And gave his doleful warning.

Delicious is the lay that sings
The haunts of happy lovers,
The path that leads them to the grove,   35
The leafy grove that covers:
And pity sanctifies the verse
That paints, by strength of sorrow,
The unconquerable strength of love;
Bear witness, rueful Yarrow!   40

But thou that didst appear so fair
To fond imagination,
Dost rival in the light of day
Her delicate creation:
Meek loveliness is round thee spread,   45
A softness still and holy:
The grace of forest charms decay'd,
And pastoral melancholy.

That region left, the vale unfolds
Rich groves of lofty stature,   50
With Yarrow winding through the pomp
Of cultivated nature;
And rising from those lofty groves
Behold a ruin hoary,
The shatter'd front of Newark's towers,   55
Renown'd in Border story.

Fair scenes for childhood's opening bloom,
For sportive youth to stray in,
For manhood to enjoy his strength,
And age to wear away in!   60
Yon cottage seems a bower of bliss,
A covert for protection
Of tender thoughts that nestle there—
The brood of chaste affection.

How sweet on this autumnal day   65
The wild-wood fruits to gather,
And on my True-love's forehead plant
A crest of blooming heather!
And what if I enwreathed my own?
'Twere no offence to reason;   70
The sober hills thus deck their brows
To meet the wintry season.

I see—but not by sight alone,
Loved Yarrow, have I won thee;
A ray of Fancy still survives—   75
Her sunshine plays upon thee!
Thy ever-youthful waters keep
A course of lively pleasure;
And gladsome notes my lips can breathe
Accordant to the measure.   80

The vapours linger round the heights,
They melt, and soon must vanish;
One hour is theirs, nor more is mine—
Sad thought! which I would banish,
But that I know, where'er I go,   85
Thy genuine image, Yarrow!
Will dwell with me, to heighten joy,
And cheer my mind in sorrow.

                    W. Wordsworth.

C   CCCVII.

THE INVITATION.

Best and brightest, come away,—
Fairer far than this fair Day,
Which, like thee, to those in sorrow
Comes to bid a sweet good-morrow
To the rough year just awake   5
In its cradle on the brake.
The brightest hour of unborn Spring
Through the winter wandering,
Found, it seems, the halcyon morn
To hoar February born;   10
Bending from heaven, in azure mirth,
It kiss'd the forehead of the earth,
And smiled upon the silent sea,
And bade the frozen streams be free,
And waked to music all their fountains,   15
And breathed upon the frozen mountains,
And like a prophetess of May
Strew'd flowers upon the barren way,
Making the wintry world appear
Like one on whom thou smilest, dear.   20

Away, away, from men and towns,
To the wild woods and the downs—
To the silent wilderness
Where the soul need not repress
Its music, lest it should not find   25
An echo in another's mind,
While the touch of Nature's art
Harmonizes heart to heart.

Radiant Sister of the Day
Awake! arise! and come away!   30
To the wild woods and the plains,
To the pools where winter rains
Image all their roof of leaves,
Where the pine its garland weaves
Of sapless green, and ivy dun,   35
Round stems that never kiss the sun;
Where the lawns and pastures be
And the sandhills of the sea;
Where the melting hoar-frost wets
The daisy-star that never sets,   40
And wind-flowers and violets
Which yet join not scent to hue
Crown the pale year weak and new;
When the night is left behind
In the deep east, dim and blind,   45
And the blue noon is over us,
And the multitudinous
Billows murmur at our feet,
Where the earth and ocean meet,
And all things seem only one   50
In the universal Sun.

                                          P. B. Shelley.

CI.   THE RECOLLECTION.   CCCVIII.

Now the last day of many days
All beautiful and bright as thou,
The loveliest and the last, is dead:
Rise, Memory, and write its praise!
Up—to thy wonted work! come, trace   5
The epitaph of glory fled,
For now the earth has changed its face,
A frown is on the heaven's brow.

We wander'd to the Pine Forest
 That skirts the Ocean's foam ;   10
The lightest wind was in its nest,
 The tempest in its home.
The whispering waves were half asleep,
 The clouds were gone to play,
And on the bosom of the deep   15
 The smile of heaven lay ;
It seem'd as if the hour were one
 Sent from beyond the skies
Which scatter'd from above the sun
 A light of Paradise !   20

We paused amid the pines that stood
 The giants of the waste,
Tortured by storms to shapes as rude
 As serpents interlaced,—
And soothed by every azure breath   25
 That under heaven is blown,
To harmonies and hues beneath,
 As tender as its own :
Now all the tree-tops lay asleep
 Like green waves on the sea,   30
As still as in the silent deep
 The ocean-woods may be.

How calm it was !—The silence there
 By such a chain was bound,
That even the busy woodpecker   35
 Made stiller with her sound
The inviolable quietness ;
 The breath of peace we drew
With its soft motion made not less
 The calm that round us grew.   40
There seem'd, from the remotest seat
 Of the white mountain waste
To the soft flower beneath our feet,
 A magic circle traced,—
A spirit interfused around,   45
 A thrilling silent life ;
To momentary peace it bound
 Our mortal nature's strife ;—
And still I felt the centre of
 The magic circle there   50
Was one fair form that fill'd with love
 The lifeless atmosphere.

We paused beside the pools that lie
  Under the forest bough;
Each seem'd as 'twere a little sky   55
  Gulf'd in a world below;
A firmament of purple light
  Which in the dark earth lay,
More boundless than the depth of night
  And purer than the day—   60
In which the lovely forests grew
  As in the upper air,
More perfect both in shape and hue
  Than any spreading there.
There lay the glade and neighbouring lawn,
  And through the dark-green wood   66
The white sun twinkling like the dawn
  Out of a speckled cloud.
Sweet views which in our world above
  Can never well be seen   70
Were imaged in the water's love
  Of that fair forest green:
And all was interfused beneath
  With an Elysian glow,
An atmosphere without a breath,   75
  A softer day below.
Like one beloved, the scene had lent
  To the dark water's breast
Its every leaf and lineament
  With more than truth exprest;   80
Until an envious wind crept by,
  Like an unwelcome thought
Which from the mind's too faithful eye
  Blots one dear image out.
—Though thou art ever fair and kind,   85
  The forests ever green,
Less oft is peace in Shelley's mind
  Than calm in waters seen!

P. B. Shelley.

CII.   BY THE SEA.   CCCIX.

It is a beauteous evening, calm and free;
The holy time is quiet as a Nun
Breathless with adoration; the broad sun
Is sinking down in its tranquillity;

The gentleness of heaven is on the Sea :   5
Listen ! the mighty Being is awake,
And doth with his eternal motion make
A sound like thunder—everlastingly.

Dear child ! dear girl ! that walkest with me here,
If thou appear untouch'd by solemn thought   10
Thy nature is not therefore less divine :
Thou liest in Abraham's bosom all the year,
And worshipp'st at the Temple's inner shrine,
God being with thee when we know it not.
                    W. Wordsworth.

CIII.   CCCX.

SONG TO THE EVENING STAR.

Star that bringest home the bee,
And sett'st the weary labourer free !
If any star shed peace, 'tis Thou
     That send'st it from above,
Appearing when Heaven's breath and brow   5
     Are sweet as hers we love.

Come to the luxuriant skies,
Whilst the landscape's odours rise,
Whilst far-off lowing herds are heard
     And songs when toil is done,   10
From cottages whose smoke unstirr'd
     Curls yellow in the sun.

Star of love's soft interviews,
Parted lovers on thee muse ;
Their remembrancer in Heaven   15
     Of thrilling vows thou art,
Too delicious to be riven
     By absence from the heart.
                    T. Campbell.

CIV.   CCCXL

DATUR HORA QUIETI.

The sun upon the lake is low,
     The wild birds hush their song,
The hills have evening's deepest glow,
     Yet Leonard tarries long.

Now all whom varied toil and care   5
　　From home and love divide,
In the calm sunset may repair
　　Each to the loved one's side.

The noble dame, on turret high,
　　Who waits her gallant knight,   10
Looks to the western beam to spy
　　The flash of armour bright.
The village maid, with hand on brow
　　The level ray to shade,
Upon the footpath watches now   15
　　For Colin's darkening plaid.

Now to their mates the wild swans row,
　　By day they swam apart,
And to the thicket wanders slow
　　The hind beside the hart.   20
The woodlark at his partner's side
　　Twitters his closing song—
All meet whom day and care divide,
　　But Leonard tarries long !

Sir W. Scott.

CV.   CCCXII.

TO THE MOON.

Art thou pale for weariness
Of climbing heaven, and gazing on the earth,
　　Wandering companionless
　　Among the stars that have a different birth,—
And ever changing, like a joyless eye   5
That finds no object worth its constancy ?

P. B. Shelley.

CVI.   CCCXIII.

TO SLEEP.

A flock of sheep that leisurely pass by
One after one ; the sound of rain, and bees
Murmuring ; the fall of rivers, winds and seas,
Smooth fields, white sheets of water, and pure sky :

I've thought of all by turns, and yet do lie   5
  Sleepless ; and soon the small birds' melodies
Must hear, first utter'd from my orchard trees,
  And the first cuckoo's melancholy cry.

Even thus last night, and two nights more I lay,
  And could not win thee, Sleep ! by any stealth :   10
So do not let me wear to-night away :

Without Thee what is all the morning's wealth ?
Come, blessèd barrier between day and day,
  Dear mother of fresh thoughts and joyous health !
                                   W. Wordsworth.

CVII.   THE SOLDIER'S DREAM.   CCCXIV.

Our bugles sang truce, for the night-cloud had lower'd,
  And the sentinel stars set their watch in the sky ;
And thousands had sunk on the ground overpower'd,
  The weary to sleep, and the wounded to die.

When reposing that night on my pallet of straw   5
  By the wolf-scaring faggot that guarded the slain,
At the dead of the night a sweet Vision I saw ;
  And thrice ere the morning I dreamt it again.

Methought from the battle-field's dreadful array
  Far, far, I had roam'd on a desolate track :   10
'Twas Autumn,—and sunshine arose on the way
  To the home of my fathers, that welcomed me back.

I flew to the pleasant fields traversed so oft
  In life's morning march, when my bosom was young ;
I heard my own mountain-goats bleating aloft,   15
  And knew the sweet strain that the corn-reapers sung.

Then pledged we the wine-cup, and fondly I swore
  From my home and my weeping friends never to part ;
My little ones kiss'd me a thousand times o'er,
  And my wife sobb'd aloud in her fulness of heart.   20

'Stay—stay with us !—rest !—thou art weary and worn !'—
  And fain was their war-broken soldier to stay ;—
But sorrow return'd with the dawning of morn,
  And the voice in my dreaming ear melted away.
                                   T. Campbell.

CVIII.   A DREAM OF THE UNKNOWN.   CCCXV

I dream'd that as I wander'd by the way
    Bare Winter suddenly was changed to Spring,
And gentle odours led my steps astray,
    Mix'd with a sound of waters murmuring
Along a shelving bank of turf, which lay   5
    Under a copse, and hardly dared to fling
Its green arms round the bosom of the stream,
But kiss'd it and then fled, as Thou mightest in dream.

There grew pied wind-flowers and violets,
    Daisies, those pearl'd Arcturi of the earth,   10
The constellated flower that never sets;
    Faint oxlips; tender blue-bells, at whose birth
The sod scarce heaved; and that tall flower that wets
    Its mother's face with heaven-collected tears,
When the low wind, its playmate's voice, it hears.   15

And in the warm hedge grew lush eglantine,
    Green cow-bind and the moonlight-colour'd May,
And cherry-blossoms, and white cups, whose wine
    Was the bright dew yet drain'd not by the day;
And wild roses, and ivy serpentine   20
    With its dark buds and leaves, wandering astray;
And flowers azure, black, and streak'd with gold,
Fairer than any waken'd eyes behold.

And nearer to the river's trembling edge
    There grew broad flag-flowers, purple prank'd with white,
And starry river-buds among the sedge,   26
    And floating water-lilies, broad and bright,
Which lit the oak that overhung the hedge
    With moonlight beams of their own watery light;
And bulrushes, and reeds of such deep green   30
As soothed the dazzled eye with sober sheen.

Methought that of these visionary flowers
    I made a nosegay, bound in such a way
That the same hues, which in their natural bowers
    Were mingled or opposed, the like array   35
Kept these imprison'd children of the Hours
    Within my hand,—and then, elate and gay,
I hasten'd to the spot whence I had come
That I might there present it—O! to Whom?
                                        P. B. Shelley.

CIX.   KUBLA KHAN.

In Xanadu did Kubla Khan
A stately pleasure-dome decree :
Where Alph, the sacred river, ran
Through caverns measureless to man
 Down to a sunless sea.   5
So twice five miles of fertile ground
With walls and towers were girdled round :
And there were gardens bright with sinuous rills
Where blossom'd many an incense-bearing tree ;
And here were forests ancient as the hills,   10
Enfolding sunny spots of greenery.

 But oh ! that deep romantic chasm which slanted
Down the green hill athwart a cedarn cover !
A savage place ! as holy and enchanted
As e'er beneath a waning moon was haunted   15
By woman wailing for her demon-lover !
And from this chasm, with ceaseless turmoil seething,
As if this earth in fast thick pants were breathing,
A mighty fountain momently was forced :
Amid whose swift half-intermitted burst   20
Huge fragments vaulted like rebounding hail,
Or chaffy grain beneath the thresher's flail :
And mid these dancing rocks at once and ever
It flung up momently the sacred river.
Five miles meandering with a mazy motion   25
Through wood and dale the sacred river ran,
Then reach'd the caverns measureless to man,
And sank in tumult to a lifeless ocean :
And 'mid this tumult Kubla heard from far
Ancestral voices prophesying war !   30

 The shadow of the dome of pleasure
 Floated midway on the waves ;
 Where was heard the mingled measure
 From the fountain and the caves.
It was a miracle of rare device,   35
A sunny pleasure-dome with caves of ice !
 A damsel with a dulcimer
 In a vision once I saw :
 It was an Abyssinian maid,
 And on her dulcimer she play'd,   40
Singing of Mount Abora.

Could I revive within me
Her symphony and song,
To such a deep delight 'twould win me
That with music loud and long,   45
I would build that dome in air,
That sunny dome! those caves of ice!
And all who heard should see them there,
And all should cry, Beware! Beware!
His flashing eyes, his floating hair!   50
Weave a circle round him thrice,
And close your eyes with holy dread,
For he on honey-dew hath fed,
And drunk the milk of Paradise.

S. T. Coleridge

CX.   THE INNER VISION.   CCCXVII.

Most sweet it is with unuplifted eyes
To pace the ground, if path be there or none,
While a fair region round the traveller lies
Which he forbears again to look upon;

Pleased rather with some soft ideal scene,   5
The work of Fancy, or some happy tone
Of meditation, slipping in between
The beauty coming and the beauty gone.

—If Thought and Love desert us, from that day
Let us break off all commerce with the Muse: 10
With Thought and Love companions of our way—
Whate'er the senses take or may refuse,—
The Mind's internal heaven shall shed her dews
Of inspiration on the humblest lay.

W. Wordsworth.

CXI.   THE REALM OF FANCY.   CCCXVIII.

Ever let the Fancy roam;
Pleasure never is at home:
At a touch sweet Pleasure melteth,
Like to bubbles when rain pelteth;
Then let wingéd Fancy wander   5
Through the thought still spread beyond her:
Open wide the mind's cage-door,
She'll dart forth, and cloudward soar.

O sweet Fancy! let her loose;
Summer's joys are spoilt by use,   10
And the enjoying of the Spring
Fades as does its blossoming;
Autumn's red-lipp'd fruitage too,   *Picture of autumn*
Blushing through the mist and dew,
Cloys with tasting: What do then?   15
Sit thee by the ingle, when   *nook*
The sear faggot blazes bright,
Spirit of a winter's night;
When the soundless earth is muffled,
And the cakéd snow is shuffled   20
From the ploughboy's heavy shoon;
When the Night doth meet the Noon
In a dark conspiracy
To banish Even from her sky.
Sit thee there, and send abroad,   25
With a mind self-overaw'd,
Fancy, high-commission'd:—send her!
She has vassals to attend her:
She will bring, in spite of frost,
Beauties that the earth hath lost;   30
She will bring thee, all together,
All delights of summer weather;
All the buds and bells of May,
From dewy sward or thorny spray;
All the heapéd Autumn's wealth,   35
With a still, mysterious stealth:
She will mix these pleasures up
Like three fit wines in a cup,
And thou shalt quaff it:—thou shalt hear
Distant harvest-carols clear;   40
Rustle of the reapéd corn;
Sweet birds antheming the morn:
And, in the same moment—hark!
'Tis the early April lark,
Or the rooks, with busy caw,   45
Foraging for sticks and straw.
Thou shalt, at one glance, behold
The daisy and the marigold;
White-plumed lilies, and the first
Hedge-grown primrose that hath burst;   50
Shaded hyacinth, alway
Sapphire queen of the mid-May;

And every leaf, and every flower
Pearlèd with the self-same shower.
Thou shalt see the field-mouse peep   55
Meagre from its cellèd sleep ;
And the snake all winter-thin
Cast on sunny bank its skin ;
Freckled nest-eggs thou shalt see
Hatching in the hawthorn-tree,   60
When the hen-bird's wing doth rest
Quiet on her mossy nest ;
Then the hurry and alarm
When the bee-hive casts its swarm ;
Acorns ripe down-pattering,   65
While the autumn breezes sing.

Oh, sweet Fancy ! let her loose ;
Everything is spoilt by use :
Where's the cheek that doth not fade,
Too much gazed at ? Where's the maid   70
Whose lip mature is ever new ?
Where's the eye, however blue,
Doth not weary ? Where's the face
One would meet in every place ?
Where's the voice, however soft,   75
One would hear so very oft ?
At a touch sweet Pleasure melteth
Like to bubbles when rain pelteth.
Let then wingèd Fancy find
Thee a mistress to thy mind :   80
Dulcet-eyed as Ceres' daughter,
Ere the God of Torment taught her
How to frown and how to chide ;
With a waist and with a side
White as Hebe's, when her zone   85
Slipt its golden clasp, and down
Fell her kirtle to her feet,
While she held the goblet sweet,
And Jove grew languid.—Break the mesh
Of the Fancy's silken leash ;   90
Quickly break her prison-string,
And such joys as these she'll bring.
—Let the wingèd Fancy roam,
Pleasure never is at home.

J. Keats.

CXII.

WRITTEN IN EARLY SPRING.

I heard a thousand blended notes
While in a grove I sate reclined,
In that sweet mood when pleasant thoughts
Bring sad thoughts to the mind.

*man is a part
of nature just
as much as flowers
& rivers etc.*

To her fair works did Nature link   5
The human soul that through me ran ;
And much it grieved my heart to think
What Man has made of Man.

Through primose tufts, in that sweet bower,
The periwinkle trail'd its wreaths ;   10
And 'tis my faith that every flower
Enjoys the air it breathes.

The birds around me hopp'd and play'd
Their thoughts I cannot measure,—
But the least motion which they made   15
It seem'd a thrill of pleasure.

The budding twigs spread out their fan
To catch the breezy air ;
And I must think, do all I can,
That there was pleasure there.   20

If this belief from heaven be sent,
If such be Nature's holy plan,
Have I not reason to lament
What Man has made of Man ?

W. Wordsworth.

CXIII.

RUTH : OR THE INFLUENCES OF NATURE.

When Ruth was left half desolate
Her father took another mate ;
And Ruth, not seven years old,
A slighted child, at her own will
Went wandering over dale and hill,   5
In thoughtless freedom, bold.

And she had made a pipe of straw,
And music from that pipe could draw
Like sounds of winds and floods ;
Had built a bower upon the green,   10
As if she from her birth had been
An infant of the woods.

Beneath her father's roof, alone
She seem'd to live ; her thoughts her own ;
Herself her own delight :   15
Pleased with herself, nor sad nor gay ;
And passing thus the live-long day,
She grew to woman's height.

There came a youth from Georgia's shore—
A military casque he wore   20
With splendid feathers drest ;
He brought them from the Cherokees ;
The feathers nodded in the breeze
And made a gallant crest.

From Indian blood you deem him sprung :   25
But no ! he spake the English tongue
And bore a soldier's name ;
And, when America was free
From battle and from jeopardy,
He 'cross the ocean came.   30

With hues of genius on his cheek,
In finest tones the youth could speak :
—While he was yet a boy
The moon, the glory of the sun,
And streams that murmur as they run   35
Had been his dearest joy.

He was a lovely youth ! I guess
The panther in the wilderness
Was not so fair as he ;
And when he chose to sport and play,   40
No dolphin ever was so gay
Upon the tropic sea.

Among the Indians he had fought ;
And with him many tales he brought
Of pleasure and of fear ;   45

Such tales as, told to any maid
By such a youth, in the green shade,
Were perilous to hear.

He told of girls, a happy rout!
Who quit their fold with dance and shout,   50
Their pleasant Indian town,
To gather strawberries all day long;
Returning with a choral song
When daylight is gone down.

He spake of plants that hourly change   55
Their blossoms, through a boundless range
Of intermingling hues;
With budding, fading, faded flowers,
They stand the wonder of the bowers
From morn to evening dews.   60

He told of the magnolia, spread
High as a cloud, high over head!
The cypress and her spire;
—Of flowers that with one scarlet gleam
Cover a hundred leagues, and seem   65
To set the hills on fire.

The youth of green savannahs spake,
And many an endless, endless lake
With all its fairy crowds
Of islands, that together lie   70
As quietly as spots of sky
Among the evening clouds.

'How pleasant,' then he said, 'it were
A fisher or a hunter there,
In sunshine or in shade   75
To wander with an easy mind,
And build a household fire, and find
A home in every glade!

'What days and what bright years! Ah me!
Our life were life indeed, with thee   80
So pass'd in quiet bliss;
And all the while,' said he, 'to know
That we were in a world of woe,
On such an earth as this!'

And then he sometimes interwove   85
Fond thoughts about a father's love,
'For there,' said he, 'are spun
Around the heart such tender ties,
That our own children to our eyes
Are dearer than the sun.   90

'Sweet Ruth! and could you go with me
My helpmate in the woods to be,
Our shed at night to rear;
Or run, my own adopted bride,
A sylvan huntress at my side,   95
And drive the flying deer!

'Beloved Ruth!'—No more he said.
The wakeful Ruth at midnight shed
A solitary tear:
She thought again—and did agree   100
With him to sail across the sea,
And drive the flying deer.

'And now, as fitting is and right,
We in the church our faith will plight,
A husband and a wife.'   105
Even so they did; and I may say
That to sweet Ruth that happy day
Was more than human life.

Through dream and vision did she sink,
Delighted all the while to think   110
That, on those lonesome floods
And green savannahs, she should share
His board with lawful joy, and bear
His name in the wild woods.

But, as you have before been told,   115
This Stripling, sportive, gay, and bold,
And with his dancing crest
So beautiful, through savage lands
Had roam'd about, with vagrant bands
Of Indians in the West.   120

The wind, the tempest roaring high,
The tumult of a tropic sky
Might well be dangerous food

For him, a youth to whom was given
So much of earth—so much of heaven,   125
And such impetuous blood.

Whatever in those climes be found
Irregular in sight or sound
Did to his mind impart
A kindred impulse, seem'd allied   130
To his own powers, and justified
The workings of his heart.

Nor less, to feed voluptuous thought,
The beauteous forms of Nature wrought,—
Fair trees and gorgeous flowers;   135
The breezes their own languor lent;
The stars had feelings, which they sent
Into those favour'd bowers.

Yet, in his worst pursuits, I ween
That sometimes there did intervene   140
Pure hopes of high intent:
For passions link'd to forms so fair
And stately, needs must have their share
Of noble sentiment.

But ill he lived, much evil saw,   145
With men to whom no better law
Nor better life was known;
Deliberately and undeceived
Those wild men's vices he received,
And gave them back his own.   150

His genius and his moral frame
Were thus impair'd, and he became
The slave of low desires:
A man who without self-control
Would seek what the degraded soul   155
Unworthily admires.

And yet he with no feign'd delight
Had woo'd the maiden, day and night
Had loved her, night and morn:
What could he less than love a maid   160
Whose heart with so much nature play'd—
So kind and so forlorn?

Sometimes most earnestly he said,
'O Ruth! I have been worse than dead;
False thoughts, thoughts bold and vain   165
Encompass'd me on every side
When I, in confidence and pride,
Had cross'd the Atlantic main.

'Before me shone a glorious world
Fresh as a banner bright, unfurl'd   170
To music suddenly:
I look'd upon those hills and plains,
And seem'd as if let loose from chains
To live at liberty!

'No more of this—for now, by thee,   175
Dear Ruth! more happily set free,
With nobler zeal I burn;
My soul from darkness is released
Like the whole sky when to the east
The morning doth return.'   180

Full soon that better mind was gone;
No hope, no wish remain'd, not one,—
They stirr'd him now no more;
New objects did new pleasure give,
And once again he wish'd to live   185
As lawless as before.

Meanwhile, as thus with him it fared,
They for the voyage were prepared,
And went to the sea-shore:
But, when they thither came, the youth   190
Deserted his poor bride, and Ruth
Could never find him more.

God help thee, Ruth!—Such pains she had
That she in half a year was mad
And in a prison housed;   195
And there, with many a doleful song
Made of wild words, her cup of wrong
She fearfully caroused.

Yet sometimes milder hours she knew,
Nor wanted sun, nor rain, nor dew,   200
Nor pastimes of the May,

—They all were with her in her cell;
And a clear brook with cheerful knell
Did o'er the pebbles play.

When Ruth three seasons thus had lain,   205
There came a respite to her pain;
She from her prison fled;
But of the Vagrant none took thought;
And where it liked her best she sought
Her shelter and her bread.   210

Among the fields she breathed again:
The master-current of her brain
Ran permanent and free;
And, coming to the banks of Tone,
There did she rest; and dwell alone   215
Under the greenwood tree.

The engines of her pain, the tools
That shaped her sorrow, rocks and pools,
And airs that gently stir
The vernal leaves—she loved them still,   220
Nor ever tax'd them with the ill
Which had been done to her.

A barn her Winter bed supplies;
But, till the warmth of Summer skies
And Summer days is gone,   225
(And all do in this tale agree)
She sleeps beneath the greenwood tree,
And other home hath none.

An innocent life, yet far astray!
And Ruth will, long before her day,   230
Be broken down and old.
Sore aches she needs must have! but less
Of mind, than body's wretchedness,
From damp, and rain, and cold.

If she is prest by want of food   235
She from her dwelling in the wood
Repairs to a road-side;
And there she begs at one steep place,
Where up and down with easy pace
The horsemen-travellers ride.   240

That oaten pipe of hers is mute
Or thrown away : but with a flute
Her loneliness she cheers ;
This flute, made of a hemlock stalk,
At evening in his homeward walk   245
The Quantock woodman hears.

I, too, have pass'd her on the hills
Setting her little water-mills
By spouts and fountains wild—
Such small machinery as she turn'd   250
Ere she had wept, ere she had mourn'd,—
A young and happy child !

Farewell ! and when thy days are told,
Ill-fated Ruth ! in hallow'd mould
Thy corpse shall buried be ;   255
For thee a funeral bell shall ring,
And all the congregation sing
A Christian psalm for thee.

                                        W. Wordsworth.

CXIV.   CCCXXI.

WRITTEN AMONG THE EUGANEAN HILLS.

Many a green isle needs must be
In the deep wide sea of Misery,
Or the mariner, worn and wan,
Never thus could voyage on
Day and night, and night and day,   5
Drifting on his dreary way,
With the solid darkness black
Closing round his vessel's track ;
Whilst above, the sunless sky
Big with clouds, hangs heavily,   10
And behind the tempest fleet
Hurries on with lightning feet,
Riving sail, and cord, and plank,
Till the ship has almost drank
Death from the o'er-brimming deep ;   15
And sinks down, down, like that sleep
When the dreamer seems to be
Weltering through eternity ;

And the dim low line before
Of a dark and distant shore
Still recedes, as ever still
Longing with divided will,
But no power to seek or shun,
He is ever drifted on
O'er the unreposing wave,
To the haven of the grave.

   Ay, many flowering islands lie
In the waters of wide Agony :
To such a one this morn was led
My bark, by soft winds piloted.
—'Mid the mountains Euganean
I stood listening to the paean
With which the legion'd rooks did hail
The Sun's uprise majestical :
Gathering round with wings all hoar,
Through the dewy mist they soar
Like gray shades, till the eastern heaven
Bursts ; and then,—as clouds of even
Fleck'd with fire and azure, lie
In the unfathomable sky,—
So their plumes of purple grain
Starr'd with drops of golden rain
Gleam above the sunlight woods,
As in silent multitudes
On the morning's fitful gale
Through the broken mist they sail ;
And the vapours cloven and gleaming
Follow down the dark steep streaming,
Till all is bright, and clear, and still
Round the solitary hill.

   Beneath is spread like a green sea
The waveless plain of Lombardy,
Bounded by the vaporous air,
Islanded by cities fair ;
Underneath Day's azure eyes,
Ocean's nursling, Venice lies,—
A peopled labyrinth of walls,
Amphitrite's destined halls,
Which her hoary sire now paves
With his blue and beaming waves.

20

25

30

35

40

45

50

55

60

Lo ! the sun upsprings behind,
Broad, red, radiant, half-reclined
On the level quivering line
Of the waters crystalline ;
And before the chasm of light,   65
As within a furnace bright,
Column, tower, and dome, and spire,
Shine like obelisks of fire
Pointing with inconstant motion
From the altar of dark ocean   70
To the sapphire-tinted skies ;
As the flames of sacrifice
From the marble shrines did rise   .
As to pierce the dome of gold
Where Apollo spoke of old.   75

Sun-girt City ! thou hast been
Ocean's child, and then his queen ;
Now is come a darker day,
And thou soon must be his prey,
If the power that raised thee here   80
Hallow so thy watery bier.
A less drear ruin then than now,
With thy conquest-branded brow
Stooping to the slave of slaves
From thy throne among the waves   85
Wilt thou be,—when the sea-mew
Flies, as once before it flew,
O'er thine isles depopulate,
And all is in its ancient state,
Save where many a palace-gate   90
With green sea-flowers overgrown
Like a rock of ocean's own,
Topples o'er the abandon'd sea
As the tides change sullenly.
The fisher on his watery way   95
Wandering at the close of day,
Will spread his sail and seize his oar
Till he pass the gloomy shore,
Lest thy dead should, from their sleep
Bursting o'er the starlight deep,   100
Lead a rapid masque of death
O'er the waters of his path.

Noon descends around me now:
'Tis the noon of autumn's glow,
When a soft and purple mist   105
Like a vaporous amethyst,
Or an air-dissolvéd star
Mingling light and fragrance, far
From the curved horizon's bound
To the point of heaven's profound,   110
Fills the overflowing sky ;
And the plains that silent lie
Underneath ; the leaves unsodden
Where the infant Frost has trodden   *Frost young fresh.*
With his morning-wingéd feet   115
Whose bright print is gleaming yet ;
And the red and golden vines
Piercing with their trellised lines
The rough, dark-skirted wilderness ;
The dun and bladed grass no less,   120 .
Pointing from this hoary tower
In the windless air ; the flower
Glimmering at my feet ; the line
Of the olive-sandall'd Apennine
In the south dimly islanded ;   125
And the Alps, whose snows are spread
High between the clouds and sun ;
And of living things each one ;
And my spirit, which so long
Darken'd this swift stream of song,— 130
Interpenetrated lie
By the glory of the sky ;
Be it love, light, harmony,
Odour, or the soul of all
Which from heaven like dew doth fall, 135
Or the mind which feeds this verse,
Peopling the lone universe.

Noon descends, and after noon
Autumn's evening meets me soon,
Leading the infantine moon   140
And that one star, which to her
Almost seems to minister
Half the crimson light she brings
From the sunset's radiant springs :

And the soft dreams of the morn   145
(Which like wingéd winds had borne
To that silent isle, which lies
'Mid remember'd agonies,
The frail bark of this lone being),
Pass, to other sufferers fleeing,   150
And its ancient pilot, Pain,
Sits beside the helm again.

Other flowering isles must be
In the sea of Life and Agony :
Other spirits float and flee   155
O'er that gulf : Ev'n now, perhaps,
On some rock the wild wave wraps,
With folded wings they waiting sit
For my bark, to pilot it
To some calm and blooming cove ;   160
Where for me, and those I love,
May a windless bower be built,
Far from passion, pain, and guilt,
In a dell 'mid lawny hills
Which the wild sea-murmur fills,   165
And soft sunshine, and the sound
Of old forests echoing round,
And the light and smell divine
Of all flowers that breathe and shine.
—We may live so happy there,   170
That the Spirits of the Air
Envying us, may ev'n entice
To our healing paradise
The polluting multitude :
But their rage would be subdued   175
By that clime divine and calm,
And the winds whose wings rain balm
On the uplifted soul, and leaves
Under which the bright sea heaves ;
While each breathless interval   180
In their whisperings musical
The inspired soul supplies
With its own deep melodies ;
And the Love which heals all strife
Circling, like the breath of life,   185
All things in that sweet abode
With its own mild brotherhood :—

They, not it, would change ; and soon
Every sprite beneath the moon
Would repent its envy vain,   190
And the Earth grow young again.

P. B. Shelley.

CXV.

ODE TO THE WEST WIND.

O wild West Wind, thou breath of Autumn's being,
Thou, from whose unseen presence the leaves dead
Are driven, like ghosts from an enchanter fleeing,
Yellow, and black, and pale, and hectic red,
Pestilence-stricken multitudes ! O thou   5
Who chariotest to their dark wintry bed
The wingéd seeds, where they lie cold and low,
Each like a corpse within its grave, until
Thine azure sister of the Spring shall blow
Her clarion o'er the dreaming earth, and fill   10
(Driving sweet buds like flocks to feed in air)
With living hues and odours plain and hill :
Wild Spirit, which art moving everywhere ;
Destroyer and Preserver ; Hear, oh hear !

Thou on whose stream, 'mid the steep sky's commotion,
Loose clouds like earth's decaying leaves are shed,   16
Shook from the tangled boughs of heaven and ocean,
Angels of rain and lightning ! there are spread
On the blue surface of thine airy surge,
Like the bright hair uplifted from the head   20
Of some fierce Maenad, ev'n from the dim verge
Of the horizon to the zenith's height—
The locks of the approaching storm. Thou dirge
Of the dying year, to which this closing night
Will be the dome of a vast sepulchre,   25
Vaulted with all thy congregated might
Of vapours, from whose solid atmosphere
Black rain, and fire, and hail, will burst : Oh hear !

Thou who didst waken from his summer-dreams
The blue Mediterranean, where he lay,   30

Lull'd by the coil of his crystalline streams,
Beside a pumice isle in Baiae's bay,
And saw in sleep old palaces and towers
Quivering within the wave's intenser day,
All overgrown with azure moss, and flowers   35
So sweet, the sense faints picturing them! Thou
For whose path the Atlantic's level powers
Cleave themselves into chasms, while far below
The sea-blooms and the oozy woods which wear
The sapless foliage of the ocean, know   40
Thy voice, and suddenly grow gray with fear
And tremble and despoil themselves: Oh hear!

If I were a dead leaf thou mightest bear;
If I were a swift cloud to fly with thee;
A wave to pant beneath thy power, and share   45
The impulse of thy strength, only less free
Than Thou, O uncontrollable! If even
I were as in my boyhood, and could be
The comrade of thy wanderings over heaven,
As then, when to outstrip thy skiey speed   50
Scarce seem'd a vision,—I would ne'er have striven
As thus with thee in prayer in my sore need.
Oh! lift me as a wave, a leaf, a cloud!
I fall upon the thorns of life! I bleed!
A heavy weight of hours has chain'd and bow'd   55
One too like thee—tameless, and swift, and proud.

Make me thy lyre, ev'n as the forest is:
What if my leaves are falling like its own!
The tumult of thy mighty harmonies
Will take from both a deep autumnal tone,   60
Sweet though in sadness. Be thou, Spirit fierce,
My spirit! be thou me, impetuous öne!
Drive my dead thoughts over the universe,
Like wither'd leaves, to quicken a new birth;
And, by the incantation of this verse,   65
Scatter, as from an unextinguish'd hearth
Ashes and sparks, my words among mankind!
Be through my lips to unawaken'd earth
The trumpet of a prophecy! O Wind,
If Winter comes, can Spring be far behind?   70

P. B. Shelley.

CXVI.

NATURE AND THE POET.

Suggested by a Picture of Peele Castle in a Storm,
painted by Sir George Beaumont.

I was thy neighbour once, thou rugged Pile!
Four summer weeks I dwelt in sight of thee:
I saw thee every day; and all the while
Thy Form was sleeping on a glassy sea.

So pure the sky, so quiet was the air!   5
So like, so very like, was day to day!
Whene'er I look'd, thy image still was there;
It trembled, but it never pass'd away.

How perfect was the calm! It seem'd no sleep,
No mood, which season takes away, or brings: 10
I could have fancied that the mighty Deep
Was even the gentlest of all gentle things.

Ah! then—if mine had been the painter's hand
To express what then I saw; and add the gleam,
The light that never was on sea or land,   15
The consecration, and the Poet's dream,—

I would have planted thee, thou hoary pile,
Amid a world how different from this!
Beside a sea that could not cease to smile;
On tranquil land, beneath a sky of bliss.   20

Thou shouldst have seem'd a treasure-house divine
Of peaceful years; a chronicle of heaven;—
Of all the sunbeams that did ever shine
The very sweetest had to thee been given.

A picture had it been of lasting ease,   25
Elysian quiet, without toil or strife;
No motion but the moving tide; a breeze;
Or merely silent Nature's breathing life.

Such, in the fond illusion of my heart,
Such picture would I at that time have made;   30
And seen the soul of truth in every part,
A steadfast peace that might not be betray'd.

So once it would have been,—'tis so no more;
I have submitted to a new control:
A power is gone, which nothing can restore;   35
A deep distress hath humanized my soul.

Not for a moment could I now behold
A smiling sea, and be what I have been:
The feeling of my loss will ne'er be old;
This, which I know, I speak with mind serene.   40

Then, Beaumont, Friend! who would have been the friend
If he had lived, of Him whom I deplore,
This work of thine I blame not, but commend;
This sea in anger, and that dismal shore.

O 'tis a passionate work!—yet wise and well,   45
Well chosen is the spirit that is here;
That hulk which labours in the deadly swell,
This rueful sky, this pageantry of fear!

And this huge Castle, standing here sublime,
I love to see the look with which it braves,   50
—Cased in the unfeeling armour of old time—
The lightning, the fierce wind, and trampling waves.

—Farewell, farewell the heart that lives alone,
Housed in a dream, at distance from the Kind!
Such happiness, wherever it be known,   55
Is to be pitied; for 'tis surely blind.

But welcome fortitude, and patient cheer,
And frequent sights of what is to be borne!
Such sights, or worse, as are before me here:—
Not without hope we suffer and we mourn.   60

W. Wordsworth.

CXVII.   THE POET'S DREAM.   cccxxiv.

On a Poet's lips I slept
Dreaming like a love-adept
In the sound his breathing kept;
Nor seeks nor finds he mortal blisses,
But feeds on the aërial kisses   5
Of shapes that haunt Thought's wildernesses.

He will watch from dawn to gloom
The lake-reflected sun illume
The yellow bees in the ivy-bloom,
 Nor heed nor see what things they be—   10
But from these create he can
Forms more real than living Man,
 Nurslings of Immortality!   *P. B. Shelley.*

CXVIII.

CCCXXV.

GLEN-ALMAIN, THE NARROW GLEN.

In this still place, remote from men,
Sleeps Ossian, in the Narrow Glen;
In this still place, where murmurs on
But one meek streamlet, only one:
He sang of battles, and the breath   5
Of stormy war, and violent death;
And should, methinks, when all was past,
Have rightfully been laid at last
Where rocks were rudely heap'd, and rent
As by a spirit turbulent;   10
Where sights were rough, and sounds were wild,
And everything unreconciled;
In some complaining, dim retreat,
For fear and melancholy meet;
But this is calm; there cannot be   15
A more entire tranquillity.

Does then the Bard sleep here indeed?
Or is it but a groundless creed?
What matters it?—I blame them not
Whose fancy in this lonely spot   20
Was moved; and in such way express'd
Their notion of its perfect rest.
A convent, even a hermit's cell,
Would break the silence of this Dell:
It is not quiet, it is not ease;   25
But something deeper far than these:
The separation that is here
Is of the grave; and of austere
Yet happy feelings of the dead:
And, therefore, was it rightly said   30
That Ossian, last of all his race!
Lies buried in this lonely place.   *W. Wordsworth.*

CXIX.   CCCXXVI

The World is too much with us; late and soon,
Getting and spending, we lay waste our powers;
Little we see in Nature that is ours;
We have given our hearts away, a sordid boon!

This Sea that bares her bosom to the moon,   5
The winds that will be howling at all hours
And are up-gather'd now like sleeping flowers,
For this, for every thing, we are out of tune;

It moves us not.—Great God! I'd rather be
A Pagan suckled in a creed outworn,—   10
So might I, standing on this pleasant lea,

Have glimpses that would make me less forlorn;
Have sight of Proteus rising from the sea;
Or hear old Triton blow his wreathéd horn.

                                    W. Wordsworth.

CXX.   CCCXXVII.

WITHIN KING'S COLLEGE CHAPEL, CAMBRIDGE.

Tax not the royal Saint with vain expense,
With ill-match'd aims the Architect who plann'd
(Albeit labouring for a scanty band
Of white-robed Scholars only) this immense

And glorious work of fine intelligence!   5
—Give all thou canst; high Heaven rejects the lore
Of nicely-calculated less or more:—
So deem'd the man who fashion'd for the sense

These lofty pillars, spread that branching roof
Self-poised, and scoop'd into ten thousand cells 10
Where light and shade repose, where music dwells

Lingering—and wandering on as loth to die;
Like thoughts whose very sweetness yieldeth proof
That they were born for immortality.

                                    W. Wordsworth.

CXXI.   ODE ON A GRECIAN URN.   CCCXXVIII.

Thou still unravish'd bride of quietness,
  Thou foster-child of silence and slow time,
Sylvan historian, who canst thus express
  A flowery tale more sweetly than our rhyme:
What leaf-fringed legend haunts about thy shape   5
  Of deities or mortals, or of both,
    In Tempé or the dales of Arcady?
What men or gods are these? What maidens loth?
  What mad pursuit? What struggle to escape?
    What pipes and timbrels? What wild ecstasy?   10

Heard melodies are sweet, but those unheard
  Are sweeter; therefore, ye soft pipes, play on;
Not to the sensual ear, but, more endear'd,
  Pipe to the spirit ditties of no tone:
Fair youth, beneath the trees, thou canst not leave   15
  Thy song, nor ever can those trees be bare;
    Bold Lover, never, never canst thou kiss,
Though winning near the goal—yet, do not grieve;
  She cannot fade, though thou hast not thy bliss,
    For ever wilt thou love, and she be fair!   20

Ah, happy, happy boughs! that cannot shed
  Your leaves, nor ever bid the Spring adieu;
And, happy melodist, unwearièd,
  For ever piping songs for ever new;
More happy love! more happy, happy love!   25
  For ever warm and still to be enjoy'd,
    For ever panting, and for ever young;
All breathing human passion far above,
  That leaves a heart high-sorrowful and cloy'd,
    A burning forehead, and a parching tongue.   30

Who are these coming to the sacrifice?
  To what green altar, O mysterious priest,
Lead'st thou that heifer lowing at the skies,
  And all her silken flanks with garlands drest?
What little town by river or sea shore,   35
  Or mountain-built with peaceful citadel,
    Is emptied of this folk, this pious morn?
And, little town, thy streets for evermore
  Will silent be; and not a soul to tell
    Why thou art desolate, can e'er return.   40

O Attic shape! Fair attitude! with brede
  Of marble men and maidens overwrought,
With forest branches and the trodden weed;
  Thou, silent form, dost tease us out of thought
As doth eternity: Cold Pastoral!   45
  When old age shall this generation waste,
    Thou shalt remain, in midst of other woe
Than ours, a friend to man, to whom thou say'st,
  'Beauty is truth, truth beauty,'—that is all
    Ye know on earth, and all ye need to know.   50

                                                J. Keats.

CXXII.   YOUTH AND AGE.   CCCXXIX.

        Verse, a breeze 'mid blossoms straying,
        Where Hope clung feeding, like a bee—
        Both were mine! Life went a-maying
            With Nature, Hope, and Poesy,
                When I was young!   5
        When I was young?—Ah, woful When!
        Ah! for the change 'twixt Now and Then!
        This breathing house not built with hands,
        This body that does me grievous wrong,
        O'er aery cliffs and glittering sands   10
        How lightly then it flash'd along:
        Like those trim skiffs, unknown of yore,
        On winding lakes and rivers wide,
        That ask no aid of sail or oar,
        That fear no spite of wind or tide!   15
        Nought cared this body for wind or weather
        When Youth and I lived in't together.

        Flowers are lovely; Love is flower-like;
        Friendship is a sheltering tree;
        O! the joys, that came down shower-like,   20
        Of Friendship, Love, and Liberty,
            Ere I was old!
        Ere I was old? Ah, woful Ere,
        Which tells me, Youth's no longer here!
        O Youth! for years so many and sweet,   25
        'Tis known that Thou and I were one,
        I'll think it but a fond conceit—
        It cannot be, that Thou art gone!

Thy vesper-bell hath not yet toll'd :—
And thou wert aye a masker bold !
What strange disguise hast now put on   30
To make believe that thou art gone ?
I see these locks in silvery slips,
This drooping gait, this alter'd size ;
But Springtide blossoms on thy lips,   35
And tears take sunshine from thine eyes !
Life is but Thought : so think I will
That Youth and I are house-mates still.

Dew-drops are the gems of morning,
But the tears of mournful eve !   40
Where no hope is, life's a warning
That only serves to make us grieve
    When we are old :
—That only serves to make us grieve
With oft and tedious taking-leave,   45
Like some poor nigh-related guest
That may not rudely be dismist,
Yet hath out-stay'd his welcome while,
And tells the jest without the smile.

S. T. Coleridge.

CXXIII.   THE TWO APRIL MORNINGS.   CCCXXX.

We walk'd along, while bright and red
Uprose the morning sun ;
And Matthew stopp'd, he look'd, and said
'The will of God be done ?'

A village schoolmaster was he,   5
With hair of glittering gray ;
As blithe a man as you could see
On a spring holiday.

And on that morning, through the grass
And by the steaming rills   10
We travell'd merrily, to pass
A day among the hills.

'Our work,' said I, 'was well begun :
Then, from thy breast what thought,
Beneath so beautiful a sun,   15
So sad a sigh has brought ?'

A second time did Matthew stop ;
And fixing still his eye
Upon the eastern mountain-top,
To me he made reply :   20

'Yon cloud with that long purple cleft
Brings fresh into my mind
A day like this, which I have left
Full thirty years behind.

'And just above yon slope of corn   25
Such colours, and no other,
Were in the sky that April morn,
Of this the very brother.

'With rod and line I sued the sport
Which that sweet season gave,   30
And to the churchyard come, stopp'd short
Beside my daughter's grave.

'Nine summers had she scarcely seen,
The pride of all the vale ;
And then she sang—she would have been   35
A very nightingale.

'Six feet in earth my Emma lay ;
And yet I loved her more—
For so it seem'd—than till that day
I e'er had loved before.   40

'And turning from her grave, I met,
Beside the churchyard yew,
A blooming Girl, whose hair was wet
With points of morning dew.

'A basket on her head she bare ;   45
Her brow was smooth and white :
To see a child so very fair,
It was a pure delight !

'No fountain from its rocky cave
E'er tripp'd with foot so free ;   50
She seem'd as happy as a wave
That dances on the sea.

'There came from me a sigh of pain
Which I could ill confine;
I look'd at her, and look'd again: 55
And did not wish her mine!'

—Matthew is in his grave, yet now
Methinks I see him stand
As at that moment, with a bough
Of wilding in his hand.   60

W. Wordsworth.

CXXIV.   CCCXXXI.

THE FOUNTAIN

A Conversation.

We talk'd with open heart, and tongue
Affectionate and true,
A pair of friends, though I was young,
And Matthew seventy-two.

We lay beneath a spreading oak,   5
Beside a mossy seat;
And from the turf a fountain broke
And gurgled at our feet.

'Now, Matthew!' said I, 'let us match
This water's pleasant tune   10
With some old border-song, or catch
That suits a summer's noon;

'Or of the church-clock and the chimes
Sing here beneath the shade
That half-mad thing of witty rhymes   15
Which you last April made!'

In silence Matthew lay, and eyed
The spring beneath the tree;
And thus the dear old man replied,
The gray-hair'd man of glee: 20

'No check, no stay, this Streamlet fears,
How merrily it goes!
'Twill murmur on a thousand years
And flow as now it flows.

'And here, on this delightful day,   25
I cannot choose but think
How oft, a vigorous man, I lay
Beside this fountain's brink.

'My eyes are dim with childish tears,
My heart is idly stirr'd,   30
For the same sound is in my ears
Which in those days I heard.

'Thus fares it still in our decay:
And yet the wiser mind
Mourns less for what Age takes away   35
Than what it leaves behind.

'The blackbird amid leafy trees,
The lark above the hill,
Let loose their carols when they please,
Are quiet when they will.   40

'With Nature never do they wage'
A foolish strife; they see
A happy youth, and their old age
Is beautiful and free:

'But we are press'd by heavy laws;   45
And often, glad no more,
We wear a face of joy, because
We have been glad of yore.

'If there be one who need bemoan
His kindred laid in earth,   50
The household hearts that were his own—
It is the man of mirth.

'My days, my friends, are almost gone,
My life has been approved,
And many love me; but by none   55
Am I enough beloved.'

'Now both himself and me he wrongs,
The man who thus complains!
I live and sing my idle songs
Upon these happy plains: 60

'And Matthew, for thy children dead
I'll be a son to thee!'

At this he grasp'd my hand and said
'Alas! that cannot be.'

—We rose up from the fountain-side; 65
And down the smooth descent
Of the green sheep-track did we glide;
And through the wood we went;

And ere we came to Leonard's rock
He sang those witty rhymes 70
About the crazy old church-clock,
And the bewilder'd chimes.

W. Wordsworth.

CXXV. THE RIVER OF LIFE. CCCXXXII.

The more we live, more brief appear
  Our life's succeeding stages:
A day to childhood seems a year,
  And years like passing ages.

The gladsome current of our youth, 5
  Ere passion yet disorders,
Steals lingering like a river smooth
  Along its grassy borders

But as the care-worn cheek grows wan,
  And sorrow's shafts fly thicker, 10
Ye Stars, that measure life to man,
  Why seem your courses quicker?

When joys have lost their bloom and breath
  And life itself is vapid,
Why, as we reach the Falls of Death, 15
  Feel we its tide more rapid?

It may be strange—yet who would change
  Time's course to slower speeding,
When one by one our friends have gone
  And left our bosoms bleeding? 20

Heaven gives our years of fading strength
  Indemnifying fleetness;
And those of youth, a seeming length,
  Proportion'd to their sweetness.

T. Campbell.

THE HUMAN SEASONS.

Four seasons fill the measure of the year;
There are four seasons in the mind of man:
He has his lusty Spring, when fancy clear
Takes in all beauty with an easy span:

He has his Summer, when luxuriously   5
Spring's honey'd cud of youthful thought he loves
To ruminate, and by such dreaming high
Is nearest unto heaven: quiet coves

His soul has in its Autumn, when his wings
He furleth close; contented so to look   10
On mists in idleness—to let fair things
Pass by unheeded as a threshold brook.

He has his Winter too of pale misfeature,
Or else he would forego his mortal nature.

J. Keats.

A DIRGE.

Rough wind, that moanest loud
  Grief too sad for song;
Wild wind, when sullen cloud
  Knells all the night long;
Sad storm whose tears are vain,   5
Bare woods whose branches stain,
Deep caves and dreary main,—
  Wail for the world's wrong!

P. B. Shelley.

THRENOS.

O World! O Life! O Time!
On whose last steps I climb,
  Trembling at that where I had stood before;
When will return the glory of your prime?
  No more—Oh, never more!   5

Out of the day and night
A joy has taken flight:
  Fresh spring, and summer, and winter hoar
Move my faint heart with grief, but with delight
  No more—Oh, never more!   10

P. B. Shelley.

CXXIX.   CCCXXXVI.

THE TROSACHS.

There's not a nook within this solemn Pass,
But were an apt confessional for One
Taught by his summer spent, his autumn gone,
That Life is but a tale of morning grass

Wither'd at eve. From scenes of art which chase   5
That thought away, turn, and with watchful eyes
Feed it 'mid Nature's old felicities,
Rocks, rivers, and smooth lakes more clear than glass

Untouch'd, unbreathed upon:—Thrice happy quest,
If from a golden perch of aspen spray   10
(October's workmanship to rival May),

The pensive warbler of the ruddy breast
That moral sweeten by a heaven-taught lay,
Lulling the year, with all its cares, to rest!

W. Wordsworth.

CXXX.   CCCXXXVII.

My heart leaps up when I behold
  A rainbow in the sky:
So was it when my life began,
So is it now I am a man,
So be it when I shall grow old   5
  Or let me die!
The Child is father of the Man:
And I could wish my days to be
Bound each to each by natural piety.

W. Wordsworth.

CXXXI.   CCCXXXVIII.

ODE ON INTIMATIONS OF IMMORTALITY FROM RECOLLECTIONS OF EARLY CHILDHOOD.

There was a time when meadow, grove, and stream,
The earth, and every common sight
    To me did seem
  Apparell'd in celestial light,
The glory and the freshness of a dream.   **5**
It is not now as it hath been of yore;—
    Turn wheresoe'er I may,
      By night or day,
The things which I have seen I now can see no more.

    The rainbow comes and goes,   **10**
    And lovely is the rose;
    The moon doth with delight
Look round her when the heavens are bare;
    Waters on a starry night
    Are beautiful and fair;   **15**
The sunshine is a glorious birth;
But yet I know, where'er I go,
That there hath past away a glory from the earth.

Now, while the birds thus sing a joyous song,
    And while the young lambs bound   **20**
    As to the tabor's sound,
To me alone there came a thought of grief:
A timely utterance gave that thought relief,
    And I again am strong.
The cataracts blow their trumpets from the steep;— **25**
No more shall grief of mine the season wrong:
I hear the echoes through the mountains throng,
The winds come to me from the fields of sleep,
    And all the earth is gay;
      Land and sea   **30**
    Give themselves up to jollity,
    And with the heart of May
    Doth every beast keep holiday;—
      Thou child of joy
Shout round me, let me hear thy shouts, thou happy
    Shepherd-boy!   **35**

Ye blesséd Creatures, I have heard the call
  Ye to each other make; I see
The heavens laugh with you in your jubilee;
  My heart is at your festival,
   My head hath its coronal,   **40**
The fulness of your bliss, I feel—I feel it all.
   Oh evil day! if I were sullen
   While Earth herself is adorning
    This sweet May-morning;
   And the children are culling   **45**
    On every side
  In a thousand valleys far and wide,
  Fresh flowers; while the sun shines warm
And the babe leaps up on his mother's arm:—
  I hear, I hear, with joy I hear!   **50**
 —But there's a tree, of many, one,
A single field which I have look'd upon,
Both of them speak of something that is gone:
   The pansy at my feet
   Doth the same tale repeat: **55**
Whither is fled the visionary gleam?
Where is it now, the glory and the dream?

Our birth is but a sleep and a forgetting;
The Soul that rises with us, our life's Star,
   Hath had elsewhere its setting **60**
    And cometh from afar;
   Not in entire forgetfulness,
   And not in utter nakedness,
But trailing clouds of glory do we come
    From God, who is our home: **65**
Heaven lies about us in our infancy!
Shades of the prison-house begin to close
    Upon the growing Boy,
But he beholds the light, and whence it flows,
   He sees it in his joy;   **70**
The Youth, who daily farther from the east
  Must travel, still is Nature's priest,
   And by the vision splendid
   Is on his way attended;
At length the Man perceives it die away, **75**
And fade into the light of common day.

Earth fills her lap with pleasures of her own;
Yearnings she hath in her own natural kind,

And even with something of a mother's mind
   And no unworthy aim,   80
  The homely nurse doth all she can
To make her foster-child, her inmate, Man,
   Forget the glories he hath known,
And that imperial palace whence he came.

Behold the Child among his new-born blisses, 85
A six years' darling of a pigmy size !
See, where 'mid work of his own hand he lies,
Fretted by sallies of his mother's kisses,
With light upon him from his father's eyes !
See, at his feet, some little plan or chart, 90
Some fragment from his dream of human life,
Shaped by himself with newly-learnéd art ;
   A wedding or a festival,
   A mourning or a funeral ;
    And this hath now his heart, 95
   And unto this he frames his song
    Then will he fit his tongue
To dialogues of business, love, or strife ;
   But it will not be long
   Ere this be thrown aside, 100
   And with new joy and pride
The little actor cons another part ;
Filling from time to time his 'humorous stage'
With all the Persons, down to palsied Age,
That life brings with her in her equipage ; 105
   As if his whole vocation
   Were endless imitation.

Thou, whose exterior semblance doth belie
   Thy soul's immensity ;
Thou best philosopher, who yet dost keep 110
Thy heritage, thou eye among the blind,
That, deaf and silent, read'st the eternal deep,
Haunted for ever by the eternal Mind,--
   Mighty Prophet ! Seer blest !
   On whom those truths do rest 115
Which we are toiling all our lives to find,
In darkness lost, the darkness of the grave ;
Thou, over whom thy Immortality
Broods like the day, a master o'er a slave,
A Presence which is not to be put by ; 120

Thou little child, yet glorious in the might
Of heaven-born freedom on thy being's height,
Why with such earnest pains dost thou provoke
The years to bring the inevitable yoke,
Thus blindly with thy blessedness at strife?   125
Full soon thy soul shall have her earthly freight,
And custom lie upon thee with a weight
Heavy as frost, and deep almost as life!

            O joy! that in our embers
            Is something that doth live,   130
            That Nature yet remembers
            What was so fugitive!
The thought of our past years in me doth breed
Perpetual benediction: not indeed
For that which is most worthy to be blest,   135
Delight and liberty, the simple creed
Of Childhood, whether busy or at rest,
With new-fledged hope still fluttering in his breast:—
            —Not for these I raise
            The song of thanks and praise;   140
        But for those obstinate questionings
        Of sense and outward things,
        Fallings from us, vanishings;
        Blank misgivings of a creature
Moving about in worlds not realized,   145
High Instincts, before which our mortal nature
Did tremble like a guilty thing surprized:
        But for those first affections,
        Those shadowy recollections,
            Which, be they what they may   150
Are yet the fountain-light of all our day,
Are yet a master-light of all our seeing;
        Uphold us, cherish, and have power to make
Our noisy years seem moments in the being
Of the eternal Silence: truths that wake,   155
            To perish never;
Which neither listlessness, nor mad endeavour,
            Nor man nor boy
Nor all that is at enmity with joy,
Can utterly abolish or destroy!   160
        Hence, in a season of calm weather
            Though inland far we be,

Our souls have sight of that immortal sea   *The eternally around us.*
   Which brought us hither ;
    Can in a moment travel thither—   165
And see the children sport upon the shore,
And hear the mighty waters rolling evermore.

Then, sing ye birds, sing, sing a joyous song !
   And let the young lambs bound
   As to the tabor's sound !   170
  We, in thought, will join your throng
   Ye that pipe and ye that play,
   Ye that through your hearts to-day
   Feel the gladness of the May !
What though the radiance which was once so bright 175
Be now for ever taken from my sight,
  Though nothing can bring back the hour
Of splendour in the grass, of glory in the flower ;
   We will grieve not, rather find
   Strength in what remains behind ;   180
   In the primal sympathy
   Which having been must ever be ;
   In the soothing thoughts that spring
   Out of human suffering ;
   In the faith that looks through death, 185
In years that bring the philosophic mind.

And O, ye Fountains, Meadows, Hills, and Groves,
Forbode not any severing of our loves !
Yet in my heart of hearts I feel your might ;
  I only have relinquish'd one delight   190
To live beneath your more habitual sway :
I love the brooks which down their channels fret
Even more than when I tripp'd lightly as they ;
  The innocent brightness of a new-born day
   Is lovely yet ;   195
The clouds that gather round the setting sun
Do take a sober colouring from an eye
That hath kept watch o'er man's mortality ;
Another race hath been, and other palms are won.
  Thanks to the human heart by which we live, 200
Thanks to its tenderness, its joys, and fears,
To me the meanest flower that blows can give
Thoughts that do often lie too deep for tears.
        W. Wordsworth.

CXXXII.

Music, when soft voices die,
Vibrates in the memory—
Odours, when sweet violets sicken,
Live within the sense they quicken.

Rose leaves, when the rose is dead, 5
Are heap'd for the beloved's bed;
And so thy thoughts, when Thou art gone,
Love itself shall slumber on.

P. B. Shelley.

NOTES.

MR. PALGRAVE'S SUMMARY OF BOOK FOURTH.

It proves sufficiently the lavish wealth of our own age in Poetry, that the pieces which, without conscious departure from the standard of Excellence, render this Book by far the longest, were with very few exceptions composed during the first thirty years of the Nineteenth century. Exhaustive reasons can hardly be given for the strangely sudden appearance of individual genius : that, however, which assigns the splendid national achievements of our recent poetry to an impulse from the France of the first Republic and Empire is inadequate. The first French Revolution was rather one result,— the most conspicuous, indeed, yet itself in great measure essentially retrogressive,—of that wider and more potent spirit which through enquiry and attempt, through strength and weakness, sweeps mankind round the circles (not, as some too confidently argue, of Advance, but) of gradual Transformation : and it is to this that we must trace the literature of Modern Europe. But, without attempting discussion on the motive causes of Scott, Wordsworth, Shelley, and others, we may observe that these Poets carried to further perfection the later tendencies of the Century preceding, in simplicity of narrative, reverence for human Passion and Character in every sphere, and love of Nature for herself :—that, whilst maintaining on the whole the advances in art made since the Restoration, they renewed the half-forgotten melody and depth of tone which marked the best Elizabethan writers :—that, lastly, to what was thus inherited they added a richness in language and a variety in metre, a force and fire in narrative, a tenderness and bloom in feeling, an insight into the finer passages of the Soul and the inner meanings of the landscape, a larger sense of Humanity,—hitherto scarcely attained, and perhaps unattainable even by predecessors of not inferior individual genius. In a word, the Nation which, after the

140

Greeks in their glory, may fairly claim that during six centuries it has proved itself the most richly gifted of all nations for Poetry, expressed in these men the highest strength and prodigality of its nature. They interpreted the age to itself—hence the many phases of thought and style they present :—to sympathize with each, fervently and impartially, without fear and without fancifulness, is no doubtful step in the higher education of the soul. For purity in taste is absolutely proportionate to strength—and when once the mind has raised itself to grasp and to delight in excellence, those who love most will be found to love most wisely.

But the gallery which this Book offers to the reader will aid him more than any preface. It is a royal Palace of Poetry which he is invited to enter :

Adparet domus intus, et atria longa patescunt—

though it is, indeed, to the sympathetic eye only that its treasures will be visible.

ABBREVIATIONS.

A.S. = Anglo-Saxon, adj. = adjective, cp. = compare, Fr. = French, Ger. = German, Lat. = Latin, l. = line, N.E.D. = New English Dictionary (Oxford), O.F. = Old French, subst. = substantive. Notes borrowed from Mr. F. T. Palgrave are enclosed in inverted commas and followed by his initials (F. T. P.). Poems in Book IV. are referred to simply by their number in this volume : poems in other Books of the *Golden Treasury* are referred to by their number in the complete edition, preceded by the letters G. T.

No. I.   *Whether on Ida's shady brow*

IT is remarkable that these lines—a complaint that there is no more poetry left in the world—should have been written so shortly before the greatest outburst of poetry that England has known since the days of Elizabeth. The poem appeared in Blake's *Poetical Sketches*, 1783, so that it preceded by 15 years the famous joint volume of Wordsworth and Coleridge, *Lyrical Ballads*, 1798. Its author, William Blake, poet, painter, designer, and mystic, lived apart from his contemporaries, who altogether failed to understand him. He read the Elizabethan poets, and was influenced by them, but, not less than Wordsworth, he went direct to Nature for inspiration. Since Wordsworth taught English readers of poetry to appreciate truth and simplicity in verse, Blake, too, has had his admirers.

Very similar in thought is Matthew Arnold's poem, *The Progress of Poesy*, especially the line, "The mount is mute, the channel dry." Compare also his lines beginning "Though the Muse be gone away."

1. Ida. There were two mountains of this name celebrated in ancient poetry, (1) the mountain in the Troad on which the three goddesses appeared to Paris, and whence the gods often watched the Trojan war, (2) the mountain in Crete on which Jupiter was fabled to have been brought up.

No. II. *Bards of Passion and of Mirth*

WRITTEN by Keats on the blank page before Beaumont and Fletcher's tragi-comedy, *The Fair Maid of the Inn.*

The poets enjoy a double immortality—on earth and in Elysium. With the sentiment may be compared the loftier and more earnest strain in which Shelley afterwards claimed immortality for the writer of these lines :

"Peace, peace ! he is not dead, he doth not sleep !"
(*Adonais*, stanzas 39 *et seq.*)

Metre.—The charm of the poem depends largely on the free, apparently careless, in reality consummately skilful, variation of the simple metre. There are four accents in each line, and the general effect is trochaic. But three lines (10, 22, 30) have an extra syllable at the beginning, and several others an extra unaccented syllable at the end. Without such variation we should have the monotonous metre that Touchstone ridicules in *As You Like It*, calling it "the very false gallop of verses," and offering to rhyme Rosalind thus, "eight years together, dinners and suppers and sleeping hours excepted."

4. double-lived, 'having two lives,' used by Keats for 'having a second life.' For the form cp. 'long-lived.'

8. parle (Fr. *parler*), same word as *parley*, which Shakespeare uses both as noun and verb. Generally 'conference with an enemy' ; here used, in accordance with its etymology, simply for 'speech.' Milton uses the form 'parle.'

11. Elysian. Compare the noble description (partly imitated from Virgil, *Aeneid*, VI. 639) in Wordsworth's *Laodamia* :

"He spake of love, such love as Spirits feel
In worlds whose course is equable and pure ;
No fears to beat away—no strife to heal—
The past unsigh'd for, and the future sure ;
Spake of heroic hearts in graver mood
Revived, with finer harmony pursued ;

Of all that is most beauteous—imaged there
In happier beauty ; more pellucid streams,
An ampler ether, a diviner air,
And fields invested with purpureal gleams :
Climes which the sun, who sheds the brightest day
Earth knows, is all unworthy to survey."

12. **Dian**, Diana, a Roman goddess, identified by the Romans themselves with Artemis, the Greek virgin goddess, whose favourite occupation was hunting : the fawn was specially connected with her, and she is sometimes represented in a chariot drawn by two fawns.

13. **tented,** dwelling under tents. It generally means 'covered with tents' as in 'the tented field' (*Othello*, I. iii.), 'tented shores' (XCVII. 54).

14. **rose-scented**, an instance of Keats' skill in the formation of compounds. How far is this a merit ? A language dies if it becomes incapable of 'growing' new words. But nothing requires greater caution than such coinage on the part of a poet. We may say that (1) he must not coin words or compounds without a good reason, (2) they must be pleasing to the ear, (3) they must not suggest any incongruous associations. Within these limits a poet may study freshness of diction.

18. **trancéd.** A 'trance' is a 'transit' or 'passage,' then 'an absence of sensation or power to feel.' So Keats apparently means 'without sense or feeling.'

20. **numbers** (Lat. *numerare*, through the French), applied to the counting of the succession of feet in a verse, and so used for 'poetry.'

21. **golden**, a favourite epithet of the poets for 'delightful,' 'precious.' So Homer speaks of 'golden Aphrodite.' We speak of 'The Golden Legend,' 'golden deeds,' 'The Golden Treasury,' etc.

28. **slumber'd,** for 'slumbering.' The licence which Keats allows himself in the invention of participial forms is not always justifiable.

cloying. The intransitive use for 'to be cloyed, satiated, is very rare, but an example is given in *N.E.D.* under date 1721.

30. **little week**, the short space of mortal life. With this description of the subjects of poetry we may compare Terence's famous profession, *Homo sum ; nihil humani a me alienum puto*, and Virgil's equally famous line, so often quoted (apart from its context) as the noblest expression of the function of poetry, *Sunt lacrimae rerum et mentem mortalia tangunt.*

No. III. *Much have I travell'd in the realms of gold*

ONE of the finest tributes ever paid by one poet to another (in this case to two others). Keats wrote it in 1815, in his twentieth year. It is the first poem in which his genius stands fully revealed. Like Shakespeare, he had "little Latin and less Greek"; or rather he had no Greek at all, though he had picked up a good deal of classical mythology in his school-days. No one contributed more than Keats to the revival of the love of the bright Hellenic spirit at the beginning of the nineteenth century: but his wonderful insight into that spirit was the gift of nature, not the fruit of learning.

Metre.—See Appendix on Sonnet.

1. **realms of gold.** The world of books is imagined as divided into kingdoms. 'Realms of gold' are regions where the explorer may hope to find gold; but the phrase had also a reference to the metaphor 'golden' as applied to books (cp. II. 21). 'Western islands' seems to suggest the Hesperides and the Atlantis of the ancients: the earthly paradise was generally imagined to lie westwards beyond the Straits of Gibraltar and the Atlantic Ocean. Westwards, too, beyond 'the Spanish Main' went the modern seekers after new 'realms of gold.' But perhaps Keats only meant the English and Latin poets as distinguished from the Greek. The poets are further represented as holding their kingdoms under Apollo, the god of music and poetry.

4. **fealty, "true service,"** from Latin *fidelitas*, through O.F. *feaute, fealte.*

6. **deep-brow'd:** see note on 'drear-nighted, XXVIII. 1.

demesne, pronounced "di-mēn." It is properly the substantive of an O.F. adjective meaning 'belonging to a lord.' The Anglo-French spelling is due to the old law-books. Possession; an estate possessed; the land subject to a king or prince.

7. **Serene,** Lat. *serenus,* 'bright,' 'clear,' of weather. Here the adj. is used as subst.

8. **Chapman** (circa 1557-1634) translated the *Iliad* and *Odyssey* into English rhyming verse, the first into long lines of seven iambic feet, the second into the ordinary ten-syllable heroic couplet. He speaks out "loud and bold," retaining much of the Homeric fire and swiftness of movement, and—when read in sufficient quantities for the impression of his crudities to wear off—may still be enjoyed. Yet, as Mr. Palgrave notes, "to find in Chapman's Homer the 'pure serene' of the original, the reader must bring with him the imagination of the youthful poet;—he must be 'a Greek himself,' as Shelley finely said of Keats."

11. **Cortez,** a mistake of Keats. It was not Cortez, the conqueror of Mexico (1485-1554), who discovered the Pacific, but Vasco Balboa, the Spanish navigator. The date of the discovery is given as September 25, 1513.

No. IV. *All thoughts, all passions, all delights*

THIS poem is taken from the second (1800) edition of the *Lyrical Ballads.* An earlier form of it, entitled *The Dark Ladie*, had appeared in *The Morning Post*, December 21, 1799. A still earlier version has been printed in an interesting little volume, *Coleridge's Poems : a Facsimile Reproduction of the Proofs and MSS. of some of the Poems,* edited by J. D. Campbell (Westminster, 1899).

The qualities that give *The Ancient Mariner* its high place in English literature are largely present here also. There is the same revival of the simplicity of the ancient ballad. There is the same subtlety of psychological analysis, so foreign to the ancient ballad, which stamps the poem as the work of a reflective philosopher. There is the same power of representing a scene vividly by a few strokes of the pen. There is the same fascination of melody, increasing the power of the poem upon us each time we re-read it.

1. We may compare the song in the *Merchant of Venice,* III. ii. :

> " Tell me where is fancy bred ?
> Or in the heart or in the head ?
> How begot, how nourished ?
>   Reply, reply.
> It is engender'd in the eyes,
> With gazing fed ; and fancy dies
> In the cradle where it lies."

(Fancy = love). Coleridge's answer is different.

17. It has often been remarked that happy youth finds a special pleasure in sad poetry or music. Cp. Wordsworth's *Ode to Lycoris,* stanza 2, " In youth we love the darksome lawn."

25. flitting, quickly coming and going.

30. brand (same root as German *brennen,* to burn), properly a burning stick or torch. Applied to a sword in quite early English, apparently from its terrible gleam when in motion.

42. crazed. To 'craze' is (1) literally, to 'break' ; (2) metaphorically, to break down in health, impair ('Till length of years and sedentary numbness craze my limbs,' Milton, *Samson Agonistes*) ; (3) to impair in intellect, drive mad.

lovely, now applied only to women or children, was less restricted in its use in older English.

45. savage den, lair of wild beasts.

53. unknowing, not knowing, seems formed by f....
There are two prefixes un, one prefixed to substan...un-fair,
and adverbs, meaning 'not,' much commoner ...
than now (e.g. un-famous, un-right, as well ...
etc.), the other prefixed to verbs to exp...closing,'
action (e.g. to un-lock). Both prefixes ...
participle, which is therefore ambi...
cases ; i.e. 'unlocked' might me...
simply 'not closed.' But the f...

with a present participle when it is a real participle, not a mere adjective.

63. **yellow.** This seems a simple epithet enough for 'forest-leaves.' Yet in nothing more than in such simple but vivid and truthful epithets does the poetry of Wordsworth and Coleridge differ from most poetry of the earlier eighteenth century. The town poets used purely conventional epithets for natural objects; Wordsworth and Coleridge expressed the impressions they had received directly from nature. To some readers this epithet 'yellow' will at once recall the landscapes of the pre-Raphaelite brotherhood of painters, who also tried to rescue art from the conventions into which it had fallen and to reproduce nature as they found it. (Coleridge was ridiculed by Byron for speaking of the 'yellow-green' in the western sky after sunset: see his ode, *Dejection.*)

66. **ditty,** from the Latin *dictatum,* past participle of *dictare,* a 'lesson,' 'exercise,' was not at first limited to verse. In the *Romaunt of the Rose* Cicero's treatise *De Amicitia* is called a ditty. Afterwards it was used chiefly of songs (in Shakespeare and other poets, often of the songs of birds), especially ballads or simple poems.

69. These 'impulses of soul and sense,' particularised in lines 71-76, are the thoughts, passions and delights of the first stanza.

73. **kindle, produce.** The verb 'kindle' in the sense of 'produce' is said to have a different origin from the same verb in the sense of 'inflame.'

76. **subdued.** Observe here and throughout the poem how skilfully Coleridge uses the repetition of words and phrases. He is never afraid of tautology. Cp. in the *Ancient Mariner* :

> " *The western wave* was all aflame,
> The day was well-nigh done !
> Almost upon *the western wave*
> Rested the *broad* bright *Sun* ;
> When that strange shape drove suddenly
> Betwixt us and the *Sun.*
> And straight the *Sun* was flecked with bars,
> (Heaven's Mother send us grace !)
> As if through a dungeon grate he peered
> With *broad* and burning face."

7... earlier version inserted a stanza here, which is worth
quo...

> While Fancy, like the midnight torch
> That bends and rises in the wind,
> ...up with wild and broken lights
> The tumult of her mind."

' Cp. to 'abash' = to 'confuse with shame,

No. V.   *O talk not to me of a name great in story*

" THE most tender and true of Byron's smaller poems " (F.T.P.). Written by him on the road between Florence and Pisa.

Metre : There are four accents in each line. The prevailing foot is an anapaest ($\smile \smile -$) for which an iambus is sometimes substituted ; and there is an extra unaccented syllable at the end of each line.

1. **story,** history.

3. **myrtle and ivy.** Milton associated these with the laurel in the opening lines of *Lycidas* :

> " Yet once more, O ye laurels, and once more
>   Ye myrtles brown, with ivy never sere."

There all three are combined to form the poet's garland, which Milton describes himself as about to assume prematurely (" I come to pluck your berries harsh and crude "). Here the myrtle and ivy are *contrasted* with the laurel. At Greek banquets a bough of myrtle was held by each guest in turn as he sang. (Cp. Aristophanes, *Clouds*, 1364, and the well-known Athenian drinking-song, 'I'll wreathe my sword in myrtle now.') The ivy was sacred to Bacchus. These two, as emblems of youthful jollity, are contrasted with the laurel, the crown of the victor.

sweet two-and-twenty. Cp. the song, 'O mistress mine,' in Shakespeare's *Twelfth Night* :

> "Come and kiss me, sweet-and-twenty,
>   Youth's a stuff will not endure."

4. **plenty,** subst. inaccurately used for adj. ' plenteous.' Derived (through French) from Latin *plenus*, ' full.'

6. **May-dew.** The dew in May was supposed to have miraculous properties ; to bathe the face in it was to secure perpetual beauty.

11. **discover,** reveal.

No. VI.   *O Brignall banks are wild and fair*

THIS and No. XXXI. are songs from Sir W. Scott's poem of *Rokeby*.

1. **Brignall,** near Barnard Castle in the North Riding of Yorkshire ; the *Greta* is a tributary of the Tees. ' Dotheboys Hall' (*Nicholas Nickleby*, chap. iv.) was 'near Greta Bridge, in Yorkshire.' For Scott's use of place-names see note on LVI. 1.

4. **Notice** the omission of the relative ' that ' at the beginning of this line. Generally speaking, poetry tends to omit relatives and conjunctions when they can be spared without injury to the sense.

25. **read, suppose, conjecture.** The radical meaning of the word (Ger. *reden*) is 'to put or place before.' From this come various meanings, *e.g.* to place before the mind, *i.e.* conjecture, imagine, consider, consult, advise; to place before others, *i.e.* declare, tell; to place writing before others, *i.e.* to speak it aloud.

26. **palfrey,** a saddle-horse. The word is in early use in English, derived through the French from the low Latin *paraveredus*, a hybrid formation from the Greek παρά, 'beside' (so 'extra'), and *veredus*, late Latin, 'a post-horse.' The modern French form is *palefroi*.

27. **ranger,** one who ranges a forest, the officer in charge of it. To 'range' meant 'to set in a rank,' so 'to scour a country with an array of armed men' (Skeat); then, to 'traverse' or 'rove over.'

28. **greenwood.** This compound (cp. 'greensward') occurs as early as Chaucer.

29. **winds,** 'blows,' the same word as the subst. 'wind.' Cp. Milton, *Lycidas*, "What time the gray-fly winds her sultry horn."

37. **brand.** See note on IV. 30.

musketoon, from It. *moschettone*, a short musket carried by cavalry in 17th and 18th centuries (Stanford).

39. **Dragoon,** orig. a kind of musket, so-called from its 'breathing fire' like a dragon; then, a cavalry soldier armed with this weapon.

40. **list,** 'listen,' 'give heed to,' an extension of an A.S. word meaning 'to desire' (cp. 'listless').

tuck, properly tuckett, a flourish on a trumpet. The word is said to be of Teutonic origin and connected with 'touch,' but it is certainly the same as the Italian word *toccata*, a prelude to a piece of music (Skeat).

47. **mickle,** a longer form of 'much.' Both forms occur in early English.

48. **would reign,** the relative 'who' is omitted.

51. **fiend,** A.S. an enemy, especially used of evil spirits. The *ignis fatuus*, or Will o' the Wisp, is meant by 'the fiend whose lantern lights the mead.' See the description of him in Milton's *L'Allegro* (where he is called 'the drudging goblin' and 'the lubber fiend'); *Comus*, l. 432; *Paradise Lost*, ix. 634-42.

No. VII.   *There be none of Beauty's daughters*

WRITTEN in 1816.

Metre : There are three accents in each of the eight lines of the stanza, except the second and fourth, which have only two. The rhythm is iambic, varied by anapaests (‿ ‿ —).

10. **Her bright chain.** The picture is of the moonbeam lying across the waters, but the thought is suggested of the mysterious influence of the moon on the tides. Cp. Walt Whitman:

> "Silently as the water follows the moon,
> With fluid steps anywhere around the globe."

No. VIII.   *I arise from dreams of thee*

A NOTE on the manuscripts of this poem, and on its composition, will be found in Mr. Buxton Forman's large edition of Shelley. Whether Shelley wrote the verses to a special Indian air is not known; they were written for his friend, Mrs. Jane Williams, who used to sing them.

Metre: Three accents in each line, the feet iambic with an anapaest sometimes substituted in the first place. Observe the effect of this initial anapaest in giving swiftness to the line. Lines where the sense requires slow movement—"I die, I faint, I fail"—are purely iambic.

11. **champak**, an Indian tree of the Magnolia genus, which has fine fragrant yellow blossoms (Stanford).

fail. This word is left without its proper rhyme in line 15. Shelley might easily have written 'pine,' but the correspondence with line 18—"I die, I faint, I fail!"—would then have been left incomplete.

12. **like sweet thoughts.** The faint sweet odours, vanishing even as we become conscious of them, are compared to the fugitive, scarcely apprehended, thoughts of a dreamer. To Shelley the world of imagination is so much more real than the material world that he is always explaining things in the real world by reference to the other. The 'dead leaves' in Autumn suggest to him "ghosts from an enchanter fleeing" (CXV. 3). The voice of the hushed city at noon is "soft like Solitude's" (LXIII. 9). Most poets, conversely, explain things in the imaginary world by images drawn from the material world.

13. **complaint.** The song of the nightingale is often so called in Elizabethan poetry, as it is called *querela* in Latin.

No. IX.   *She walks in beauty, like the night*

WRITTEN in 1814 in honour of a cousin, "the beautiful Mrs Wilmot."

8. **Had,** would have.

9. **raven,** black like the raven's.

14. **eloquent,** explained by the lines that follow.

No. X. *She was a phantom of delight*

COMPOSED in 1804. In 1802, Wordsworth had married Mary Hutchinson, who in childhood had been his fellow-pupil in a dame's school at Penrith. It was she undoubtedly who inspired the poem, of which Wordsworth tells us that "it was written from my heart as is sufficiently obvious." An interesting account of the poet's wife and also of his sister, Dorothy Wordsworth, will be found in De Quincey's *Lake Reminiscences* (Vol. II., pp. 236, 282, of the 1896 edition of the Collected Writings). De Quincey says that Mrs. Wordsworth "furnished a remarkable proof how possible it is for a woman neither handsome nor even comely according to the rigour of criticism—nay, generally pronounced very plain—to exercise all the practical fascination of beauty, through the mere compensatory charms of sweetness all but angelic, of simplicity the most entire, womanly self-respect and purity of heart speaking through all her looks, acts, and movements."

We may compare the exquisite lines that Tennyson wrote at the close of his life in dedicating his last book to his wife ("There on the top of the down"), and Browning's beautiful tributes to his wife, *By the Fireside, One Word More*, and the invocation ("O lyric love") in *The Ring and the Book*.

No. XI. *She is not fair to outward view*

HARTLEY COLERIDGE, son of S. T. Coleridge, was born in 1796 and died in 1849. He was buried at Grasmere, where his grave is near Wordsworth's. He was the child in whose honour Coleridge wrote the fine poem, *Frost at Midnight*:

"I was reared
In the great city, pent 'mid cloisters dim,
And saw nought lovely but the sky and stars.
But thou, my babe ! shalt wander like a breeze
By lakes and sandy shores, beneath the crags
Of ancient mountains, and beneath the clouds
Which image in their bulk both lakes and shores
And mountain crags : so shalt thou see and hear
The lovely shapes and sounds intelligible
Of that eternal language, which thy God
Utters, who from eternity doth teach
Himself in all, and all things in Himself. . . .
Therefore all seasons shall be sweet to thee. . . ."

Wordsworth also celebrated his beautiful childhood in exquisite verse, the lines *To H. C., Six Years Old*, in which he foretold that Nature would preserve for him "by individual right, A young lamb's heart among the full-grown flocks." (See also CXXXI. 85-128.)

There is something inexpressibly sad about the futility of a life begun under such splendid auspices. Hartley Coleridge's life was almost entirely one of failure, though he wrote some charming poems, of which one has attained the honour of a place in this collection.

No. XIII. *She dwelt among the untrodden ways.*

ON the four poems that follow (XIII.-XVI.) Mr. Aubrey de Vere writes (*Essays chiefly on Poetry*, Vol. I., p. 152):

"That these poems are love-poems is certain: whether they were founded on reality, the poet has left unrecorded.

"No one was less disposed than Wordsworth to minister to that vulgar curiosity which in these days respects no sanctuary. The egotism with which his poetry has been charged was commonly of a wholly different sort: the "Mind of Man" he speaks of as

'My haunt, and the main region of my song:'

in studying human nature, his own breast was the nearest mirror of humanity into which he could look; and it is a human, not an individual interest in himself that is so frankly revealed in his philosophical verse. He was confidential on subjects respecting which others have nothing to confide; but confidences such as those in which some poets have been profuse would have been against his instincts."

If these poems had never been written, we might perhaps have felt that there was something lacking in Wordsworth—that infinite tenderness which is perhaps the most deeply poetic thing in poetry. This depth of emotion is not inconsistent with—rather it is essentially connected with—the severest self-restraint in expression. How little these lines *say* as compared with the much that they *imply*!

The "Lucy" series contains one other poem, a very striking one, not included in *The Golden Treasury*. It begins "Strange fits of passion have I known." See also the little poem beginning, "Among all lovely things my love had been."

2. Dove. The 'place where' is not important, and there is nothing to be gained by trying to identify it. There is a beautiful river Dove in Derbyshire, a tributary of the Trent, and there is a Dove Crag on the small lake of Brother's Water in Westmoreland. But

"Be Yarrow stream unseen, unknown !
    It must, or we shall rue it;
We have a vision of our own,
    Ah, why should we undo it ?"

No. XIV. *I travell'd among unknown men*

11. **Wheel**, the spinning wheel, worked by the hand, once to be found in every well-ordered English household, now entirely obsolete owing to the introduction of machinery. "I could write a treatise of lamentation upon the changes brought about among the cottages of Westmoreland by the silence of the spinning wheel. During long winter nights and wet days, the wheel upon which wool was spun gave employment to a great part of a family. The old man, however infirm, was able to card the wool, as he sat in the corner by the fireside; and often, when a boy, have I admired the cylinders of carded wool which were softly laid upon each other by his side. Two wheels were often at work on the same floor; and others of the family, chiefly little children, were occupied in teasing and cleaning the wool to fit it for the hand of the carder." (Wordsworth.)

13. **thy nights concealed.** A superfluous addition if we look at the bare prosaic fact, and yet just the most exquisite touch in the poem.

14. **bowers.** The word first means 'dwelling' (O.E.); (2) 'a vague poetic word for an idealized abode, not realized in any actual dwelling': cp. Milton, 'The bower of earthly bliss'; (3) an inner apartment, especially a lady's private apartment or boudoir; (4) a place closed in with trees, a leafy covert, arbour. It is a favourite word with Wordsworth (cp. XV. 10), and with Scott (XXXIII. 5.) The latter uses it in sense (3); Wordsworth in a sense which here at least vaguely combines (2), (3) and (4).

No. XV. *Three years she grew in sun and shower*

WORDSWORTH's poetry is full of 'the education of Nature.' For that education as experienced in his own life, see especially *The Prelude* and *Lines composed a few miles above Tintern Abbey.* Again, we may compare the influence of life-long contact with Nature upon the shepherd Michael in Wordsworth's story of that name, and contrast the fatal influence of tropical Nature upon a sensuous temperament as conceived by him in the poem *Ruth* (CXIII. in this volume).

Of the sixth stanza of this poem and of X. 15-16, Ruskin says (*Sesame and Lilies*, Lecture II., of Queens' Gardens): "There are two passages of that poet who is distinguished, it seems to me, from all others—not by power, but by exquisite rightness—which point you to the source, and describe to you, in a few syllables, the completion of womanly beauty."

12. **kindle or restrain.** Observe the correspondence to 'law and impulse' in line 8.

16. breathing balm. 'Breathing' is used here as a participial adjective intransitive.   Compare for the thought,

> "And balmy drops in summer dark
> Slide from the bosom of the stars."
>
> —*Tennyson.*

We may contrast the voluptuous influence of tropical Nature described in *Ruth* (CXIII. 133-138).

17. silence. Cp.

> "The silence that is in the starry sky,
> The sleep that is among the lonely hills."

19. the floating clouds. Cp. XCIV., "I wander'd lonely as a cloud That floats on high o'er vales and hills."

state, prop. 'condition,' especially the condition of high rank ; here 'stateliness,' 'magnificence.'

27. secret, Latin *secretus*, 'far-withdrawn.' So Milton 'On the secret top Of Oreb or of Sinai,' which Bentley strangely emended to 'On the sacred top.'

29. Observe how beautifully the 'murmuring sound' of rivulets and waterfalls is reproduced in this line.   Cp. a wonderful passage in a letter of T. E. Brown's which describes the rivulets on a Swiss Alp : "The grass seems to be all flowers, and the flowers to be all grass : the closest-grained math I ever beheld ; and through it everywhere, led by careful hands, go singing, hissing rather, like sharp silver scythes, the little blessed streams." (*Letters of T. E. Brown*, Vol. I., p. 77.)   Here the kind of rill and kind of sound, are different, and the onomatopoeic effect in the language is correspondingly different.

31. vital. The epithet recalls us to line 13.   "There are deadly feelings of delight ; but the natural ones are vital, necessary to very life."   Ruskin, *Sesame and Lilies.*

35. She and I.   Observe that Nature is still the speaker.

42. never more.   From Sophocles, with his πανύστατον δὴ κοὔποτ' αὖθις ὕστερον—"For the last, last time and never again hereafter "—in the dying speech of Ajax, the pathos of this inexorable 'never more' recurs often in poetry.

No. XVI.   *A slumber did my spirit seal*

THERE is no denial here of the immortality so nobly proclaimed by Wordsworth himself in his *Ode* (CXXXI.) ; only the contrast inevitably forcing itself upon the mourner between the loved human form as it was and as it is.   Similarly, after Hallam's death, Tennyson's mind is pre-occupied with the thought of the

ship bringing home the mortal remains (*In Memoriam*, Cantos
IX.-XIX.), especially such lines as :

> " And hands so often clasped in mine
> Should toss with tangle and with shells,"

or

> " And dead calm in that noble breast
> Which heaves but with the heaving deep."

With this perfect elegy of eight lines may be compared W. S.
Landor's lines in memory of Rose Aylmer :

> " Ah, what avails the sceptred race !
> Ah, what the form divine !
> What every virtue, every grace !
> Rose Aylmer, all were thine.
> Rose Aylmer, whom these wakeful eyes
> May weep, but never see,
> A night of memories and sighs
> I consecrate to thee."

The two poems are alike in their self-restraint, so characteristic
of the best classical poetry.   Wordsworth's elegy Mr. Aubrey
de Vere describes as " a dirge which those who confound the
passionate with the exclamatory will do well to pass by, but
which to others will represent, in its stern brevity, the tragic
rising to the terrible."

7. **diurnal.**   Cp. Wordsworth's description of skating :

> " Still the solitary cliffs
> Wheeled by me—even as if the earth had rolled
> With visible motion her diurnal round."

Observe the added weight and dignity given by the use of
' diurnal ' instead of the commonplace ' daily.'

No. XVII.   *I meet thy pensive, moonlight face*

HENRY FRANCIS LYTE (1793-1847), the author of this poem and
LXXIII., was an English clergyman, curate of Lymington, Hamp-
shire, and Charlton, Devonshire, and afterwards vicar of Lower
Brixham.   He is chiefly remembered as the author of several
well-known hymns, " Abide with me, fast falls the eventide,"
" Pleasant are Thy courts above," " Jesus, I my cross have
taken."

1. **moonlight.**   A face full of brightness and happiness is often
said to be ' full of sunshine.'   So a face of calm, thoughtful
beauty is here compared to moonlight.   With this lover's vision
of his dead love—dreamt of, however, as living,—compare the
vision of a living love in Tennyson's *Maud* :

> " Cold and clear-cut face, why come you so cruelly meek,
> Breaking a slumber in which all spleenful folly was drown'd,

Pale with the golden beam of an eyelash dead on the cheek,
Passionless, pale, cold face, star-sweet on a gloom profound ;
Woman-like, taking revenge too deep for a transient wrong
Done but in thought to your beauty, and ever as pale as before,
Growing and fading and growing upon me without a sound.
Luminous, gem-like, ghost-like, death-like, half the night long,
Growing and fading and growing, till I could bear it no more."

14. **more sad and fair.** The combination of epithets is obscure.
Perhaps the meaning is, 'In days which, even when fuller of
pain, were dearer to me than the present.'

No. XVIII. *A chieftain to the highlands bound*

T. CAMPBELL (1777-1844) won his chief fame as a poet by *The
Pleasures of Hope*, a didactic poem in heroic couplets, which he
published at the age of twenty-one. It was admired beyond its
deserts—though it contains good poetic stuff—by a generation
not yet ready to appreciate the far greater poetry of Wordsworth
and Coleridge. Campbell himself learnt much from them and
from Scott, and wrote not a few short poems and two fairly long
ones, *O'Connor's Child* and *Gertrude of Wyoming*, that are not
unworthy to be read along with theirs. In the reaction which
has followed his popularity he has suffered unduly.

Lord Ullin's Daughter has all the four qualities which Matthew
Arnold found to be the main characteristics of Homer, rapidity,
plainness of thought, plainness of diction, and within its compass
nobility. There can scarcely be higher praise for a ballad.
Shelley's poem, *The Fugitives* ('The waters are flashing') very
closely resembles this one in subject : the difference in treatment
makes a comparison of the two poems a very instructive lesson.

Metre : The trochaic rhyme-ending (*e.g.* shrieking, speaking)
is admittedly difficult to manage with dignity in English. The
treatment of it here is very successful. It helps the rapidity of
the narrative, which is further assisted by the occasional double
rhyme (lines 31, 45, 55). The same metre is used by Wordsworth in the Yarrow poems (XCVIII. and XCIX.), and with equal
skill, though for a very different subject.

5. **Lochgyle,** generally known as Loch-na-Keal, on the west
coast of Mull. The island of Ulva is opposite the mouth of the
loch. Loch is a Gaelic word, used both for a narrow arm of the
sea (like the Norwegian fiords) and an inland lake.

15. **bonny, handsome, fair, blythe.** A corruption of the
French *bonne*, fem. of *bon*, 'good.'

20. **winsome,** from the A.S., pleasant, lovely.

26. **water-wraith.** A wraith (Scandinavian word) was an
apparition in the likeness of a person supposed to be seen just

before or just after his death. See the wonderful description of the wraith of King James I. of Scotland in Rossetti's *King's Tragedy*. Compare also XCIX. 31-2 (Wordsworth, quoting the old ballad), "The water-wraith ascended thrice, And gave his doleful warning"; and LXXIV. 11-12, "The fishers have heard the water-sprite, Whose screams forebode that wreck is nigh."

No. XIX.   *Oft I had heard of Lucy Gray*

IF there are any persons who still maintain the eighteenth century doctrine so strenuously combated by Wordsworth, that the chief difference between poetry and prose lies in the diction—not in the thought, but in the drapery of the thought—they will probably see nothing whatever to admire in *Lucy Gray*. Some too, whose love of poetry is less shallow than this, and who care for poetry because, and in proportion as, it seems to them more elevated than prose, and who, therefore, without confusing the inner spirit and the external trappings, demand that the two shall correspond in dignity and nobility, may cavil at the unadorned simplicity of this poem. Wordsworth has abandoned in it all the external helps of dignified and unfamiliar language, or pathetic and lofty association, which a poet may justifiably use to enhance the impressiveness of his theme. He has chosen to rely on the absolute and sufficient pathos of the story—the tragedy of a young and beautiful life lost within such close proximity to those who could have saved it and would so cheerfully have given their own lives to save it. He sets down the plain facts with that simplicity which seems so easy but is really the perfection of art; so that we see the whole sequence of events in a series of pictures unsurpassed in literature for vividness. If that is not enough for us, if the unutterable pathos does not move us, he will do no more for us—add no more to disguise from us our own callousness to the appeal. Yes, just one thing more he will do—spiritualize the incident by showing us that even Lucy's peasant neighbours cannot associate the thought of death with a being so full of life and unselfish joy. If one of the great functions of poetry is to 'awake the mind from the lethargy of custom' to the infinite depth below the surface of common every-day things, Wordsworth has abundantly fulfilled it here.

The poem was written in 1799; the incident on which it was founded occurred near Halifax in Yorkshire.

Metre: Observe how the very simple metre is saved from monotony by an occasional line where the natural emphasis does not fall on the verse accent or even within the same foot; *e.g.* 'She dwèlt on a wïde mòor' where the emphasis is on the three marked syllables.

19. **minster**, the same word as 'monastery,' from the late Latin *monasterium*, but used as the name of several English

cathedral churches. Here as in LVI. Wordsworth is indifferent to 'local colour': there is no 'minster' near Halifax.

21. hook, a curved iron instrument for cutting or lopping.

26. wanton, playful, sportive, unrestrained: "the true sense is unrestrained, uneducated, not taken in hand by a master." (Skeat.)

No. XX. *Why weep ye by the tide, ladie*

THE first stanza of this ballad is ancient. The others were written, like XLI., for Campbell's *Albyn's Anthology* in 1816. Scotch words: sall = shall, sae = so, loot = let, fa' = fall, wilfu' = wilful, ha' = hall, a' = all, kirk = church, baith = both, awa' = away, wi' = with.

12. Langley-dale, in county of Durham, five miles north of Barnard Castle.

19. mettled, spirited, "Absolutely the same word as *metal*, though the difference in sense is now indicated by a difference in the spelling. The allusion is to the temper of the *metal* of a sword-blade." (Skeat.)

managed, trained. To 'manage' is to 'handle' (cp. Ital. *mano*, hand), and was first used of the control of horses.

20. palfrey. See note on VI. 26.

25. morning-tide. 'Tide' properly means 'time' (which word is from the same root); the use of it for the flux and reflux of the sea is derived from this. Cp. "Alike to him was time or tide," in *Lay of the Last Minstrel*, I. xxi.

30. bower. See note on XIV. 14.

No. XXI. *The fountains mingle with the river*

THE source of Shelley's poem has been found in a French song of eight lines, "Les vents baisent les nuages."

Metre: The poem is written in trochaic lines of four accents, except that every fourth line has only three accents. Further, an extra syllable is allowed at the beginning of the line, as in the first and third lines (The foúntains míngle wíth the ríver); and the final trochee may be reduced to a single long syllable, as in lines 6 and 8 (Whý not Í with thíne?).

No. XXII. *How sweet the answer Echo makes*

A VERY simple but singularly musical poem—one of the most perfect of Moore's 'Melodies,' as they are appropriately named. There is an onomatopoeic effect in it, which is difficult to analyse—as if the smooth swift ripple of the long lines gave us the very sound 'of horn or lute or soft guitar,' and the short lines the answering echoes.

This is the first of a group of poems connected with evening or night (XXII.-XXV.). Another such group begins at CII.

No. XXIII. *Ah! County Guy, the hour is nigh*

THIS song is from *Quentin Durward*, Chapter IV.

1. **county.** Count, Earl. "Apparently an adoption of Anglo-French *Counte*, or O.F. and Ital. *Conte*, with unusual retention of final vowel, confused in form with *county*" [the domain of a Count] (*N.E.D.*).

3. **bower.** See note on XIV. 14.

7. **confess,** either 'acknowledge,' or 'attest,' as in Pope's "The voice divine confess'd the warlike maid."

No. XXIV. *Gem of the crimson-colour'd Even*

COMPARE CIII., also by Campbell.

5. **pensile,** hanging. Shenstone speaks of 'pensile woods.'

6. **tear of twilight,** a somewhat euphuistic expression for the dew. But cp. Coleridge in CXXII. 40, and Moore in XXXVIII. 1.

7. **So due, etc.,** *i.e.* so faithfully do you return at the appointed hour to the sunset sky.

11. **sure,** *i.e.* 'it is sure that,' 'it must be that.'

23. **wanton.** Cp. XIX. 26.

30. **embalms,** makes balmy.

33. **winnow'd,** fanned. Generally it is used of grain separated from chaff by fanning, and this modern sense is also the commonest in early English. Campbell's use may have been suggested by Milton, *Paradise Lost*, Bk. V.:

> "Then with quick fan
> Winnows the buxom air, till within soar
> Of tow'ring eagles, to all the fowls he seems
> A phoenix."

No. XXV. *Swiftly walk over the western wave*

PERSONIFICATIONS of Day, Night, Sleep, and Death are common enough in the English poets in imitation of classical poetry, but they are apt to be frigid. The remarkable thing about Shelley's personifications is that they are more real to him than their ancient counterparts were to the great majority of the classical poets themselves. Perhaps the best help to the appreciation of such a poem as this—the very stuff of dreams woven into tissue of the most delicate hues—would be the study of some of the allegorical paintings of Burne Jones.

Metre: To call the metre irregular might be misleading, for there is no more perfect piece of melody in the book. But it is difficult to reduce it to rule, beyond saying that the first, third, fourth, fifth, and sixth lines of each stanza contain four accents, while the second and seventh contain two. The rhythm is sometimes dactylic (swiftly walk), sometimes trochaic (wéstern), whilst in some lines the effect is iambic (Where áll the lóng and lóne daylíght), though perhaps we should in such cases regard the line as trochaic, not counting the first syllable, and taking the last syllable by itself: in the dactylic lines the last syllable certainly goes by itself. A monosyllabic foot seems even to be admitted into the middle of a line (Thy bróther | Déath | cáme and | críed).

2. **Spirit of Night.** Night is personified in Euripides' play of Orestes (Electra's prayer, lines 174-177). Compare Tennyson's 'young Night divine' in *The Palace of Art*, and Longfellow's *Hymn to the Night*.

. **eastern cave.** Cp. c. 44-5.

> " When the night is left behind
> In the deep east, dim and blind."

9. **Star inwrought.** The dark sky is the mantle of Night with stars woven into its texture.

13. **opiate,** bringing forgetfulness.

17. **rode,** more picturesque than 'rose' or 'mounted.' Light is imagined as a horseman or a charioteer, as Phoebus and Aurora drive their steeds in the ancient poets.

19. **his.** Day is masc. in this line, fem. in l. 11.

22. **Thy brother Death.** Sleep is personified as the brother of Death in *Iliad* XIV. 231, ἔνθ' Ὕπνῳ σύμβλητο κασιγνήτῳ Θανάτοιο. Virgil too makes Death the brother of Sleep—*Consanguineus Leti Sopor*—but his Death and Sleep are shapes of terror in the entrance to the lower world and represent 'drugged sleep' and 'violent death,' *Aen.* VI. 278. Tennyson, *In Memoriam*, Canto 68, follows Homer:

> " When in the down I sink my head,
> Sleep, Death's twin brother, times my breath."

Similarly Shelley himself in the opening lines of *Queen Mab*:

> " How wonderful is Death,
> Death and his brother Sleep."

24. **filmy-eyed.** A whole picture in an epithet. Such coinage of a picturesque compound is more characteristic of Keats than of Shelley.

No. XXVI.   *Why art thou silent?   Is thy love a plant*

IN XXVI.-XXXIV. we have a group of poems devoted to 'The pains of love'—especially the sadness of love that meets with unfaithfulness.

Wordsworth wrote this poem in 1835. "In the month of January, when Dora and I were walking from Town End, Grasmere, across the vale, snow being on the ground, she espied, in the thick though leafless hedge, a bird's nest half-filled with snow. Out of this comfortless appearance arose this sonnet, which was, in fact, written without the least reference to any individual object" (Wordsworth's note). It recalls his earlier poem, "There is a change and I am poor" (1806).

7. Even my least generous wishes have only sought for what you could give without lessening your own happiness.

13. eglantine, sweet brier.   Cp. the description of an arbour in Spenser, *Faerie Queene*, II. v. 29:

"Through which the fragrant eglantine did spread,
    His prickling arms, entrayled with roses red,
    Which daintie odours round about them threw."

Milton in *L'Allegro*, 48, and Shelley in CVIII. 16, seem to use 'eglantine' for 'honeysuckle.'

No. XXVII.   *When we two parted*

FIRST published in 1816.

Metre : Dactylic. The first line of each couplet consists of two dactyls, the second of which is often shortened into a trochee (Whén we two párted). In two lines of the last stanza it is shortened still further, but the following line in each case begins with an extra syllable which takes the place of the dropped one. The second line of each couplet consists of a dactyl followed by a single long syllable. All the lines, as is usual in lyric metres, admit of an extra unaccented syllable—or even two syllables—at the beginning (In silence and teárs).

7-8. The first draft of these lines was

"Never may I behold
    Moment like this."

The superiority of the later version is self-evident; and a comparison of the two should help to convince those who think that revision and the taking of pains are inconsistent with poetic inspiration. It would have been well if Byron, whom Sir W. Scott oddly described as wielding his pen with the negligent ease of a person of quality, had revised more often and more carefully.

14. **light**, lightly spoken of or lightly esteemed, the opposite of Lat. *gravis*, so often applied to character.

18. **a knell**, *i.e.* 'and the sound is as a knell to mine ear.' The construction is what would be called in Greek grammar 'accusative in apposition to the sentence,' like Ἑλένην κτάνωμεν Μενέλεῳ λύπην πικράν.

No. XXVIII.   *In a drear-nighted December*

1. **drear-nighted.** This epithet combines two practices which are specially characteristic of Keats amongst the English poets, (1) the invention of compounds, (2) the formation of an adjective from a substantive by means of a participial termination.   Mr. W. T. Arnold, in the introduction to his edition of Keats, points out that both practices may be defended by many examples, though perhaps no poet uses them so freely as Keats.   In coining 'drear-nighted' Keats may be said to be only following the analogy of 'good-natured.'   Shakespeare has 'sceptred sway,' Milton has 'tower'd cities,' 'squadron'd angels,' and many more, Gray has 'storied urn,' even Wordsworth (following Milton) has 'pillar'd shade.'

On Keats' use of 'drear,' Mr. W. T. Arnold remarks that the word is, or was, frequent in the work of only one other poet, Chatterton.   "The word is also used three times by Coleridge, once in the famous line, 'A grief without a pang, dark, void and drear'; once at least by both Shelley and Tennyson; and of late years has become comparatively common."

4. **green felicity**, the happy time of their greenness.   The bold use of this epithet recalls the equally audacious and equally successful employment of the same word in Marvell's *Thoughts in a Garden* (G. T. CXLII.):

> "Annihilating all that's made
> To a green thought in a green shade."

There is an interesting verbal parallel in Euripides, *Bacchae*, 866, νεβρὸς χλοεραῖς ἐμπαίζουσα λείμακος ἀδοναῖς.

5. **undo**, the opposite of 'to do,' especially in Early English to open that which has been fastened, a sense in which the word is still common; then, generally, to 'annul,' 'destroy.'

6. **sleety.** Adjectives in *y* are "so numerous as to be a distinct feature in Keats' style" (W. T. Arnold).

12. **Apollo.** See note on CXIV. 75.

14. **fretting**, the ruffling of their crystal surface.   So 'fretted' means 'ruffled' in CXXXI. 88, "Fretted by sallies of his mother's kisses."   'To fret' properly means 'to eat' (cp. the German,

fressen), then 'to corrode,' and metaphorically 'to vex.' The word 'fret' used in architecture and music is of different origin.

15. petting. There is a substantive 'pet' and an adjective 'pettish,' but the verb seems to be of Keats' own coining. A 'pet' in the sense of 'a fit of peevishness' is probably derived from 'pet,' a 'darling,' because darlings naturally become peevish.

20. writhed, *i.e.* 'who writhed.' For the omission of the relative cp. VI. 4. The harshness of the juxtaposition of 'writhed' with the unaccented ending and 'passéd' with the accented ending is the solitary blemish in this lovely poem.

21. Cp. Tennyson, *Locksley Hall*, "This is truth the poet sings, That a sorrow's crown of sorrow is remembering happier things." Tennyson was thinking of Dante, *Inferno*, V. 121-3:

> "Nessun maggior dolore
> Che ricordarsi del tempo felice
> Nella miseria."

Mr. Churton Collins (*Illustrations of Tennyson*, p. 63) quotes parallel passages from Thucydides, Pindar, Boethius, and others.

No. XXIX. *Where shall the lover rest*

THE song occurs in *Marmion*, Canto III., where 'the air' is described as 'wild and sad,' like "the lament of men Who languish'd for their native glen." To Marmion, who had betrayed Constance Beverley, the words are specially ominous, and they are recalled by him at the hour of death (Canto VI., stanza xxxii.).

Metre.—Dactylic. The first line of each couplet contains two dactyls, the second a dactyl followed by a trochee. An extra unaccented syllable is allowed at the beginning of the line, *e.g.* "(Her) wíng shall the | eágle flap." But the metrical triumph of the song is the magnificent rendering of the rush of flight and pursuit in the third stanza. The sense of irresistible speed is conveyed by the way in which the metre ignores the ordinary breaks between the lines: "Í'n the lost | báttle, Borne | dówn by the | flý'ing, Where míngles war's | ráttle with | gróans of the | flý'ing." Scott may not consciously have manipulated his metre with this object. More probably he was simply guided by instinct. If so, it was the instinct of a poet.

9. Eleu loro, apparently a Gaelic lament, like the Greek ὀτοτοῖ.

12. laving, more properly a transitive verb meaning 'to wash' or 'cleanse.' So Milton, "But as I rose out of the laving stream."

27. rattle, the confused noise of war.

No. XXX.   *O what can ail thee, knight-at-arms*

"Awakening up, he took her hollow lute,—
    Tumultuous,—and, in chords that tenderest be,
He play'd an ancient ditty, long since mute,
    In Provence call'd, 'La belle dame sans merci.'"
                                  Keats, *Eve of St. Agnes*, st. **xxxiii.**

In a note on the above (*Longer English Poems*, p. 412), Mr.
J. W. Hales says: "It would seem to have been rather the name
of the old poem, than the old poem itself, that inspired Keats'
piece. The old poem, written originally by Alain Chartier in
the early 15th century, translated into English by Sir Richard
Ros, consists mainly of a somewhat prolix conversation between
an obdurate lady and her lover, at the close of which she goes
away indifferent to dance and play, he desperate to tear his hair
and die. A copy of the English version may be seen in Chalmers'
British Poets, vol. i. 518, and also in *Political, Religious, and
Love Poems*, ed. by Mr. Furnivall for the Early English Text
Society. For some account of Alain Chartier, see Besant's *Early
French Poetry*, chap. i."

Mr. F. T. Palgrave thought Keats "not quite himself in this
imitative ballad, which, alone among his poems, is admirable
rather for the picturesqueness of the whole than for the equal
wealth of the details also." But detailed ornament would
scarcely have been in keeping with the ballad style. For Keats'
possible debt to Coleridge, see note on *Kubla Khan*, **cix.** 16.

2. **palely.** The adverb should more properly have been an
adjective, an epithet of the knight. It is substituted, not so
much for metrical reasons as from a fondness, characteristic of
Keats, for unusual modes of expression.

4. **And no birds sing.** Four very simple monosyllables; but
in this place they are an instance of the stupendous effect which
a great poet can produce from the simplest materials. Some of
the finest lines in English poetry (*e.g.* the last two of Wordsworth's great ode, **cxxxi.**, and much of Shakespeare's sonnet,
"That time of year thou mayst in me behold," **xxxviii.** in
Book I.) are almost or entirely monosyllabic. Pope's dislike
for monosyllables, "Ten low words oft creep in one dull line,"
has not been shared by our greatest poets.

6. **woe-begone.** The original phrase was 'him was woe-begone,'
i.e. 'to him had woe closed round,' from the obsolete verb
'bego'='encompass,' but the later construction occurs in
Chaucer (*N. E. D.*).

18. **zone**, girdle.

19. **as**, as if. Cp. **lxxii.** 7 and **cxiv.** 74. An archaism: the
'if' was not needed when the force of the subjunctive was livelier.

21. **pacing,** moving with measured steps. 'Pace' is the same word as 'pass'; Lat. *passus.*

26. **manna-dew,** Hebrew. See Exodus, xvi. 15. "It is impossible to name any natural product that will answer to the requirements of the Scriptural narrative in regard to this heaven-sent food" (*Cambridge Companion to the Bible*).

29. **elfin** is the adjective of 'elf,' a little sprite, though it is often itself used as a substantive.

35. **latest,** not simply 'last' but with an allusion to the fact—doubtless familiar to Keats as a medical student—that vitality is lowest in the hours just before dawn. Cp. "The dead dark hour before the dawn When sick men die," Lewis Morris, *Epic of Hades.*

41. **gloam.** There is a substantive 'gloaming,' evening twilight, and also a verb 'to gloam,' to grow dark, both chiefly found in Scotch writers, but apparently of English origin and connected with 'glow' and 'gloom.' The word 'gloaming' is still used in the Yorkshire dialect. The form 'gloam' as substantive is Keats' own invention.

42. **gapéd,** *i.e.* 'I saw (that) their lips gaped,' the verb not the participle, unless we are to suppose that the participle is inaccurately formed, like 'slumber'd' in II. 28.

No. XXXI. *A weary lot is thine, fair maid*

LIKE VI., this song is from *Rokeby*. It was suggested to Scott by an old Scotch ballad, from which he borrowed a verse:

> "He turn'd him round and right about,
>   All on the Irish shore,
> He gave his bridle-reins a shake,
>   With Adieu for evermore,
>   My dear!
>   Adieu for evermore!"

The whole ballad is given by Scott in the notes to *Rokeby*. These are the "charming lines of Scott's"—only, as we have seen, they are not Scott's—from which Clive Newcome made a sketch to relieve his feelings after a memorable disappointment. Thackeray, *The Newcomes*, chap. liii.

3. **braid,** to bind the hair with a 'braid' or ribbon.

4. **rue,** Greek, ῥυτή, a plant of bitter taste, sometimes called 'herb of grace' because it symbolised repentance. Cp. *Hamlet*, IV. v. 182, "We may call it herb of grace o' Sundays."

7. **Lincoln green.** "Lincoln at one time dyed the best green

of all England, and Coventry the best blue" (Dr. Brewer). Cp.
the ballad of *The Outlaw Murray*:

> "Thereat he spyed five hundred men
>   Shooting with bows on Newark lea;
> They were a' in ae livery clad
>   O' the Lincoln green sae gay to see."

12. **fain**, adverb, 'joyfully.'

No. XXXII. *When the lamp is shatter'd*

IT would be difficult to find, either in earlier or later English
poetry, a dirge so full of music as this, where the sound not
merely helps the sense, but seems even fuller of meaning than the
actual words.

Metre.—Anapaestic. The first line of each couplet contains
two feet with an extra unaccented syllable at the end, the second
contains three feet. An iambus is often substituted for an
anapaest. When the lámp | is shát | tered | The li'ght | in the
dúst | lies déad.

19. The weaker of the two lovers is left single, left alone.
This is better than taking 'singled' to mean 'selected.'

20. A very obscure line. If the text is really what Shelley
wrote, it seems to mean 'To endure to feel as a burden that
which was once cherished as a possession.' Mr. F. H. Dale
suggests to me a brilliant emendation, 'To endure *that* it once
possest'—*i.e.* 'To endure (the thought) that ...,' also an elliptical
expression, but a far more natural one. In this case the thought
is the one expressed by Keats in XXVIII.

23. **the frailest**, *i.e.* the human heart. Cp. Wordsworth,
Laodamia:

> "Mightier far
> Than strength of nerve and sinew, or the sway
> Of magic, potent over sun and star,
> Is love—though oft to agony distrest,
> And though his favourite seat be feeble woman's breast."

30. **eagle**, adjective, perched in a lofty and dangerous position,
such as an eagle might choose. Cp. Tennyson, *Demeter*, 'I
stared from every eagle peak.'

No. XXXIII. *O lover's eyes are sharp to see*

THIS and the following poem are founded on the same legend,
which is best given in the words of Scott's note: "There is a
tradition in Tweeddale, that when Neidpath Castle, near Peebles,
was inhabited by the Earls of March, a mutual passion subsisted
between a daughter of that noble family, and a son of the Laird

of Tushielaw, in Ettrick Forest. As the alliance was thought unsuitable by her parents, the young man went abroad. During his absence, the lady fell into a consumption; and at length, as the only means of saving her life, her father consented that her lover should be recalled. On the day when he was expected to pass through Peebles, on the road to Tushielaw, the young lady, though much exhausted, caused herself to be carried to the balcony of a house in Peebles, belonging to the family, that she might see him as he rode past. Her anxiety and eagerness gave such force to her organs, that she is said to have distinguished his horse's footsteps at an incredible distance. But Tushielaw, unprepared for the change in her appearance, and not expecting to see her in that place, rode on without recognizing her, or even slackening his pace. The lady was unable to support the shock; and, after a short struggle, died in the arms of her attendant."

For Neidpath, see also LXXXVII. It now belongs to the Earl of Wemyss.

5. bower. See note on XIV. 14.

13. sultry, hot, feverish.

hectic. ἑκτικός, 'habitual,' from ἕξις, a 'habit' of body, was applied to fevers by Galen; hence 'hectic' means feverish, consumptive.

21. kenn'd, recognised.

26. glancing, transitive, i.e. 'casting quickly or obliquely.' Generally intransitive.

27. spoke, for 'spoken,' past participle.

No. XXXIV.   *Earl March look'd on his dying child*

12. Ellen. Campbell's poems are too often marred by inexact rhymes. There are several in *Lord Ullin's Daughter* (XVIII.).

No. XXXV.   *Bright Star! would I were stedfast
as thou art*

"THIS beautiful sonnet was the last word of a youth, in whom, if the fulfilment may ever safely be prophesied from the promise, England lost one of the most rarely gifted in the long roll of her poets. Shakespeare and Milton, had their lives been closed at twenty-five, would (so far as we know) have left poems of less excellence and hope than the youth who, from the petty school and London surgery, passed at once to a place with them of 'high collateral glory'" (F.T.P.).

It was written after landing on the Dorset coast at the beginning of his voyage to Italy, Autumn, 1820, when "the bright beauty of the day and the scene revived for a moment the poet's drooping heart."

4. **Eremite**, the same word as 'hermit,' from Gk. ἐρημία, 'a desert.' Originally the two forms were used indiscriminately, but from about the middle of the 17th century they have been differentiated in use, 'hermit' being the ordinary and popular word, while eremite (always spelt without the unetymological *h*) is used either poetically or rhetorically or with special reference to its primitive use in Greek (*N. E. D.*). *Nature's Eremite* is the moon.

6. In a poet who knew no Greek the resemblance to Euripides is the more striking : Θάλασσα κλύζει πάντα τἀνθρώπων κακά, *Iph. Taur.* 1193, "The sea cleanses all the ills of men." With 'hung aloft' in l. 2 we may compare *Alcestis*, 450, ἀειρομένας παννύχου σελάνας, "When all night long the moon is lifted high."

13. **tender-taken**, gently drawn, a happily formed compound.

No. XXXVI. *When I have fears that I may cease to be*

WRITTEN not later than January, 1818, soon after the completion of *Endymion*. The most Shakespearean of the sonnets of the poet who has sometimes been said to have had more of Shakespeare's spirit than any other modern writer. The likeness to Shakespeare is a thing to be felt rather than analysed, but one or two striking resemblances may be noted : (1) the beginning—compare the openings of several of Shakespeare's finest sonnets, "When I have seen by Time's fell hand defaced," "When in disgrace with fortune and men's eyes," "When in the chronicle of wasted time," "When to the sessions of sweet silent thought" (all in *Golden Treasury*, Book I.) ; (2) the scheme of rhymes is Shakespearean, not Italian ; (3) the couplet ending is especially Shakespearean ; (4) the rhythm—a peculiarly stately iambic ; (5) the rich imagery ; (6) the richness of the language. Matthew Arnold, in applying the epithet Shakespearean to Keats' work, expressly says that he means "not imitative of Shakespeare," but having "that rounded perfection and felicity of loveliness of which Shakespeare is the great master" ; but in this sonnet the resemblance is closer than usual.

The greatness of the thought in this sonnet should be borne in mind by those who are tempted to judge Keats unfavourably because of some lapses in his poetry and in his letters to Fanny Brawne.

3. **charact'ry**, written symbols. Cp. Shakespeare, *Jul. Caes.* II. i. 308, 'All the charactery of my sad brows,' *i.e.* 'all the signs of care graven in my sad brow.'

6. **a high romance,** the mystery of the universe, of endless space and endless time. Compare Kant's saying, 'Two things fill me with awe, the grandeur of the starry heavens without, and the grandeur of the moral law within.'

8. **hand of chance,** the hand of the poet directed by unseen influence, doing its best things as if "by chance"—θείᾳ τύχῃ ἄνευ νοῦ, as Plato says in the *Ion*. It was the complaint of Socrates that the poets could not explain their inspired utterances.

11. **faery,** magical, transporting me out of myself.

No. XXXVII. *Surprized by joy—impatient as the wind*

WORDSWORTH'S daughter, Catharine, died in 1812 at the age of three. De Quincey, who was devoted to the child, has left some account of her in his *Reminiscences*. This sonnet to her memory was written many years after her death, and is a proof of the strength of Wordsworth's affections.

1. **surprized,** suddenly overtaken.

No. XXXVIII. *At the mid hour of night, when stars are weeping, I fly*

"IT is impossible not to regret that Moore has written so little in this sweet and genuinely national style." (F.T.P.)

Metre.—Four accents in each line. The feet are indifferently anapaests or iambi.

1. **weeping.** The stars were supposed to distil dew. Cp. Tennyson, *In Memoriam*, xvii.:

> "And balmy drops in summer dark
> Slide from the bosom of the stars."

So Shelley, *Adonais*, l. 91, "starry dew." See also XXIV. 6 and CXXII. 40.

8. **orison,** prayer, from Lat. *orare*, 'to pray,' through O.F.

9. Suggested by a passage in Montaigne : "There are countries where they believe that the souls of the blest live in all manner of liberty in delightful fields; and that what we call Echo is those souls repeating the words we utter" (Moore's note).

No. XXXIX. *And thou art dead, as young and fair*

"A MASTERLY example of Byron's command of strong thought and close reasoning in verse:—as the next is equally characteristic of Shelley's wayward intensity." (F.T.P.)

The absolute simplicity of the language and the large proportion of monosyllables are remarkable, as is also the solemn elegiac cadence of the verse, suited to the expression of a grief that does not rebel, but sadly accepts the ruling of destiny.

18. That what I loved is now nothingness.

30. lours, frowns. Cp. 'lowering,' A.V. of Matthew xvi. 3.

60. a faint embrace. Cp. *Soph. Ant.* 1236, ἐς δ' ὑγρὸν ἀγκῶν' ἔτ' ἔμφρων παρθένῳ προσπτύσσεται, "and still breathing clasps the maiden in a faint embrace."

71. endears, properly transitive, 'makes dear to me,' and so it may be here, governing 'more': but it may possibly be intransitive, 'is more dear to me.'

No. XL. *One word is too often profaned*

WRITTEN to Jane Williams, to whom also were dedicated two other poems in this collection, XCIII. (*With a guitar*) and CI. (*The Recollection*).

Metre.—There are three accents in the first line of each couplet, two in the second. The feet are anapaests and iambi subtly mingled.

1. One word, love. One feeling, worship. One hope, the desire of the moth for the star (l. 13).

8. that must mean "love." Shelley's wish to keep this word back till the second stanza has led him into some obscurity of expression.

No. XLI. *Pibroch of Donuil Dhu*

"THIS is a very ancient pibroch belonging to Clan Macdonald, and supposed to refer to the expedition of Donald Balloch, who, in 1431, launched from the Isles with a considerable force, invaded Lochaber, and at Inverlochy defeated and put to flight the Earls of Mar and Caithness, though at the head of an army superior to his own. The words of the set theme or melody, to which the pipe variations are applied, run thus in Gaelic:—

"*Piobaireachd Dhonuil Dhuidh, piobaireachd Dhonuil* (ter); *Piob agus bratach air faiche Inverlochi.*"

"The pipe-summons of Donald the Black, the pipe summons of Donald;

The war-pipe and the pennon are on the gathering-place at Inverlochy" (Scott's note).

There is a magnificent description of such a summons and of the gathering of the clans in *The Lady of the Lake*, Canto iii.

Metre.—First line two dactyls; second line dactyl and trochee. In the second stanza the metre disregards the division between the lines, as in the third stanza of XXIX.: the effect is the same—an irresistible swiftness. In the first and third lines of the third stanza anapaests are substituted for dactyls: the change produces a slower movement appropriate to the stern solemnity of the lines.

1. **Pibroch**, from Gaelic *piobaireachd*, 'pipe-music,' a wild piece of martial music for performance on the bagpipes.

8. **Gentles**, men of 'gentle' or noble birth.

11. **War-pipe**, the bag-pipe, the national Scotch instrument for martial music.

pennon, same word as 'pennant' (see note on LVIII. 3), a pointed flag formerly borne at the end of a spear or lance; or, in wider sense, used simply for 'flag.'

12. **Inverlochy**, near Fort William, Inverness. Montrose defeated Argyll here in 1645.

13. **plaid** (Gaelic word), a rectangular piece of woollen cloth worn as a garment by the Scotch Highlanders. The plaid was woven with the 'Tartan' or arrangement of colours indicating the clan.

24. **targes**, shields, from Lat. *tergum*, through French. 'Target' is the same word.

40. **knell**, sound as a bell, toll. The verb is older than the substantive.

No. XLII. *A wet sheet and a flowing sea*

ALLAN CUNNINGHAM (1784-1842) began life as a stonemason's apprentice, and afterwards became clerk of the works to Chantrey, the sculptor. His writings in prose and verse are not, as a rule, of a very high order; but this sea-song holds a permanent place in English literature.

1. **sheet**, a rope by which a sail is handled. The original sense is 'projection' or that which *shoots* out, then a corner, especially of a garment or of a cloth; after which it was extended to mean a whole cloth or sheet. The nautical senses are found in the cognate Scandinavian words (*Skeat*). *Flowing*, advancing, rising. This sense is chiefly common in the phrase 'ebb and flow.'

2. **follows**. A following wind is obviously a favourable one. Compare the Latin *secundus*, 'favourable,' derived from *sequor*, 'to follow.' Virgil combines the original and derivative senses in *Aeneid* I. 156: *Flectit equos curruque volans dat lora secundo.*

8. **lee**, on the sheltered side, away from the wind; Scandinavian word.

11. **snoring.** So the breeze is sometimes said to 'mutter' or 'growl.'

14. **tight,** water-tight; but it also expresses trimness, completeness.

17. **hornéd,** crescent-shaped.

No. XLIII. *Ye Mariners of England*

THIS stirring sea-song was written by Campbell to the tune of an older song, 'Ye Gentlemen of England,' composed by Martin Parker, 1630.

Metre.—Observe the rapidity given by the double rhyme in the seventh line of each stanza. Compare the similar effect in lines 31, 45, 55, of *Lord Ullin's Daughter* (XVIII.).

15. **Blake,** Robert (1599-1657). The great English Admiral who won several victories over the Dutch and afterwards over the Spaniards in the time of the Commonwealth.

Nelson, Horatio. Lord Nelson, the greatest of all English Admirals, born 1758, killed at the battle of Trafalgar Bay, in which he defeated the French and Spanish fleets, October 21, 1805.

21. **bulwarks,** originally the bole or trunk of a tree, then a rampart or fortification made of the trunks of trees. The Paris *boulevards* are broad streets occupying the site of ancient ramparts. The word is specially used (as in XLIV. 11) of the railboards or defences of a ship.

22. **steep,** adj. for subst., the cliffs. Cp. Milton, *Hymn on Nativity*, "The steep of Delphos"—a phrase afterwards used by Gray.

25. **native oak,** the 'wooden walls of old England,' the wooden ships, superseded by ironclads, which in turn have been replaced by vessels built of steel.

31. **meteor,** metaphor for simile: 'the flag of England shall still strike terror into her enemies like a terrible meteor, a sign of evil omen, burning in the midnight sky.'

No. XLIV. *Of Nelson and the North*

ONE of the noblest patriotic songs in the language, full of martial ardour, yet inspired with a magnanimity that is conspicuously absent from many popular war-poems. The metre is magnificently handled, and the solitary blemish in the poem is the introduction of the mermaid.

The battle of the Baltic was fought off Copenhagen on April 2nd, 1801. "It resulted in the breaking up of the northern coalition against England, which had been one of Napoleon's most cherished schemes. After safely passing Cronenberg Castle, Nelson persuaded Parker to commence the attack without delay. Two days were spent by Nelson in sounding the King's Channel, which lies between Copenhagen and a large shoal, and is only three-quarters of a mile broad. Along the land side of this channel the Danes had ranged nineteen ships and floating batteries. Everything being in readiness, Nelson made the signal for action early in the morning of the 2nd. The action began at ten o'clock. Riou, with the frigates, at once attacked the Crown Batteries, and maintained the unequal contest for three hours, until he was killed. The battle raged for three hours without any apparent advantage being gained, and Sir Hyde Parker made the signal for recall. Nelson, affecting not to see it, continued the action, and about two o'clock the greater part of the Danish fire ceased. It was impossible, however, to take possession of the ships that struck, because they were protected by the batteries on shore. Nelson, wishing to save further bloodshed, sent ashore a flag of truce, saying that he must be allowed to take possession of the prizes, if only for the sake of the wounded men on board of them ; and during the next day, Good Friday, the work still went on. The following days were spent by Nelson in maturing the negotiations, and on the 9th he succeeded in concluding an armistice for fourteen weeks, his object being to gain time to attack the Russians. The opportune death of the Czar Paul rendered any active hostility with that country unnecessary, and the armistice resulted in a treaty between England and the Northern Powers." —*Dictionary of English History*, Low and Pulling.

Metre.—The feet are iambi varied with anapaests. The fifth line of the stanza presents some difficulty. Probably it is meant to consist of four feet, the last being an anapaest. But though there are always four emphatic syllables in each line, they do not always coincide with the verse accent, or respect the division into feet ; *e.g.* the emphasis in lines 5, 32 requires us to read

Ǎnd hěr ǎr͞ms | ǎlong | thě dē͞e'p | pro͝o'udlў shon'e.
Théir sho͝o'ts | ǎlong | thě dē͞e'p | slo͝o'wlў boo'm.

The fine metrical effect obtained is ample justification for the irregularity : the poet's instinct in a case like this is absolutely sound, more to be trusted than rules. For a similar irregularity compare Wordsworth in XIX. 6.

8. **Prince.** The Crown Prince of Denmark.

10. **leviathans,** identified in most translations of the Bible with the whale, and so by Milton, *Paradise Lost,* I. 201, "That sea-beast Leviathan, which God of all his works Created hugest that swim the ocean-stream." The Hebrew word was used of any huge monster.

11. **bulwarks :** see note on XLIII. 21.

14. Mr. Aubrey de Vere first pointed out to me in a letter the effect of the touch of exactness in this line, "giving the hour as it was doubtless given by Nelson himself in his despatch." It increases the impressiveness of the narrative by making it seem more real to us.

21. the fleeter, so much the more quickly.

24. adamantine, iron. The rarer word, from the Greek, properly meaning 'not to be subdued or broken,' conveys an idea of implacable, resistless fate, that would not have been given by the simpler epithet.

26. hurricane eclipse, like the sudden blotting out of the sun by a wild storm of wind. Prof. Herford has remarked the presence of Hebraic imagination in this and other lines of Campbell.

29. havoc, destruction, perhaps originally a hunting term.

30. a feeble cheer, governed by 'sent back.'

37. Nelson wrote a letter addressed "To the brothers of Englishmen, the Danes," and sent it under a flag of truce to the Crown Prince. "Lord Nelson has directions to spare Denmark when no longer resisting; but if the firing is continued on the part of Denmark, Lord Nelson will be obliged to set on fire all the floating batteries he has taken, without having the power of saving the brave Danes who have defended them." See account of battle in Mahan's *Influence of Sea-Power upon the French Revolution and Empire*, vol. II., ch. xiii.

53. funeral, here an adjective, not quite the same as 'funereal,' which means simply 'deathlike,' 'mournful': 'fires of funeral light' means 'fires that lit up death.' Cp. 'fires of death,' LII. 7.

57. blaze, *i.e.* of illuminations.

58. in light, in brilliantly lighted banqueting-halls.

63. Elsinore, a sea-port on the sound of Denmark (Danish name, Helsingör) opposite the Swedish town of Helsingborg. It is the scene of *Hamlet.* Campbell shows a poet's instinct in his choice of the lofty-sounding name.

66. Cp. Thucydides II. 42, funeral speech of Pericles, δἰ ἐλαχίστου καιροῦ τύχης ἅμα ἀκμῇ τῆς δόξης μᾶλλον ἢ τοῦ δέους ἀπηλλάγησαν, "In an instant, at the height of their fortune, they passed away from the scene, not of their terror, but of their glory."

67. Riou, commander of the *Amazon* frigate in the battle. "During the night of April 1 Riou was in almost constant attendance on Nelson; and in the last instructions prior to the battle of Copenhagen the frigates and small craft were placed under his orders 'to perform such service as he is directed by

Lord Nelson'" (*Dict. of Nat. Biog.*). He was killed by a cannon-shot in the battle, and Nelson in his despatch wrote that the country had sustained an irreparable loss.

70. The mermaid brings a note of artificiality and unreality into a poem that is otherwise full of reality. Campbell might have defended himself by pleading the example of Milton, who introduced a dolphin into *Lycidas* (*G. T.* LXXXIX. 164), but the dolphin, though its appropriateness is open to dispute, has a justification that is lacking to the mermaid here: the mermaid is a solitary figure, the dolphin in *Lycidas* has a good deal of mythological company. For a similar reason the sea-nymphs of *The Tempest* (*G. T.* LXV.) do not make a valid precedent.

No. XLV.   *Stern Daughter of the Voice of God*

THOSE who appreciate the greatness of this poem will be in a position to give the right answer to the old question 'whether didactic poetry is a mistake.' Moral teaching does not become poetry by being cut up into lengths and furnished with rhymes, but it may be made poetry if it is infused with passion and imagination. The *Ode to Duty* is a great poem, not primarily because of the soundness of its philosophy, but because the poet has given to the abstract conception of Duty 'the consecration and the poet's dream,' and out of an abstraction has created 'a form more real than living man, Nursling of immortality.' But a poem artistically great might still—like some of Shelley's—be morally unsound: it is the soundness of its philosophy that makes the value of the *Ode to Duty* for mankind.

The following extracts are from Mr. Aubrey de Vere's comments on the poem (*Essays chiefly on Poetry*, vol. I. pp. 179-183): "It affirms that between the lower and higher sections of man's nature there commonly exists an antagonism, and that the condition of man's life is a militant condition. A few happier spirits may stand outside the battle, and, led on by an inner law of unconscious goodness, may, at least for an indefinite period, advance along a flower-strewn path of virtue: but even these are insecure; the path of virtue is, for the most part, a rough and thorny path, and the children of men can only find peace while they tread it in obedience to a Law challenging them from above. To find true freedom they must subject themselves to a noble bondage. ...

"The chief excellence of this poem, in its moral bearings, consists in the absolute spontaneousness of its 'good confession' that Duty is the one thing that gives dignity to life. The poet does not speak of the excesses into which human nature falls when apart from such a guide, but of 'omissions':

'I deferred
The task imposed, from day to day.'

It is in the 'quietness of Thought' that he repudiates the 'unchartered freedom' which tires, and demands instead the liberating yoke of that subjection which is at once 'victory and law.' He looks around him, and from every side the same lesson is borne in upon him. It is because they obey law that the flowers return in their seasons and the stars revolve in their courses; the law of Nature is to inanimate things what Duty is to man. The peasant who had only half learned his lesson in science might imagine that the law of gravitation was but a burden that binds man to earth. The philosopher knows that amid the boundless fields of the creation it is that which gives to everything its proper place, its motion, and its rest."

With this ode should be compared a later poem of Wordsworth's, the *Happy Warrior*. In its account of the man

" Who, doomed to go in company with Pain,
  And Fear, and Bloodshed, miserable train !
  Turns his necessity to glorious gain "

it "illustrates by an example the principle which the earlier poem affirms."

There are several variations of reading in different editions of the Ode. The most important variants are:

15, 16. " May joy be theirs while life shall last !
              And Thou, if they should totter, teach them
                  to stand fast."

24. " Yet find that other strength according to their need."

31. " The task imposed from day to day."

1. **Daughter of the Voice.** This is a Hebrew expression, 'Bath-col,' according to De Quincey, *Autobiography*, vol. I., p. 123, 1896 edition. "The daughter of a voice meant an echo, the original sound being viewed as the mother, and the reverberation, or secondary sound, as the daughter" (De Quincey's note).

37. **uncharter'd,** I am weary of a freedom that is not, like the freedom of a true citizen, regulated by a Charter which defines his rights and privileges.

39. **change their name,** be fixed on different objects.

45. **flowers laugh.** Cp. the famous attribution of laughter, ἀνήριθμον γέλασμα, to the sea by Aeschylus; also XCIV. 14, "Outdid the sparkling waves in play"; and *Isaiah*, LV. 12, "The trees of the field shall clap their hands." Shelley imitated Wordsworth's expression in *Adonais*, l. 441, "A light of laughing flowers along the grass is spread."

48. Cp. the description in Soph. *O. T.* 863 *seq.*, of the νόμοι ὑψίποδες, οὐρανίαν δι' αἰθέρα τεκνωθέντες, ὧν Ὄλυμπος πατὴρ μόνος, "laws established on high, whose birth-place is the heaven above, whose sire is Olympus alone."

53. **lowly wise.** The phrase comes from Milton, *Paradise Lost*, VIII. 173, "Be lowly wise." *Lowly* is an adverb as in *All's Well that Ends Well*, II. ii., "I will show myself highly fed and lowly taught."

55. **confidence of reason**, confidence that rests on reason and has therefore a sound basis.

56. **light of truth**, as opposed to superstitious fear.

No. XLVI. *Eternal Spirit of the chainless Mind*

"BONNIVARD, a Genevese, was imprisoned by the Duke of Savoy in Chillon on the lake of Geneva for his courageous defence of his country against the tyranny with which Piedmont threatened it during the first half of the seventeenth century. This noble sonnet is worthy to stand near Milton's on the Vaudois massacre." (F.T.P.) Wordsworth's Sonnet to Toussaint l'Ouverture, with its magnificent ending

> "Thou hast great allies ;
> Thy friends are exaltations, agonies,
> And love, and man's unconquerable mind,"

should also be remembered in this connection.

Byron's well-known poem, the *Prisoner of Chillon*, was written before he heard the story of Bonnivard. It was suggested by his first sight of the prison, and the story is his own invention.

1. The line is suggested by Pope's "Eternal sunshine of the spotless mind," *Eloisa to Abelard*, l. 209.

No. XLVII. *Two voices are there ; one is of the sea*

SWITZERLAND was usurped by the French under Napoleon in 1800.

The next five poems (XLVII.—LI.) are perhaps the finest of Wordsworth's splendid series of political sonnets—patriotic in the best sense ; the work of one whose very love of his country makes him deeply sensitive to her fame and afraid lest his own generation should do anything to diminish the glory of their noble heritage.

No. XLVIII. *Once did she hold the gorgeous East in fee*

THE republic of Venice, so powerful in the Middle Ages, had long become "the shade of that which once was great," when it was finally crushed by Napoleon in 1797, and handed over by him the same year after the treaty of Campo Formio to Austria.

1. **in fee** (A.S. *feoh* ; connected with 'fief' and 'feudal'), as a fee or fief, an estate held from a superior under certain conditions, especially on condition of military service.

7. Compare cxiv. 76-86. "The going out of the Doge from the Lido to wed the sea," afterwards called the Sposalizio del Mare, was a festival instituted to commemorate the victory of the Doge Orseolo over the Dalmatians in 998. Under the dukedom of Ziani and the patronage of Pope Alexander III., in 1178, the ceremonial became more elaborate. It was performed annually on the Feast of the Ascension, and not only encouraged the Venetians to hope for success in every maritime enterprise, but, under the Pope's sanction, it had the effect of proclaiming to Europe the supremacy of Venice over the Adriatic. For an account of the ceremony, see any history of Venice.

No. XLIX. *O friend ! I know not which way I must look*

"WHILE leading men to pierce below the artificial and conventional to the natural man and natural life, as Rousseau did, Wordsworth still cherished the symbols, the traditions, and the great institutes of social order. Simplification of life and thought and feeling was to be accomplished without summoning up the dangerous spirit of destruction and revolt. Wordsworth lived with nature, yet waged no angry railing war against society. . . . Communion with nature is, in Wordsworth's doctrine, the school of duty."—Mr. John Morley in his Introduction to Wordsworth's *Poetical Works*.

10. This is idolatry, *i.e.* to be guilty of these is to be guilty of worshipping the idol of wealth. Cp. *Colossians*, III. 5, "covetousness, which is idolatry."

12. the good old cause, devotion to country combined with simplicity in the home. The thought is like Horace's *Privatus illis census erat brevis, commune magnum.*

13. fearful, afraid to do wrong.

No. L. *Milton ! thou should'st be living at this hour*

"IT is interesting to know that it was with Milton before him as a model that Wordsworth first experimented in sonnet-writing; for undoubtedly there passed from the elder poet to the younger something more than the mere rhythm and cadence of his lines; there passed also the heroic style, and what underlies heroic style—dignity of thought, passion of conviction, self-restraint."—*Quarterly Review*, Oct., 1900.

3. altar, sword, and pen. A definite reference to classes—the clergy, the soldier, the student.

4. fireside, domestic life (cp. 'household laws' in the last sonnet). **hall and bower,** knights and ladies.

8. **manners, character,** Lat. *mores,* as in William of Wykeham's motto, 'Manners makyth man.'

11. **naked,** *i.e.* cloudless. So 'bare' in LXXX. 28, 'When night is bare,' and in CXXXI. 13, 'When the heavens are bare.'

14. **lowliest duties.** So in *Ode to Duty,* XLV. 53, 'lowly wise.

No. LII.   *On Linden, when the sun was low*

THE first of a group of four poems dealing with war. *Hohenlinden* and *After Blenheim* show the terrible side of battle, the waste of life, the wanton misery of warfare. The two poems that come after these reveal another aspect : *Dulce et decorum est pro patria mori.*

Hohenlinden, though it is said to have been originally rejected by a Scotch newspaper as 'not up to the editor's standard,' has enjoyed a thoroughly deserved popularity from the time of its first publication. Sir W. Scott was fond of quoting it. He declaimed it to Leyden (Lockhart's *Life of Scott,* vol. VI. p. 326) who remarked, "Dash it, man, tell the fellow that I hate him, but, dash him, he has written the finest verses that have been published these fifty years." Campbell's reply, when Scott reported this, was, "Tell Leyden that I detest him, but I know the value of his critical approbation."

1. **Linden,** Hohen Linden, 'High Lime-trees,' a village in Upper Saxony. Here Napoleon's general, Moreau, defeated the Austrians under Archduke John on December 3rd, 1800. Moreau's army was posted on the plateau between the Iser and the Inn, the Austrian army on the right bank of the Inn. The Austrians advanced amidst drifting snow, and attacked with great fury ; but the French received considerable reinforcements under Ney, and the Austrians were totally routed. The latter lost 8000 killed and wounded, and 11,000 prisoners ; the French loss was 5000 killed and wounded.

7. **fires of death.** Cp. XLIV. 53, 'fires of funeral light.'

13. **riven,** split, cloven (Danish word).

22. **war-clouds,** clouds of smoke. **dun,** dusky, gloomy.

23. **Frank,** the French. France received its name from the Franks, one of the tribes of a Germanic confederation formed in the third century A.D. **Hun,** here used to describe the Austrians, inhabitants of Austro-Hungary.

24. **canopy,** covering (from the Greek, through mediaeval Latin and French).

27. **Munich,** capital of Bavaria.

No. LIII. *It was a summer evening*

ROBERT SOUTHEY (1774-1843), the friend of Coleridge and Wordsworth, had a distinguished literary career, and attained the Poet Laureateship. His lives of Nelson and John Wesley rank as classics. It is not likely that his longer poems will find many admirers again, but this poem, together with *The Scholar* (LXIV.) and *The Holly Tree*, holds a secure place.

Blenheim is a village in Austria, on the northern bank of the Danube. The great battle was fought on August 13, 1704, during the third campaign of the War of the Spanish Succession. Marshals Tallard and Marsin were in command of the forces of Louis XIV. The Duke of Marlborough and Prince Eugene commanded the allies. Their victory frustrated the plans of Louis, who had hoped to strike at the heart of the Austrian power by menacing Vienna.

28. **wonder-waiting**, expecting to hear some marvel, a happily-invented compound.

38. **yon little stream**, the Nebel, a small tributary of the Danube.

44. **childing**, a woman with child. The verb 'to child' is found in old English, and Shakespeare speaks of 'the childing Autumn' for 'the fruitful Autumn.'

55. "Marlborough, seeing the weakness of the French centre, threw his cavalry across the Nebel, and after a terrific struggle cut the French line in two. Meanwhile, on the right, Eugene only saved the battle by the steadiness of his Prussian infantry…. The allies are computed to have lost 11,000 men out of an army of 52,000; the French altogether 40,000 out of 60,000, including 14,000 prisoners" (*Dictionary of Eng. History*).

No. LIV. *When he who adores thee has left but the name*

THE lines commemorate the fate of Robert Emmett, one of the most disinterested leaders in the sad Irish insurrection of 1803.

Metre.—Four accents in the first, three in the second line of each couplet. The feet are indifferently anapaests and iambi.

1. **thee**, addressed to Ireland.

10. **of my reason**, of mature years, when man is supposed to be guided by reason.

No LV. *Not a drum was heard, not a funeral note*

CHARLES WOLFE (1791-1823), an Irish clergyman, who died of consumption in his thirty-first year. His famous poem first appeared in an Irish newspaper, and various pretenders laid claim to the distinction of its authorship.

The battle of Corunna (January 16, 1809), between the English and French, was fought during the Peninsular War at the close of Sir John Moore's retreat from Madrid pursued by Soult. Moore defeated the French, and carried out the embarkation of his troops with but little loss, but was himself killed in the battle. The story should be read in Napier's *Peninsular War*. The poem is one that goes straight to the heart, even of those who care little for poetry in general. It expresses with perfect sincerity and directness a pathos that all can feel. Without any seeking after picturesque phrases, or straining after rhetorical effect, it sets the scene before us with wonderful vividness—the hurried march, the hasty digging of the grave, the dim light of moon and lantern, the simple nobility of the dead, the anguish of the last farewell. Like Wordsworth's elegy (XVI.) it is a model of grief ennobled by manly reticence.

Metre.—As in the preceding poem, except for the extra short syllable which gives a trochaic ending to the second line of each couplet. Occasionally a single long syllable is substituted for the first foot: this gives a dactylic effect, *e.g.* it would be possible to scan l. 21, Líghtly they'll | tálk of the | spírit that's | góne, but the metrical structure of the rest of the poem shows that the true scansion is, Líght | ly they'll tálk | of the spír | it that's góne.

10. wound. Cp. LII. 30.

30. field of his fame. See note on XLIV. 66. Cp. XLIII. 13.

No. LVI. *In the sweet shire of Cardigan*

A SERIES of poems now follow (LVI.-LXII) dealing with the pathos of old age, the contrast with youth and strength, the sweetness and sadness of memory.

This poem, composed in 1798, was written in strict adherence to Wordsworth's theory that there ought to be no difference between the diction of poetry and of prose, that the language used in a poem of humble life ought to be just such language as the persons represented would naturally use, and that the nobility of a poem ought to be due entirely to the thought without aid from the words. As we shall see (LXXVIII.) Wordsworth's greatest poetical triumphs are won when the true instinct of a poet leads him to abandon his theory. That theory, if it needs any refutation, is amply refuted in the *Biographia Literaria* of Coleridge, who shows exactly where the truth lies between the opposite doctrines of Wordsworth and the eighteenth century poets. *Simon Lee* has undoubtedly suffered from the theory. The defence we made of *Lucy Gray* (XIX.) will not hold here: that poem, though simplicity itself, was never commonplace. *Simon Lee* is open to this charge, and to the

charge of diffuseness and of a carelessness that even suffers such
a rhyme as 'woman' and 'common.' In palliation of these
faults we may say that the poem is modelled on the old ballads,
which freely admit such blemishes. That it has fine qualities
which far outweigh its faults scarcely needs to be said. Much
will be forgiven for the sake of the description of the hunt,
the pathetic picture of the strong man brought low, and the
exquisite beauty of the last four lines. Whatever diffuseness
there may have been before, there is none at the close, which
offers a splendid example of Wordsworth's self-restraint and concentrated thought—the quality so conspicuous in XIII.

In a note prefixed to the poem many years afterwards, Wordsworth tells us that the incident was a fact, and that the expression about the hounds, "I dearly love their voice," was word for
word from the old man's own lips.

1. **Cardigan**, one of the western counties of Wales. But from
Wordsworth's note, above referred to, we learn that the huntsman really lived in Somerset, on the Quantocks (CXIII. 246), 'a
little way from the entrance to Alfoxden Park.' Alfoxden was
Wordsworth's home in 1797-8, Coleridge being at that time
settled at Nether Stowey, a few miles away.

Prof. Herford (*Age of Wordsworth*, p. 188) happily contrasts
the indifference to precise locality which Wordsworth shows here
and in *Lucy Gray* (XIX.) with Scott's use of "the subtle aroma of
place-names." "To Scott the actual scenery of a story was part
of its life-blood; it died if transplanted."

20. **stone-blind**, blind as a stone, completely blind through
exhaustion. Spenser uses the expression 'stone-dead.' 'Sand-
blind' is used for 'half-blind' in *Merchant of Venice*, Act II. Sc. ii.

23. **chiming**, sounding in harmony, properly used of the
musical harmony produced from a set of bells tuned to a
musical scale and struck by hammers.

No. LVII. *I have had playmates, I have had companions*

CHARLES LAMB (1775-1835), the friend of Coleridge from boyhood, the author of *Essays of Elia*, and the joint author with his
sister of *Tales from Shakespeare*, the best loved of English
humourists and letter-writers, composed little poetry; but the
three poems inserted in this collection (LVII., LXIX., LXXV.) are all
of remarkable beauty.

The Old Familiar Faces seems to be a genuine bit of auto-
biography. It was written in 1798. The 'friend of my bosom'
was Coleridge; the friend whom Lamb had left 'like an ingrate,'
Charles Lloyd. See J. D. Campbell's Biographical Introduction
to *Coleridge's Poetical Works*, p. xliii.

Metre.—So perfect is the music of this exquisite poem that few readers, in all probability, observe any metrical irregularity in it. Yet it would be difficult or impossible to reduce it to any rule. Like most of the verse of a later poet, Walt Whitman, it seems obedient only to an inner law, the sound everywhere responding to the feeling with no aid or constraint from metrical rules. It is so far more regular than Walt Whitman's poems that the lines are of fairly equal length, that there is a caesura or 'break' in each line, and that the movement is on the whole dactylic.

5. **cronies,** intimate companions ; derived from 'crone,' an old woman, especially a witch who chants or 'croons' incantations.

11. **ingrate,** adj. and subst., ungrateful, from Lat. *ingratus* through Fr. *ingrat.*

No. LVIII.   *As slow our ship her foamy track*

THIS is one of Moore's *Irish Melodies* : LXII., on the same theme, is from his collection of *National Airs.*

3. **pennant.** Here a long narrow flag pointed at the end, and hung at the mast-head or yard-arm-ends in ships of war. See note on XLI. 11.

No. LIX.   *There's not a joy the world can give like that it takes away*

Metre.—Each iambic line of seven feet is practically divided into two lines by the caesura at the end of the fourth foot. The iambi are varied by anapaests. The poem is full of simple and obvious, but very gracefully managed, metaphors. In spite of their rapid succession, no sense of incongruity is aroused.

No. LX.   *There is a Flower, the lesser Celandine*

WRITTEN in 1804. Wordsworth had already, in 1802, dedicated two longer but less perfect poems to the same flower. In the note prefixed to the earlier verses, he writes : "It is remarkable that this flower, coming out so early in the spring as it does, and so bright and beautiful, and in such profusion, should not have been noticed earlier in English verse. What adds much to the interest that attends it is its habit of shutting itself up and opening out according to the degree of light and temperature of the air."

2. Cp. in the second of the two earlier poems:

> "Blithe of heart, from week to week
>   Thou dost play at hide-and-seek;
>   While the patient primrose sits
>   Like a beggar in the cold,
>   Thou, a flower of wiser wits,
>   Slipp'st into thy sheltering hold;
>   Liveliest of the vernal train
>   When ye all are out again."

20. spleen, ill-humour, vexation, from a Greek word denoting that part of the stomach which was supposed to be the seat of anger: cp. the use of 'bile,' 'melancholy.'

21-4. The last stanza is somewhat obscure. The young man is the favourite of the prodigal, Youth; the old man is the pensioner of the miser, Age. We waste the many gifts of Youth, and have afterwards to be content with scanty gifts from Old Age. In the case of the flower Youth and Age are again prodigal and pensioner. In the first 1802 poem the celandine is described as "Spreading out thy glossy breast Like a careless Prodigal; Telling tales about the sun When we've little warmth, or none."

No. LXI. *I remember, I remember*

THOMAS HOOD (1798-1845), journalist and writer of humorous sketches in prose and verse, wrote also several poems that have earned, by their truth and pathos, a place beside the work of far greater poets. His best-remembered pieces are this and *The Bridge of Sighs* (LXVII.), *The Song of the Shirt* and *Eugene Aram.*

Metre.—A beautiful variation of a very simple metre—the couplet of four iambic feet followed by three. In the first line of each stanza four trochees are substituted. The effect is a peculiarly haunting wistfulness.

16. A good example of that poetic self-restraint, implying so much more than it actually expresses, referred to in the notes on XIII. and LVI.

No. LXII. *Oft in the stilly night*

Metre.—Though it may seem involved at a first glance, the metre is really very simple. Each stanza of 14 lines really contains two four-line stanzas with a stanza of 6 short lines interposed.

1. stilly, a variation of 'still' found in other poets also, but too obviously existing *metri gratia* to be altogether acceptable. A coinage like 'sleety' (XXVIII. 6) has a justification that 'stilly' cannot plead.

2. **slumber's chain.** The metaphor occurs as early as Sophocles, *Ajax*, 675, ὁ παγκρατὴς ὕπνος | λύει πεδήσας οὐδ᾽ ἀεὶ λαβὼν ἔχει, "All-powerful sleep releases those whom he has fettered and keeps not his captives for ever."

21. We may recall the picture of Dido in the 'banquet-hall deserted,' dreaming of Aeneas: *absens absentem auditque videtque* (*Aeneid* iv. 83).

No. LXIII.   *The sun is warm, the sky is clear*

A LANDSCAPE very characteristic of Shelley. The whole scene, as in some of Turner's paintings, appears bathed in iridescent light. Compare other landscapes by the same poet in C., CI., CXIV.

The poem was written in December, 1818. The following extract from a letter to Thomas Love Peacock, dated Naples, December 22, 1818, may describe the day and the scene: "We set off an hour after sunrise one radiant morning in a little boat; there was not a cloud in the sky, nor a wave upon the sea, which was so translucent that you could see the hollow caverns clothed with the glaucous sea-moss, and the leaves and branches of those delicate weeds that pave the unequal bottom of the water. As we approached, the heat, and especially the light, became intense. We then coasted the bay of Baiae to the left, in which we saw many picturesque and interesting ruins; but I have to remark that we never disembarked but we were disappointed—while from the boat the effect of the scenery was inexpressibly delightful. The colours of the water and the air breathe over all things here the radiance of their own beauty."

Metre.—A variation of the Spenserian stanza, the only difference being that the first eight lines have four iambic feet instead of five. The ninth line, as in Spenser, is an Alexandrine (six feet). The scheme of rhymes is *a b a b b c b c c.*

5. This line was omitted in the *Posthumous Poems*, in which, and in Mrs. Shelley's subsequent editions, the line before ends with *light*, probably, as Mr. Forman says, through the transcriber or printer having run two lines into one.

9. For the simile, see note on VIII. 12.

10. **untrampled,** a poetical variation for 'untrodden.'

21. **content, surpassing wealth.** Compare Sir E. Dyer's poem, 'My mind to me a kingdom is,' especially the second stanza:

> "Content I live, this is my stay;
>   I seek no more than may suffice;
> I press to bear no haughty sway;
>   Look, what I lack my mind supplies.
> Lo! thus I triumph like a king,
> Content with that my mind doth bring."

22. the sage. The reference may be to the Stoic doctrine that 'the wise man alone is free, and not only free but even a king': cp. Diogenes Laertius, Bk. vii., Cicero *Pro Murena*, xxix. 61.

27. On a careless reading this line will seem unmetrical. Read carefully and slowly—as befits the solemn contrast with the preceding line—it is peculiarly impressive:

To mé | that cúp | has beén | déalt in | anóth|er meás|ure.

33. A remarkable anticipation (as J. A. Symonds points out in his *Life of Shelley*) of Shelley's own death by drowning. Cp. the last stanza of *Adonais*:

> " The breath whose might I have invoked in song
>   Descends on me; my spirit's bark is driven
>   Far from the shore, far from the trembling throng
>   Whose sails were never to the tempest given;
>   The massy earth and sphered skies are riven!
> I am borne darkly, fearfully afar;
>   Whilst, burning through the inmost veil of Heaven,
>   The soul of Adonais, like a star,
> Beacons from the abode where the Eternal are."

36. Acting on the principle announced in his preface, that it is right to make such an omission "when the piece could be thus brought to a closer lyrical unity," Mr. Palgrave has excised the fifth stanza to be found in all editions of Shelley. That stanza is in every way inferior to the rest, and the poem gains much by its exclusion. Excisions have also been made in two others of Shelley's poems, o. and cxiv.

LXIV. *My days among the Dead are past*

Perhaps the best commentary on this beautiful poem is supplied by the following extract from Macaulay:

" Just such is the feeling which a man of liberal education naturally entertains towards the great minds of former ages. The debt which he owes to them is incalculable. They have guided him to truth. They have filled his mind with noble and graceful images. They have stood by him in all vicissitudes, comforters in sorrow, nurses in sickness, companions in solitude. These friendships are exposed to no danger from the occurrences by which other attachments are weakened or dissolved. Time glides on; fortune is inconstant; tempers are soured; bonds which seemed indissoluble are daily sundered by interest, by emulation, or by caprice. But no such cause can affect the silent converse which we hold with the highest of human intellects. That placid intercourse is disturbed by no jealousies or resentments. These are the old friends who are never seen with new faces, who are the same in wealth and in poverty, in glory and

in obscurity. With the dead there is no rivalry. In the dead
there is no change. Plato is never sullen. Cervantes is never
petulant. Demosthenes never comes unseasonably. Dante never
stays too long. No difference of political opinion can alienate
Cicero. No heresy can excite the horror of Bossuet."

There is a fine passage in Bishop Hall to the like effect; given
in *Foliorum Centuriae*, No. 210.

LXV.   *Souls of Poets dead and gone*

Metre.—As in II.

2. Elysium. See note on II. 11.

4. Mermaid Tavern, "the club-house of Shakespeare, Ben
Jonson, and other choice spirits of that age" (F.T.P.).

6. Canary, wine from the Canary islands, off the N.W. coast
of Africa. This wine was very highly esteemed in Shakespeare's
time.

9. generous (from Lat. *generosus*, high-born, through Fr.),
when applied, as here, to wine or food, combines a variety of
notions—excellent, abundant, invigorating.

10. Robin Hood, the most famous of English outlaws and free-
booters. He is said to have lived from 1160 to 1247, and to have
been originally Earl of Huntingdon; but, having outrun his
fortune, he was outlawed, and thenceforward lived by plundering
rich men. Sherwood Forest was his favourite haunt. His company consisted of as many as a hundred archers, and his chief
companions were Little John, Friar Tuck, and Maid Marian.
He is the hero of some of the earliest English ballads and a
character in Scott's *Ivanhoe*.

12. bowse (Teutonic), also spelt 'bouse' and 'booze,' to drink
long and deeply.

17. sheepskin, parchment.

18. you, the dead poets.

22. Zodiac, an imaginary broad belt in the heavens, within
which the apparent motions of the sun, moon, and the planets
known to the ancients, are confined; divided into twelve parts
or 'signs,' named from the constellations or groups of stars
through which the sun appears successively to pass. One of
these signs, entered by the sun on Aug. 22, is *Virgo*, with which
perhaps Keats playfully identifies the Mermaid.

LXVI.   *Proud Maisie is in the wood*

"Scott has given us nothing more complete and lovely than this
little song, which unites simplicity and dramatic power to a wild-

wood music of the rarest quality. No moral is drawn, far less any conscious analysis of feeling attempted : the pathetic meaning is left to be suggested by the mere presentment of the situation. A narrow criticism has often named this, which may be called the Homeric manner, superficial, from its apparent facility ; but first-rate excellence in it is in truth one of the least common triumphs of Poetry. This style should be compared with what is not less perfect in its way, the searching out of inner feeling, the expression of hidden meanings, the revelation of the heart of Nature and of the Soul within the Soul—the analytical method, in short—most completely represented by Wordsworth and by Shelley." (F.T.P.)

This song is the last utterance of Madge Wildfire in the *Heart of Midlothian.*

Metre.—Two dactyls in each line, but the second dactyl of the second line is often shortened to a trochee, and a good deal of freedom is permitted in the way of extra short syllables, *e.g.* Prŏud Māisĭe 's | ĭn thĕ wŏod | Wālkĭng sŏ | eārly.

1. Maisie, Mary.

7. braw (Scottish), handsome, fine-looking.

LXVII. *One more Unfortunate*

Metre.—Dactylic. The metre, with its short lines and dactylic rhymes (of which there are very few in the English language) is a difficult one to handle with dignity. To have succeeded in a poem of such length, "fashioned so slenderly," is no small poetic triumph. Hood has made the very frailty and delicacy of his metre finely expressive of the frailty and delicacy of the life so sadly thrown away.

10. cerements, grave-clothes ; properly, a cloth dipped in melted wax (Lat. *cera*) or some gummy matter, in which dead bodies were formerly wrapped.

22. mutiny, rebellion against the laws of life. Socrates in the *Phaedo* speaks of suicide as a desertion of the post at which God has placed us, or a running away from prison.

78. lave, wash. The use is not quite the same as in XXIX. 12. In both cases the properly transitive verb is made intransitive by the omission of the object, but there the implied object is 'the shores,' here it is the reflexive pronoun.

86. decently, becomingly (Lat. *decet*).

96. contumely, four syllables : the accent is generally placed on the first, Hood seems to place it on the second. From Lat. *contumelia,* through French, insolence, contemptuous speech.

No. LXVIII.   *Oh snatched away in beauty's bloom*

13. **unteach.** Cp. Lat. *dedoceo*. For the prefix *un*, see note on IV. 53.

No. LXIX.   *When maidens such as Hester die*

COMPARE R. Browning's poem, *Evelyn Hope*.

11. **rate**, measure.

17. **Quaker rule**, the strict way of life followed by the Quakers, the name commonly given to members of the Society of Friends, a sect of English Protestants founded by George Fox, 1650.

21. **prying**, scrutinizing narrowly, enquiring into everything.

32. **fore-warning**, of the happiness of another life.

No. LXX.   *If I had thought thou couldst have died*

"WOLFE resembled Keats, not only in his early death by consumption and the fluent freshness of his poetical style, but in beauty of character:—brave, tender, energetic, unselfish, modest. Is it fanciful to find some reflex of these qualities in the *Burial* and *Mary*? Out of the abundance of the *heart* ... " (F.T.P.).

No. LXXI.   *He is gone on the mountain*

Coronach (Scottish), a dirge.

Metre.—Dactyl followed by trochee. An extra unaccented syllable—or even two syllables—is admitted at the beginning of the line. Once—in the last line but one—an extra syllable is admitted in the body of the line; the words should be hurried over proportionately: the intention is to express the swift bursting of the bubble. It should scarcely be necessary to point out that the metrical charm of a song largely depends on such variations, when they are introduced as skilfully as by Scott here and in XXIX. But so little was the experiment appreciated by contemporary critics that the *Quarterly Review* indulged in feeble pleasantries on Scott's failure to make the lines of this poem scan.

15. **in flushing**, full of vigour. The subst. is formed from the adj. 'flush,' meaning 'fresh,' abundant,' esp. used of a river whose waters are high, on a level with the banks.

17. **correi** or **corrie** (Scottish), a covert on a hillside.

18. **cumber**, trouble, perplexity. The verb is commoner in the sense of 'to obstruct,' as in " Why cumbereth it the ground ? ";

the adjectives 'cumbersome,' 'cumbrous,' are derivatives. Skeat says 'cumber' is corrupted from Lat. *cumulus*, a heap, by the change of *l* into *r*, and the insertion of *b*. Cp. Ger. *kummer*, trouble, rubbish.

No. LXXII. *We watch'd her breathing thro' the night*

7. as, as if. See note on xxx. 19.

8. eke (Teutonic; cp. Ger. *auch*), to add to, to protract, spin out.

No. LXXIII. *I saw her in childhood*

"THIS book has not a few poems of greater power and more perfect execution than *Agnes*, and the extract which we have ventured to make from the deep-hearted author's *Sad Thoughts* (XVII.). But none are more emphatically marked by the note of exquisiteness" (F.T.P.).

Metre.—Dactyl and trochee in the first line, dactyl and long syllable in the second line, of each couplet. An extra unaccented syllable at the beginning of each line. This extra syllable becomes two in lines 10, 26, and 32, to compensate for the docking of the trochee in the preceding line.

14. moonlight. So in XVII. 1, 'thy pensive, moonlight face.'

No. LXXIV. *O listen, listen, ladies gay*

ONE of the finest of Scott's ballads. It has not the simplicity and artlessness of the genuine old ballad; the effects are deliberately sought, the picturesque details painted in with great care; but the pictures are vivid, the rhythm is masterly, and there is something Homeric about the way in which the story is made, as in LXVI., to convey its own pathos without any words of comment.

The ballad divides itself into four parts: First, the minstrel's proem (ll. 1-4); second, the scene on the shore of the stormy firth—the struggle between Rosabelle's filial affection and the forebodings of her counsellors (ll. 5-24); third, the picture of the ominous light seen in Roslin Chapel (ll. 25-44); fourth, the sequel, connecting the two scenes described in the main part of the poem.

There are some interesting notes on *Rosabelle* in the "Suggestions on the Teaching of English" prefixed to Professor J. W. Hales' *Longer English Poems*.

Metre.—Observe the variations in the last stanza: the double rhyme in lines 49, 51 (as in *Lord Ullin's Daughter*, XVIII. 31, 45,

55); and the three accents instead of four in line 50. It would be possible to scan this line on the principle explained in the metrical note on CVIII., but it is probably a mere irregularity, such as is often found in the old ballads.

3. Cp. Campbell, *O'Connor's Child*:

> " Sad was the note, and wild its fall,
> As winds that moan at night forlorn,
> Along the isles of Fion-Gall,
> When, for O'Connor's child to mourn,
> The harper told ... "

7. Ravensheuch, the raven's crag. The word *heuch* or *heugh* is used by Burns.

8. firth or frith, a narrow inlet of the sea, esp. at the mouth of a river, *e.g.* the firth of Forth, the firth of Clyde. It is the same word as the Norwegian *fiord*, perhaps also as the Lat. *fretum*.

10. inch, Keltic word for 'island.'

11. Water-Sprite. See note on 'water-wraith," XVIII. 26.

13. gifted Seer, gifted with 'second sight,' the power to see the future. A belief in this power long prevailed in the Highlands of Scotland. It is often mentioned in Scott (*e.g.* in his *Legend of Montrose*), and is described in Dr. Johnson's *Journey to the Hebrides*.

18. Roslin, on the river North Esk, south of Edinburgh. There is a modern castle, but the ruin of the ancient one is still standing, as also Roslin Chapel, founded in 1445 or 1450 by Sir William St. Clair, baron of Roslin and earl of Orkney.

21. the ring. "A ring was suspended, not tightly fastened, but so that it could easily be detached, from a horizontal beam resting on two upright posts. The players rode at full speed through the archway thus made, and as they went under, passed their lance-points, or aimed at passing them, through the ring, and so bore it off. See Ellis's *Brand's Popular Antiquities*, re-edited by Hazlitt." (Prof. Hales.)

30. ruddied. 'Ruddy' is now only used as an adjective, and the verb was doubtless an archaism even in Scott. Cp. Spenser, *Faerie Queene*, II. i., " Her cheeks, like apples which the sun had rudded."

32. Hawthornden. Here lived, 1585-1649, the poet William Drummond.

35. sable shroud. Cp. Milton, *Lycidas*, 22, "And bid fair peace be to my sable shroud." In Elizabethan English 'shroud' is used for any covering or shelter, not being confined as now to the clothing of the dead. Cp. *Ode on Nativity*, l. 218.

36. panoply (Greek), full suit of armour.

38. sacristy, a room in a church where the sacred vessels and vestments are kept; from Low Latin, *sacristia*, derived from *sacer*, ' holy.'

pale, enclosure ; from Lat. *palus.*

39. pillar. The beauty of the ' Apprentice's Pillar ' in Roslin Chapel is famous.

41. pinnet, a variation of ' pinnacle,' a high turret.

44. high, high-born.

46. chapelle. The form is intended to have an antique sound, as ' ladye' in l. 6 to have an antique look.

50. candle, book, knell. For the connection of these three with the service for the dead, Prof. Hales quotes *Hamlet*, v i., the priest's words about Ophelia :

> " Her obsequies have been as far enlarged
> As we have warranty ...
> ... She is allowed her virgin crants,
> Her maiden strewments, and the bringing home
> Of bell and burial ...
> We should profane the service of the dead
> To sing a requiem and such rest to her
> As to peace-parted souls " ;

and Dunbar's *Will of Maister Andro' Kennedy* :

> " I will no priestis for to sing
>   Dies illa, dies irae,
> Nor yet no bellis for to ring
>   Sicut solet semper fieri ;
> But a bagpipe to play a spring
>   Et unum alewisp ante me,
> Instead of torches for to bring
>   Quatuor lagenas cervisiae "—

i.e. four flagons of beer.

51. sea-caves rung. Cp. the sea dirge in Shakespeare's *Tempest*, given in *G. T.* LXV. :

> " Sea-nymphs hourly ring his knell :
>   Hark ! now I hear them,—
>   Ding, dong, bell ! "

No. LXXV. *I saw where in the shroud did lurk*

In its rhythm and diction, and above all in its quaint conceits, this poem of Charles Lamb wonderfully recalls the work of seventeenth century poets. There is indeed in Mr. Beeching's *Lyra Sacra* an anonymous seventeenth century poem on the same theme of an infant's death—"He did but float a little way Adown the stream of time"—that, to one judging from internal evidence alone, would seem to have far less right to be attributed to that period.

12. **glasses of mortality**, the eye of a mortal, here compared to a window or pair of spectacles.

21. **Promethean.** Prometheus was fabled by the Greeks to have brought down fire from heaven as a gift to mortals. The legend of his punishment by Zeus for this offence forms the subject of the tragedy of *Prometheus Bound* by Aeschylus, and of Shelley's *Prometheus Unbound.* Cp. *Othello,* v. ii. 10:

> "But once put out thy light,
> Thou cunning'st pattern of excelling nature,
> I know not where is that Promethean heat
> That can thy light relume."

22. **moons**, months.

38. **economy**, from Gk. οἰκονομία, household management; applied also to the management of the affairs of a nation, as in 'political economy.' Here the meaning is : Heaven seems to be wasteful of human life; the seeming waste doubtless has its explanation, but we do not know what it is. Cp. Tennyson, *In Memoriam,* cantos liv.-lvi.

39. **clerks**, scholars, from Lat. *clericus.* The name reminds us that the clergy were at one time the only educated class of the community in Western Europe. When education spread to other classes, *clericus* was applied to every educated man, even though not a deacon or priest. Cp. the expression 'clerical error' for an unintentional slip in a written composition.

missed the mark, failed to explain satisfactorily.

41. **ephemeral**, from Gk. ἐφήμερος, lasting only for a day.

42. **Crones.** See note on LVII. 5.

No. LXXVI. *A child's a plaything for an hour*

"FROM *Poetry for Children* (1809), by Charles and Mary Lamb. This tender and original little piece seems clearly to reveal the work of that noble-minded and afflicted sister, who was at once the happiness, the misery and the life-long blessing of her equally noble-minded brother." (F.T.P.) In 1796 Mary Lamb "worn down to a state of extreme nervous misery by attention to needle-work by day and to her mother by night" went mad and stabbed her mother to death. She was placed in an asylum, and her reason gradually returned to her. But the malady recurred at intervals in after-life. She knew when an attack was approaching; and

Charles, "obtaining leave of absence from the East India office, *as if for a day's pleasure*, might be seen escorting his sister, both in tears, to the accustomed asylum in the neighbourhood of London."

No. LXXVII. *Where art thou, my beloved Son*

RUSKIN, *Modern Painters*, Vol. III., Pt. IV., ch. iii., uses this poem to illustrate the difference between 'historical or simply narrative art' and great imaginative art. The power of the poet is 'the power of assembling, by the help of the imagination, such images as will excite noble emotions.' In the strictest sense, the poet cannot create; he can only use the materials supplied to him by experience; his creative power, his imagination, shows itself in the selection and combination of such materials. By the side of Wordsworth's imaginative poem, Ruskin places Saussure's plain narrative of a parallel fact from real life :

"Nothing surprised me more than a woman of Argentière, whose cottage I went into to ask for milk, as I came down from the glacier of Argentière, in the month of March, 1764. An epidemic dysentery had prevailed in the village, and, a few months before, had taken away from her, her father, her husband, and her brothers, so that she was left alone, with three children in the cradle. Her face had something noble in it, and its expression bore the seal of a calm and profound sorrow. After having given me milk, she asked me whence I came, and what I came there to do, so early in the year. When she knew that I was of Geneva, she said to me, 'She could not believe that all Protestants were lost souls; that there were many honest people among us, and that God was too good and too great to condemn all without distinction.' Then, after a moment of reflection, she added, in shaking her head, 'But that which is very strange is that of so many who have gone away none have ever returned. I,' she added, with an expression of grief, 'who have so mourned my husband and my brothers, who have never ceased to think of them, who every night conjure them with beseechings to tell me where they are, and in what state they are! Ah, surely, if they lived anywhere, they would not leave me thus! But, perhaps,' she added, 'I am not worthy of this kindness, perhaps the pure and innocent spirits of these children,' and she looked at the cradle, 'may have their presence, and the joy which is denied me.'"—Saussure, *Voyages dans les Alpes*, chap. xxiv.

The Affliction of Margaret may be compared—as has already been done by Mr. Swinburne in *Essays and Studies*—with Tennyson's *Rizpah*, another poem of a mother's anguish.

20. as hath been said, as detractors alleged.

29. **Neglect me!** Was I indignant at the thought of his neglect?

50. The late Mr. F. Myers in his *Life of Wordsworth* (*English Men of Letters Series*) examines this stanza in connection with Wordsworth's theory that poetry ought to give "a selection of the language really spoken by men" with "metre superadded." Mr. Myers shows (p. 107) the complexity of the music on which this stanza depends for its power—the slow rhythm resulting from a large proportion of strong accents and long vowels, and the subtle alliterations of the letters *d, h, m, th* in the first four lines. He dwells, too, on the choice of words: *inheritest* and *summoned* are not words that "a poor widow, even at Penrith," would employ; "they are used to intensify the imagined relation which connects the missing man with (1) the wild beasts who surround him, and (2) the invisible Power which leads; so that something mysterious and awful is added to his fate. This impression is heightened by the use of the word *incommunicable* in an unusual sense, 'incapable of being communicated *with*' instead of 'incapable of being communicated'; while the expression 'to keep an incommunicable sleep' for 'to lie dead' gives dignity to the occasion by carrying the mind back along a train of literary associations of which the well-known ἀτέρμονα νήγρετον ὕπνον of Moschus may be taken as the type."

No. LXXVIII. *Waken, lords and ladies gay*

Metre.—Observe how the sound echoes to the sense in line 7, where two dactyls, 'Merrily, merrily,' are substituted for two trochees, to be said or sung in the time that would ordinarily be occupied by two trochees.

4. Perhaps the best modern account of an old English hunt 'with hawk and horse and hunting-spear,' is to be found in *The Diary of Master William Silence*, a book that deals very fully with the field sports of Shakespeare's time.

12. **diamonds of dew.** Cp. CXXII. 39, "Dew-drops are the gems of morning."

29. **baulk** or **balk,** baffle, frustrate; properly, to separate by 'balks' or beams, to partition off.

No. LXXIX. *Ethereal minstrel! pilgrim of the sky!*

THE five poems (LXXIX.-LXXXIII.) in praise of birds, written by the three greatest poets of the period, Wordsworth, Shelley and Keats, will help the reader to compare the very different genius, character and method of their three authors. Wordsworth's song never soars so far as to be oblivious of the earth and the common life of men. Like his own skylark he is 'true to the kindred points of Heaven and Home,' rising to a splendid height at times, but always to bring some lesson down. In every aspect of Nature, in every bird and flower, he finds 'thoughts that lie deep'; and everywhere he hears 'the still sad music of humanity. Shelley's song is as different from Wordsworth's as his skylark is different. It mounts 'in profuse strains' of an art so facile that it may well seem 'unpremeditated.' It soars till earth is lost sight of, a very 'cloud of fire,' beautiful but impalpable, floating and running 'like an unbodied joy.' The poet is 'hidden' —not revealed—in the dazzling, rather than illuminating, 'light' of his thoughts. Keats, once more, is like the nightingale of his imagining—'pouring forth his soul abroad' in an ecstasy that wears out his frail body prematurely; and no finer or truer description of the special note of romance that is characteristic of his poetry could be given than in the words he uses of the nightingale's song—

> The same that oft-times hath
> Charm'd magic casements, opening on the foam
> Of perilous seas, in faery lands forlorn.

Shelley saw the resemblance—writing in his elegy on Keats of "Thy spirit's sister, the lorn nightingale."

No. LXXX. *Hail to thee, blithe Spirit*

Metre.—Trochaic. Three trochees in the first line, two trochees and long syllable in the second line, of the couplet. For the third couplet of each stanza is substituted a single long line, only differing from the couplet in that (1) it admits an extra unaccented syllable at the beginning, (2) it is only rhymed at the end, (3) the break in the middle is not always observed.

2. **wert.** The rhymes are—doubtless intentionally—very freely handled throughout the poem. Tennyson's practice was much stricter, and modern criticism is apt to be severe upon loose rhyming. But we must remember (1) that rhymes which are faulty now may sometimes have been accurate in Shelley's time, pronunciation having changed, (2) that rhymes which have once been accepted tend to become traditional in the poets after they have ceased to be accurate. The rhyme of 'wert' and 'heart,' *e.g.*, used by Shelley here, occurs in Daniel, the Elizabethan poet whom Coleridge admired, and was probably correct in his time. As for the form *wert*, "'wast' is not found in the oldest English; it is quite a late form, not older than the fourteenth century. The O.E. form was *were*, from which we have formed, after the analogy of 'shall' and 'will,' *wert*, which is sometimes, but wrongly, used for the subjunctive *were* (second person singular) as 'If thou, that bidst me be content, wert grim' (*King John*, III. i.)."—Morris, *Historical Outlines of English Accidence*, p. 182.

7. **from the earth,** closely with 'higher': the lark has already left the ground.

15. **unbodied joy,** a disembodied 'spirit of delight,' one of those abstractions which to Shelley were more real than material things. Cp. the impersonations in *Adonais*, stanzas ix.-xiii. Some editors strangely emend to 'embodied.'

20. Cp. Tennyson, "Till drowned in yonder living blue The lark becomes a sightless song."

22. **silver sphere,** the star of l. 18.

28. **bare,** without clouds. So Wordsworth in cxxxi. 13, "The moon doth with delight Look round her when the heavens are bare."

55. **faint.** Cp. VIII. 9-12, "The wandering airs they faint."

66. **chorus hymeneal,** marriage song, from Hymen (Greek) the god of marriage.

82. **deem,** think, believe.

86. Cp. *Hamlet*, IV. iv. 37:

> " Sure he that made us with such large discourse,
>   Looking before and after, gave us not
>   That capability and godlike reason
>   To fust in us unused."

Gray observes the same fact as Shelley, but in a different spirit:

> " 'Tis man alone that joy descries
>   With forward and reverted eyes" (*G. T.* CLII.).

96. **measures,** music. Cp. CIX. 33, "Where was heard the mingled measure."

No. LXXXI.   *Beneath these fruit-tree boughs that shed*

THIS differs from Wordsworth's other bird-poems in that it is simply descriptive and expressive of unreflecting delight.

15. **revels of the May.** See note on CXXII. 3.

18. **paramours,** lovers, formed from an adverbial French phrase, *par amour*, just as 'debonair' is: see note on LXXXV. 7.

21. **a Presence.** Cp. LXXX. 15; LXXXII. 15-16.

No. LXXXII.   *O blithe new-comer ! I have heard*

THE cry of the cuckoo brings back for a while to Wordsworth the time

> "When meadow, grove and stream,
> The earth and every common sight
>   To me did seem
> Apparell'd in celestial light."

(See the opening of his great ode, CXXXI.) This lyric was written in 1804. In 1837, the same sound, heard at Laverna in Italy, in the neighbourhood of the monastery of St. Francis, awoke graver reflections: it seemed to him then the voice of a prophet—"of one crying amid the wilderness."

An earlier address to the cuckoo—"Hail, beauteous stranger of the grove!"—by Michael Bruce, is said to have been a favourite poem with Wordsworth, and may have suggested to him this loftier lyric. It will be found in Trench's *Household Book of English Poetry.*

12. **visionary hours,** the hours of youth—hours of 'the visionary gleam,' 'the glory and the dream' (CXXXI. 56-57).

No. LXXXIII. *My heart aches and a drowsy numbness pains*

"WRITTEN in the spring of 1819, and one of the six or eight among his poems so unique and perfect in style, that it is hard to see how any experience could have improved them" (F. T. P.).

The Ode was inspired by the song of a nightingale that had built its nest close to the house of a friend in Hampstead. The bird's song, we are told, "often threw Keats into a sort of trance of tranquil pleasure. One morning he took his chair from the breakfast-table, placed it on the grass-plot under a plum-tree, and sat there for two or three hours with some scraps of paper in his hands." Thus the Ode was written.

Metre.—Ten iambic lines to each stanza. The charm of the verse depends partly on the inevitable, yet unmonotonous, recurrence of the rhymes, partly on the effect of the shortened eighth line in producing a momentary pause that heightens the force of the full music of the last two lines.

4. **Lethe,** the river of forgetfulness, in the under-world, as imagined by the Greeks.

7. **Dryad,** a nymph inhabiting a tree and watching over it; from Gk. δρῦς, an oak.

12. **deep-delved.** The epithet, as Mr. W. T. Arnold points out, was probably suggested by Milton's lines *On the Death of a Fair Infant*—"Or that thy beauties lie in wormy bed, Hid from the world in a *low-delved* tomb."

13. **Flora,** Roman—originally Sabine—goddess of the Spring and of flowers.

14. **Provençal song,** the poetry of the troubadours, the court-poets of the twelfth century. The language which they used was the Romanic language of southern France, sometimes called the *langue d'oc.* Provence is the Roman *Provincia.* The

Provençal language ceased to be used for literary purposes in the fourteenth century.

sunburnt mirth, epithet transferred from the people to their mirth. The force of the epithet, like '*warm* South,' is to give the idea of genial Nature favouring the merriment.

16. **Hippocrene**, Greek, 'the fountain of the steed': the fount of the Muses, which was struck out of Mount Helicon by the hoof of the winged horse, Pegasus. Keats writes as if the spring ran wine.

17. **winking**, twinkling, *i.e.* breaking and sparkling. The original use is the ordinary one, 'moving the eyelids quickly.'

26. **spectre-thin**, thin as a spectre. Keats coins another compound of 'thin' differently in CXI. 57, 'winter-thin,' thin from its winter sleep.

32. **Bacchus**, the ancient god of wine, was fabled to have driven a team of tigers or lynxes round the world. Cp. Virgil, *Aen.* vi. 805, *Liber, agens celso Nysae de vertice tigres.*

pards, leopards, substituted by poetic licence for the tigers or lynxes of the legend.

37. **Fays**, the proper form of the word, though 'fairies' is more common. 'Fairy' is derived from 'fay,' and properly means 'enchantment,' in which sense the O.F. form 'faerie' is sometimes used in modern English. Cp. the adj. 'faery' as employed by Keats in XXXVI. 11, and below l. 70.

42. **soft incense**, scented blossoms.

43. **in the scented darkness**, try to distinguish the several odours.

46. **eglantine.** See note on XXVI. 13.

51. **darkling**, adv., in the dark. "As the wakeful bird sings *darkling*" (Milton).

60. **requiem**, a hymn or mass sung for the repose of the soul of the dead: the first word of the Roman Catholic hymn, *Requiem aeternam dona eis, Domine,* "Give eternal rest to them, O Lord." So 'dirge' is derived from *dirige*, the first word of another hymn.

64. **clown**, peasant. Apparently this was the original sense of the word, though the meaning 'jester' is as old, or almost as old, in literature.

66. **Ruth.** See *The Book of Ruth*, ch. ii.

70. **faery lands.** The expression recalls the Greek φιλορνις δαιμόνων ἀναστροφή, 'haunt of demigods, dear to birds' (Aeschylus, *Eumenides*, 23), but the epithet 'forlorn' adds a modern romantic note.

No. LXXXIV. *Earth has not anything to show more fair*

To any one who has ever looked upon such a scene, this sonnet will bring it back with wonderful vividness, steeped in a glow of sunshine, like a painting of Turner. Yet it is noteworthy how vague the details are as compared with those of a picture : the form and arrangement of the 'ships, towers, domes, theatres and temples' are supplied by the reader's memory or imagination—not indicated by the poet.

Prof. Herford (*Age of Wordsworth*, p. 162) notes as one of the limitations of Wordsworth that his imagination was not greatly touched by cities. "If anything in them yielded poetry, it was their moments of self-oblivion (*Stray Pleasures, Power of Music, Star-gazers*), their pining rustics (*Farmer of Tilsbury Vale*, 1803, *Poor Susan*, 1797), their early morning splendour (*Westminster Bridge*, 1802), their crises of heroism and martyrdom (*Zaragoza*, 1809). But at Grasmere he gave both profounder and more varied expression to his specific vision."

With Wordsworth's vision of London, F. W. H. Myers finely compared Sterling's imagination of it on his dying-bed : "not as full of noise and dust and confusion, but as something silent, grand and everlasting."

No. LXXXV. *To one who has been long in city pent*

THIS expression of simple delight in the charm of open country, by the poet whom Byron unfairly upbraided with being 'a Cockney,' is a fitting pendant to the great poet of Nature's confession that beauty is not absent from the city.

1. A reminiscence of Milton, *Paradise Lost*, ix. 445 :

"As one who, long in populous city pent,
   Where houses thick and sewers annoy the air,
   Forth issuing on a summer's morn to breathe
   Among the pleasant farms and villages
   Adjoined, from each thing met conceives delight."

7. debonair, elegant : Fr. *débonnaire*, i.e. *de bon aire*, of good extraction, and hence of good disposition. A Miltonic word. Cp. "So buxom, blithe and debonair," *L'Allegro*, 24.

8. languishment, languor. The word is used by Spenser and by Wyatt.

10. Philomela and Procne in the Greek legend were two sisters, who were changed, the one into a nightingale, the other into a swallow. Cp. Sir P. Sidney's poem, "The nightingale as soon as April bringeth," *G. T.* XLVII.

13. The image in the last two lines is in the manner of Shelley rather than of Keats. Cp. the exquisite lines on an angel's tear in *Adonais*, st. x.

No. LXXXVI.   *I met a traveller from an antique land*

THE best of the few sonnets that Shelley wrote. The sonnet demands too much concentration and self-restraint to be adapted to his wayward and essentially lyrical genius, that 'singing still does soar.'

Ozymandias is a Greek form of an Egyptian name. Shelley probably invented the inscription. 'Vast and trunkless legs of stone' are common enough in Egypt. But, as an Egyptologist friend, Mr. J. G. Milne, writes to me, "No traveller in Shelley's day could have translated a hieroglyphic inscription, and the inscription as given is not Egyptian in conception."

8. The sculptor's hand that mock'd the sneer and frown, and the heart of Ozymandias that fed the sneer and frown. 'Hand' and 'heart' are governed by 'survive.' We can still read the king's scorn and the sculptor's scorn of him: but king and sculptor—where are they?

No. LXXXVII.   *Degenerate Douglas! oh, the unworthy lord*

FOR Neidpath, see XXXIII. and note.
"The fact was told me by Walter Scott" (Wordsworth's note). The sonnet was written in 1803 on the same tour that produced XC., XCI., XCVIII., and CXVIII.

No. LXXXVIII.   *O leave this barren spot to me*

3-4. Cp. Wordsworth's description of the Borrowdale yew-trees:
> "A pillar'd shade,
> Upon whose grassless floor of red-brown hue
> By sheddings from the pining umbrage tinged
> Perennially—beneath whose sable roof
> Of boughs, as if for festal purpose, decked
> With unrejoicing berries—ghostly shapes
> May meet at noontide."

10. amber, the resin of extinct pine-trees, which when heated gives forth a fragrant odour. So Campbell applies the term to 'honey.' The resemblance between the two substances accounts for Virgil's prophecy—*Et durae quercus sudabunt roscida mella.*

22. The practice of carving the beloved name on the trunks of trees is frequently alluded to in ancient and modern poetry. Cp. Virgil, *Eclogues*, x. 54, *Crescent illae, crescetis amores*; Shakespeare, *As you Like it*, III. ii. 9:
> "Run, run, Orlando, carve on every tree
> The fair, the chaste and unexpressive she."

26. ravish'd, carried away in spite of itself, enraptured.

No. LXXXIX.   *Yes, there is holy pleasure in thine eye*

"INTENDED more particularly for the perusal of those who may
have happened to be enamoured of some beautiful Place of
Retreat, in the Country of the Lakes" (Wordsworth).

1. Another reading: "Well may'st thou halt, and gaze with
brightening eye!"

No. XC.   *Sweet Highland Girl, a very shower*

THIS poem—like *The Reaper* (XCI.) and *Glen Almain* (CXVIII.)—
was one of the fruits of Wordsworth's tour in the Highlands
with his sister Dorothy, August, 1803.   On the shore of Loch
Lomond the travellers encountered two girls.   "One of the
girls," writes Miss Wordsworth in her Journal, "was exceed-
ingly beautiful; and the figures of both of them, in grey plaids
falling to their feet, their faces only being uncovered, excited
our attention before we spoke to them; but they answered us so
sweetly that we were quite delighted, at the same time that
they stared at us with an innocent look of wonder.   I think I
never heard the English language sound more sweetly than from
the mouth of the elder of these girls, while she stood at the gate
answering our inquiries; her face was flushed with the rain;
her pronunciation was clear and distinct, without difficulty, yet
slow, as if like a foreign speech."

Though Wordsworth did not write love poems, as the term is
commonly understood (see note on XIII.), no poet has given us
more exquisitely tender and beautiful pictures of girlhood and
womanhood.   This poem and XCI. should be read by the side of
"She was a phantom of delight" (X.) and the four Lucy poems
(XIII.-XVI.).   Wordsworth returned to the subject of the Highland girl in a later poem, *The Three Cottage Girls*, in which he
sets her by the side of a Swiss and an Italian maid.   Still later,
in 1843, he wrote that "the sort of prophecy with which the
verses conclude, has, through God's goodness, been realized;
and now, approaching the close of my seventy-third year, I have
a most vivid remembrance of her and the beautiful objects with
which she was surrounded."

15. light of common day.   Cp. CXXXI. 76.

25. sense, good sense.

42. brook'd, A.S., endured, borne.

60. Mr. Myers recalls (*Life of Wordsworth*, p. 120) Virgil,
Eclogue x. 35, *Atque utinam ex vobis unus vestrique fuissem Aut
custos gregis aut maturae vinitor uvae.*

No. XCI.   *Behold her, single in the field*

15. Those who have had the good fortune to sail among the Hebrides (the islands off the N.W. coast of Scotland) in calm weather will understand the beauty and truth of the expression, ' the silence of the seas.'

19-20. Lines that have often been quoted—like lines 69-70 in the *Ode to a Nightingale*, LXXXIII.—as containing in an unusual degree that new romantic note that was first clearly heard in English poetry in the *Lyrical Ballads* of 1798. It is the note that modern readers have often found in Virgil—a suggestiveness reaching far beyond the obvious meaning of the words into depths that speech cannot plumb, mystery, poignant pathos, haunting melody.

No. XCII.   *At the corner of Wood Street, when daylight appears*

IN spite of the real beauty and pathos of the conception, this poem falls considerably below the level of the two that have preceded it.   The chief reason for the inferiority lies probably in the choice of a metre.   Mr. Theodore Watts-Dunton, in his *Encyclopaedia Britannica* article on Poetry, remarks that Wordsworth and Keats always fall below their best when they choose an anapaestic metre.   He acutely supplies the reason : the slower iambic metre in English is better adapted for statement, narrative, description, anapaestic or dactylic rhythm for poetry that symbolises or suggests.

1. Wood Street, Lothbury, Cheapside, all in the heart of London.

No. XCIII   *Ariel to Miranda :—Take*

THE last charge given to Ariel, the attendant 'airy spirit' of Prospero, in the 'mighty verses' of the *Tempest*, was to watch over the ship that conveyed Ferdinand and Miranda to Naples, where their marriage was to be solemnised.   Shelley imagines that Ariel's care for Miranda did not end here.   She has lived other lives since then, and now she is re-incarnated as Shelley's friend, Jane Williams (see note to c.).   Ariel, who is a 'tree-spirit'—Prospero had rescued him from a 'cloven pine,' where the witch Sycorax had imprisoned him (*Tempest*, I. ii.)—comes to her as the spirit of music in a guitar, craving only

> For his service and his sorrow
> A smile to-day, a song to-morrow.

An interesting account of the writing of this lyric, illustrating Shelley's feverish heat of composition, is given by the poet's friend, Trelawney; quoted in J. A. Symonds' *Life of Shelley*, p. 165.

Metre.—The same as the trochaic metre of Keats' three poems, II., LXV., CXI., but the proportion of lines beginning with an extra unaccented syllable is so much larger as to give a different effect. It is interesting to compare the very different music that different poets draw from the same verse. Shelley probably chose this metre here because it was used by Prospero in his Epilogue, but he was also influenced—as still more in O., *The Invitation*—by the rhythm of Milton's *L'Allegro*. The dainty and delicate handling of the metre is exquisitely adapted to the theme. This is the most Horatian of Shelley's poems, but there is also a glamour about it that the *curiosa felicitas* of Horace never attains.

8. This recalls the Platonic doctrine of the alternation of opposites. All opposites, according to Socrates in the *Phaedo*,—*e.g.* less, greater; sleeping, waking; life, death—are generated out of each other.

24. **interlunar swoon**, 'interval of the moon's invisibility' (F.T.P.). Cp. Milton, *Samson Agonistes*, 87:

> "Silent as the moon,
>   When she deserts the night,
>   Hid in her vacant *interlunar* cave."

75. **mysterious sound**, the music of the spheres. See the account in Plato, *Republic*, bk. x. Plato got the notion from Pythagoras. Cp. Milton, *Hymn on the Nativity*, l. 125 (*G. T.* LXXXV.)—

> "Ring out, ye crystal spheres!
>   Once bless our human ears
>   If ye have power to touch our senses so."

Cp also *Merchant of Venice*, v. i. 61—

> "There's not the smallest orb which thou behold'st
>   But in his motion like an angel sings,
>   Still quiring to the young-eyed cherubim."

90. "For our beloved *Jane* alone" (Shelley's MS.). The reading *one* for *our*, found in some editions of *G. T.*, appears to be an emendation of Mr. Palgrave's, afterwards withdrawn.

No. XCIV. *I wander'd lonely as a cloud*

WRITTEN at Town-end, Grasmere, 1804. "The daffodils grew and still grow on the margin of Ullswater, and probably may be seen to this day as beautiful in the month of March, nodding their golden heads beside the dancing and foaming waves" (Wordsworth). These were doubtless the daffodils of which Dorothy Wordsworth wrote in her Journal, April 15, 1802: "When we were in the woods below Gowbarrow Park we saw a few daffodils close to the water-side. As we went along there were more, and yet more ; and at last, under the boughs of the trees, we saw there was a long belt of them along the shore. I never saw daffodils so beautiful. They grew among the mossy stones about them ; some rested their heads on the stones as on a pillow ; the rest tossed, and reeled, and danced, and seemed as if they verily danced with the wind, they looked so gay and glancing."

Mr. Aubrey de Vere (*Essays chiefly on Poetry*, p. 165) has remarked how little of detail the poem contains—only 'the margin of a bay and the long galaxy of daffodils': the addition of details would have injured the singleness of effect. "The poet saw the daffodils because he saw little else, and he saw them in such sort that both for him and his readers henceforth

> They flash upon that inward eye
> Which is the bliss of solitude."

It is remarkable, by the way, that this famous couplet—suggested to the poet by Mrs. Wordsworth, and certainly her chief contribution to his works—was condemned by Coleridge (*Biographia Literaria*, ch. xxii.). Sensitive as he was to the exquisite pleasure that can be given by form and colour, Coleridge felt that the expression 'the inward eye' should be reserved for higher uses, for purely mental or spiritual delight. This was the objection of a philosopher, and has been shared by few of Wordsworth's readers. Few poems have done so much to increase the enjoyment of natural beauty by suggesting to minds less quick to receive impressions than a poet's that they can indefinitely augment their delight by cultivating the habit of thus remembering—in a spirit different from that of Keats' lyric— 'passéd joy.'

1. Byron touched this simile in *The Prisoner of Chillon*, but without adorning it :

> Lone, as a solitary cloud,
> A single cloud on a sunny day,
> While all the rest of heaven is clear,
> A frown upon the atmosphere,
> That hath no business to appear
> When skies are blue, and earth is gay.

No. XCV. *With little here to do or see*

RUSKIN, *Modern Painters*, Vol. II. (Pt. III., sec. ii., ch. iv.), quotes from this poem "two delicious stanzas of Fancy regardant (believing in her creations) followed by one of heavenly imagination." The stanzas are the third, fifth, and sixth. He proceeds : "Observe how spiritual, yet how wandering and playful, the fancy is in the first two stanzas, and how far she flies from the matter in hand; never stopping to brood on the character of any one of the images she summons, and yet for a moment truly seeing and believing in them all; while in the last stanza the imagination returns with its deep feeling to the heart of the flower, and *cleaves fast* to that."

5. **Common-place**, (1) a memorandum of something that is likely to be often referred to; (2) a customary remark, trite saying; (3) used, as here, for anything occurring frequently or habitually.

9. **dappled**, variegated with spots of another colour, by the daisies. Cp. Shakespeare, 'The gentle day Dapples the drowsy east with spots of grey.'

11. **types**, emblems, symbols.

17. **port**, bearing: from Lat. *porto*, 'to carry,' through French. Cp. Goldsmith, *Traveller*, "Pride in their port, defiance in their eye, I see the lords of humankind pass by."

22. **starveling**. Cp. Shakespeare, *Henry IV.*, Part I., ii. 1. 76, "If I hang, old Sir John hangs with me, and thou knowest he is no starveling." The diminutive suffix is contemptuous.

25. **Cyclops**. The Cyclōpes are a race of one-eyed giants in Greek mythology. The most famous of them is Polyphemus, whom Odysseus (Ulysses) encountered.

30. **boss**, the knob in the centre of a shield.

34. **star**. Shelley has the same image in c. 40, cVIII. 10, 11.

39. **who**. The antecedent is implied in *his = of him*.

42. **reveries**, dreamings, random fancies or meditations: from French *rêver*, to dream.

No. XCVI.   *Season of mists and mellow fruitfulness*

A POEM full of wonderful pictures and of a rich, solemn music. It leaves us with a sense of the joy of autumn—labour ended, perfection attained—and the sadness of autumn—the passing away of beauty and of life; the tears that come unbidden to the eye in gazing at 'the happy autumn fields.'

Metre.—Eleven iambic lines of five feet in the stanza; the scheme of rhymes varies a little in the three stanzas.

7. **plump**, to swell out (active). Keats found the verb in Chapman. "By whose side Pallas stood his crookt age streitning, His flesh more plumping and his looks enlightning," *Odyssey*, bk. xxiv.

12. The influence of this stanza may perhaps be traced in some of the descriptions in M. Arnold's *Scholar-Gipsy*.

15. **winnowing.** See note on XXIV. 33, 'winnow'd by the gentle air.' Here 'winnowing wind' = the wind that separates the corn from the chaff.

17. **drowsed,** made drowsy. This transitive use of the verb is found in Philemon Holland's *Livy*, 1600 A.D., "When as wine had drowned and *drowsed* the understanding."

fume, sleepy smell : Lat. *fumus*, smoke.

18. **swath,** a row of mown grass ; here, the row to be mown next.

25. **barred clouds,** bars of clouds, or clouds with stripes or streaks like bars.

bloom, touch with a soft, warm glow. Keats seems to have coined the verb from the subst. N. E. D. quotes from Prof. Tyndall (1860) the sentence, "Heaps of snow ... as the day advanced, *bloomed* with a rosy light."

28 **sallows,** willows : from Lat. *salix*, through French.

30. **hilly bourn,** hill bounding the view. 'Bourn' is Fr. *borne*, a limit. Cp. "That undiscovered country, from whose bourn No traveller returns," *Hamlet*, III. i.

32. **croft,** A.S., a small piece of enclosed land adjoining a dwelling-house.

No. XCVII. *When first the fiery-mantled Sun*

CAMPBELL, in the year 1800, saw something of actual warfare, though not as a combatant. The experience gives reality to his poems on war. The martial note is genuine, and his sense of the horror of bloodshed true and deep.

It is possible that Campbell was influenced, consciously or unconsciously, in this *Ode to Winter* by Coleridge's fine *Ode to the Departing Year*, written and published at the end of 1796.

Metre.—This is not irregular, as in so-called 'Pindaric' odes. The stanzas strictly correspond to each other, and the scheme of rhymes and feet presents no difficulty. The opening of *L'Allegro* may have suggested the rhythm and the impersonations of the first stanza.

11. **Calpe,** the ancient name for Gibraltar.

21. **Lofoden.** The Lofoden Islands, off the N.W. coast of Norway, are famous for their maelstroms or whirlpools. As in his choice of the word 'Elsinore' (XLIV. 63), Campbell shows his appreciation of a noble-sounding name.

23. **Runic Odin.** Odin, the chief god of the Scandinavian mythology, is called *Runic* because celebrated in the Edda or book of Runic poetry. 'Rûn' is Teutonic for mystery, and the word was applied to the first alphabet known to the northern tribes.

27. **deflowering.** Cp. LXXX. 53, 'By warm winds deflowered.'

29. **light's Lord,** the sun.

54. **tented.** See note on II. 13.

No. XCVIII.   *From Stirling Castle we had seen*

IN September, 1803, on their way back from that tour in the Highlands that led to the composition of *To the Highland Girl of Inversneyde* (XC.), *The Reaper* (XCI.), and *Glen Almain* (CXVIII.), Wordsworth and his sister Dorothy walked down the vale of Tweed from Neidpath (LXXXVII.) to Clovenford. Here, if at all, they should have turned aside to Yarrow. "A short walk to the ridge of the hill behind Yare, and the whole of Yarrow vale would have lain at their feet. They debated about it, and determined to reserve the pleasure for a future day" (Principal Shairp, Lecture on 'The Three Yarrows' in *Aspects of Poetry*).

Eleven years later (1814), Wordsworth visited Yarrow, and wrote the poem that comes next in this collection. Seventeen years after this (1831) he crossed the border again to see Sir Walter Scott once more before the latter set out from Tweedside 'in hope of recruiting his shattered health in Italy.' On that occasion Wordsworth wrote *Yarrow Revisited*, an interesting poem, but inferior to the two lyrics inserted here.

Metre.—See note on XVIII.

6. **marrow,** old and provincial English and Scottish, possibly a corruption of French *mari*, from Lat. *maritus*, a husband; 'husband,' 'companion.' Frequent in the Yarrow ballads from its usefulness as a rhyme. Wordsworth here applies it to his companion—his sister Dorothy.

8. **Braes,** slopes, a Scottish word. So Burns in "Ye banks and braes o' bonnie Doon" (*G. T.*, CLVII). Also frequent in the Yarrow ballads.

9. **frae,** Scottish, 'from.'

17. **Gala Water,** a tributary of the Tweed. **Leader haughs,** the flat alluvial land by the side of the river Leader. Dryburgh, in the Abbey of which Sir W. Scott was afterwards buried.

20. **lintwhites,** a provincial form of 'linnet,' used also by Tennyson in "Her song the lintwhite swelleth."

21. **Tiviot-dale,** the valley of the Tiviot or Teviot in Roxburghshire; a tributary of the Tweed.

33. **holms** (A.S. and Danish), a low flat tract of rich land by the side of a river. Tennyson has "The soft wind blowing over meadowy holms."

37. **strath.** "In Scotland a valley of considerable size, often having a river running through it, and giving it its distinctive appellation; as *Strathspey*, *Strathearn*, etc.; *Strathmore*, or the great valley" (Imperial Dict.).

43. **Saint Mary's Lake,** three miles long and one-half mile in extreme breadth, on the borders of the two counties of Selkirk and Peebles. Yarrow Water flows out of it. It is mentioned in the old ballad of *The Douglas Tragedy*:

> "Till bye and rade the Black Douglas
> And O but he was rough!
> For he pu'd up the bonnie briar
> And flang't in St. Mary's Lough."

Cp. *Lay of the Last Minstrel*, Canto II. st. xxxiii; Canto IV. st. viii.

No. XCIX. *And is this—Yarrow?—This the stream*

"Yarrow," says Principal Shairp in his *Aspects of Poetry* (Lecture on 'The Three Yarrows') is "the inner sanctuary of the whole Scottish border." "Ballad after ballad comes down loaded with a dirge-like wail for some sad event, made still sadder for that it befell in Yarrow." Wordsworth has not taken pains to be exact in details. As Principal Shairp points out, he has confused the lady 'flower of Yarrow' with the 'slaughtered youth' for whom so many ballads had sung lament. Mary Scott of Dryhope, the real 'Flower of Yarrow,' never 'lay bleeding' in Yarrow Vale; she became the wife of Wat of Harden, and the mother of a wide-branching race. But *The Dowie Dens o' Yarrow*, the oldest ballad of the district, tells of a knight slain treacherously by his wife's brother, and one version of it ends:

> "O haud your tongue, my father dear!
> Ye mind me but of sorrow;
> A fairer rose did never bloom
> Than now lies cropp'd on Yarrow."

Three of the Yarrow ballads may be read in *The Golden Treasury*, Book III., *Lament for Flodden* (CLXII.), Logan's version of *The Braes of Yarrow* (CLXIII.), and *Willy Drowned in Yarrow* (CLXIV). The ballad that was specially in Wordsworth's mind was another version of *The Braes*, by Hamilton, beginning "Busk ye, busk ye, my bonny, bonny bride." Another powerful Yarrow ballad is *The Douglas Tragedy*, to be found in Scott's *Minstrelsy of the Scottish Border*. The spirit of all the Yarrow legends finds perfect expression in Wordsworth's fifth stanza. As for the description of the actual place given in lines 45-48, Principal Shairp's emphatic testimony may be quoted: "You look on Yarrow, you repeat those four lines over to yourself, and you feel that the finer, more subtle essence of nature has never been more perfectly uttered in human words." These two poems are a proof that if Wordsworth did not often use "the subtle aroma of place-names" (see note on LVI.) he yet understood it.

13-16. These lines, as also 43, 44 in the preceding poem, give very beautiful expression to the charm of reflection in still waters. It is interesting to compare Shelley, c. 33 and CI. 53-80.

17-20. A characteristic touch of accurate observation of nature.

31. Water-wraith. See note on XVIII. 26.

48. melancholy. The word 'dowie' in *The Dowie Dens of Yarrow* means 'melancholy.'

55. Newark Castle, formerly a royal hunting seat in Ettrick Forest; celebrated in Scott's *Lay of the Last Minstrel*, where many of the names mentioned in the two Yarrow poems will be found. Cp. in the Introduction to the *Lay* :

"He passed where Newark's stately tower
Looks out from Yarrow's birchen bower ; "

and the couplet with which the *Lay* ends :

"And Yarrow, as he rolled along,
Bore burden to the minstrel's song."

64. The thoughts are the offspring of chaste affection.

83. Cp. Bishop King's lovely little poem, "Like to the falling of a star," which ends, "The dew dries up, the star is shot, The flight is past ;—and Man forgot." Cp. also Psalm XC.

No. C.   *Best and brightest, come away*

IN the volume of Shelley's *Posthumous Poems*, published in 1824 by Mrs. Shelley, parts of this poem and the next appeared as one composition under the title of *The Pine Forest of the Cascine near Pisa.* The division into two poems with separate titles, though not found in print till the second edition of 1839, was Shelley's own ; but the title given by Mrs. Shelley has interest as fixing the locality of the verses. The poems were addressed, like XL. and XCIII. to Mrs. Williams, who, with her husband, was much in Shelley's company during the last year of his life.

The scene is more real and definite, more truly that of the earth we know, than in most of Shelley's descriptions, though there is still a luminousness, an 'Elysian glow,' characteristic of the poet. We may compare the real forest described here with the vast ideal forests of *Alastor* and *Prometheus Unbound.*

After line 28, Mr. Palgrave has omitted a passage, the tone of which is too sharply contrasted with the rest of the poem. Such a liberty of excision is the more permissible in the case of Shelley, he wrote quickly, and did not live to prune his own work.

Metre.—See note on XCIII.

3. There is an echo of the rhythm and even the rhymes of *L'Allegro*:

> Then to come in spite of sorrow,
> And at my window bid good-morrow (l. 45, 46).

Just below 'The brightest hour of unborn Spring' may be an echo of 'The frolic wind that breathes the Spring' in *L'Allegro* (l. 18), and the mythology a reminiscence of the mythology which opens both *L'Allegro* and *Il Penseroso*. The influence of these two poems of Milton on later poetry is very remarkable. We have traced it already in Shelley (XCIII.) and Campbell (XCVII.), and it will be apparent again in Keats (CXI.).

9. halcyon. The days when the halcyons or kingfishers—Greek, ἀλκυών—were breeding were supposed to be supernaturally calm. They were in mid-winter. Cp. Milton, *On Morning of Nativity*, line 68, "While birds of calm sit brooding on the charmed wave" (*G. T.*, LXXXV.). For the ancient legend of the halcyons see Ovid, *Metamorphoses*, Book XI., or Lucian's charming little dialogue Ἀλκυὼν ἢ περὶ Μεταμορφώσεως.

33. Another picture of reflection in still water. There is a fuller one in the next poem, lines 53-80. Cp. Wordsworth in XCVIII. 44, and XCIX. 15.

40. "The daisy-star that never sets" is so called because it can be found at all seasons of the year. The same thought recurs in CVIII. 10-11, "Daisies, those pearl'd Acturi of the earth, The constellated flower that never sets." The daisy (A.S. *dæges-eáge*, day's eye) got its name because it opens and closes its flower with the daylight. Cp. Chaucer, "The daisie or els the eye of the daie."

41. wind-flowers, the *anemone nemorosa*: cp. CVIII. 9.

45. Cp. XXV., first stanza.

47. multitudinous. Shelley was doubtless thinking of Macbeth's words: "This my hand will rather The multitudinous seas incarnadine, Making the green one red," *Macbeth*, II. ii. 61.

50-51. An expression of Shelley's pantheistic creed. See note on CXIV. 136.

No. CI. *Now the last day of many days*

2. thou, the lady to whom the poem is addressed. The fuller title in Shelley's works is *To Jane—The Recollection*. See note to preceding poem.

32. The ocean-woods. The idea of these fascinated Shelley. See *Ode to the West Wind* (CXV.), third stanza.

36. **with.** So in Mr. W. M. Rossetti's edition; in other editions of Shelley the reading is *by*.

43. **soft flower.** What this was we learn from the four lines to be found in the first version of the poem and omitted from the second :

> " Were not the crocuses that grew
>   Under the ilex tree
> As beautiful in scent and hue
>   As ever fed the bee ? "

53-80. Another exquisite picture of reflections in still water, more elaborate than the two by Wordsworth in XCVIII. 43-44, XCIX. 13-16, or Shelley's own in C. 33.

74. **Elysian.** See note on II. 11.

No. CII. *It is a beauteous evening, calm and free*

WORDSWORTH'S ' sweet calm ' and his ' healing power,' which Matthew Arnold commemorated in *Obermann* and in *Memorial Verses*, are exemplified in this sonnet. This picture of a tranquil sunset—the work of one at peace with God and man and Nature —may be contrasted with the stormy sunrises and sunsets in which Shelley delights. We may further compare Wordsworth's companion picture of a peaceful sunrise in the sonnet *Upon Westminster Bridge* (LXXXIV.). That was written on his way to France in September, 1802 ; this on the beach near Calais in the same autumn. See also Milton's famous description of evening, *Paradise Lost*, IV. 598.

12. **Abraham's bosom,** *St. Luke*, xvi. 22. It was a common expression among the Jews to signify the blessedness of heaven. " The imagery is that of a banquet at which the occupant of the seat next the host would be said to be on his bosom."

14. The thought seems partly to be that of the *Ode to Duty*, second stanza (XLV.)—the " Glad hearts ! without reproach or blot, Who do thy work and know it not "—but still more that of the *Ode on Intimations of Immortality*—" Heaven lies about us in our infancy " (CXXXI. 66).

No. CIII. *Star that bringest home the bee*

COMPARE Collins, *Ode to Evening* (*G. T.*, CLXXXVI.), and Campbell's own " Gem of the crimson-coloured Even," one of the other group of evening songs (XXII.-XXV.) contained in this book. Compare also this beautiful fragment of Sappho : Έσπερε, πάντα φέρων, ὄσα φαίνολις ἐσκέδασ' αύως, φέρεις οἶν, φέρεις αἴγα, φέρεις ἄπυ ματέρι παῖδα. " Evening, thou that bringest all that bright morning scattered ; thou bringest the sheep, the goat, the child back to her mother."

7. **luxuriant.** The epithet suggests the 'fatness' of dew. Cp 'the rich and balmy eve,' IV. 72.

15. **remembrancer.** Cp. Cowper, *On my Mother's Picture*, l. 11, "Faithful remembrancer of one so dear."

No. CIV. *The sun upon the lake is low*

RUSKIN (*Modern Painters*, Vol. III., Pt. IV., ch. xvi.) notes as characteristic of Scott's landscapes the fact that he never allows his feelings to colour his descriptions. He never indulges in the 'pathetic fallacy' by which other poets represent Nature as sympathising in the joy or sorrow of themselves or their characters. Here the peace and joy of evening are contrasted with the lover's disappointment. The same thing may be observed in *A Serenade* (XXIII.).

14. **level,** from the setting sun. In *Hohenlinden* (LII. 21) Campbell applies the same epithet to the *morning* sun.

16. **plaid.** See note on XLI. 13.

No. CV. *Art thou pale for weariness*

THE fascination of the moon is strong in Shelley's poetry. Compare another exquisite fragment, beginning "And like a dying lady"; the lyric dialogue between Moon and Earth in *Prometheus Unbound*, Act IV., and the lines about the Moon in *The Cloud*. Compare also Sir Philip Sidney's lovely sonnet, "With how sad steps, O Moon, thou climb'st the skies!" (*G.T.*, LVIII.), the first two lines of which Wordsworth used, with due acknowledgment, as the opening of a sonnet of his own; and Milton's *Il Penseroso*, ll. 67-72.

4. **a different birth.** Science has confirmed Shelley's description, representing the moon as a fragment detached from the earth.

No. CVI. *A flock of sheep that leisurely pass by*

WITH this beautiful invocation of sleep compare Sir P. Sidney's sonnet, "Come, Sleep: O Sleep! the certain knot of peace" (*G.T.*, XL.), the famous speech of the King in Shakespeare's *II. Henry IV.*, Act III., Sc. i.; and the lines in Coleridge's *Ancient Mariner* (Part V.):

> " Oh sleep ! it is a gentle thing,
> Beloved from pole to pole !
> To Mary Queen the praise be given !
> She sent the gentle sleep from heaven
> That slid into my soul."

But "the sound of rain and bees murmuring" and "the fall of rivers" were probably suggested to Wordsworth by the description of the house of Morpheus in Spenser's *Faerie Queene*, I. i. 41—

> "And, more to lulle him in his slumber soft,
> A trickling streame from high rock tumbling doune,
> And ever-drizling rain upon the loft,
> Mixt with a murmuring winde, much like the soune
> Of swarming bees, did cast him in a swoune";

and by *Il Penseroso*, ll. 141-146 (*G. T.* CXLV.):

> "Hide me from day's garish eye,
> While the bee with honey'd thigh
> That at her flowery work doth sing,
> And the waters murmuring,
> With such consort as they keep
> Entice the dewy-feather'd sleep."

See also Chaucer's description of the cave of Morpheus in the *Book of the Duchess*:

> "There were a few wells
> Came running fro the cliffs adoune,
> That made a deadly sleeping soune";

and Beaumont and Fletcher's *Valentinian*, v. ii.:

> "Care-charming Sleep, thou easer of all woes,
> Brother to Death, sweetly thyself dispose
> On this afflicted prince. Fall like a cloud
> In gentle showers: give nothing that is loud
> Or painful to his slumbers: easy, sweet,
> And *as a purling stream*, thou son of Night,
> Pass by his troubled senses; sing his pain
> *Like hollow murmuring wind, or silver rain*."

Metre.—The distribution of pauses in this sonnet is worth studying. The effects are very subtle.

4. Any one who has observed the effect of 'white sheets of water' in lighting up such sombre landscapes as those of the fen country of East Anglia on a winter afternoon will appreciate the beauty of this line. Wordsworth had always loved such sights. In the first book of *The Prelude* he tells how he sometimes stood in boyhood on "The sands of Westmoreland, the creeks and bays Of Cumbria's rocky limits," by the light of the rising moon:

> "Even while mine eye hath moved o'er many a league
> Of shining water, gathering as it seemed
> Through every hair-breadth in that field of light
> New pleasure like a bee among the flowers."

In the previous line 'the fall of rivers' recalls another passage from the same book of *The Prelude*, Wordsworth's tribute to the Derwent:

> " One, the fairest of all rivers, loved
> To blend his murmurs with my nurse's song,
> And, from his alder shades and rocky falls,
> And from his fords and shallows sent a voice
> That flowed along my dreams."

No. CVII. *Our bugles sang truce, for the night-cloud had lower'd*

SEE introductory note to XCVII.

Metre.—Anapaestic. The occasional substitution of an iambus in the first foot checks the rapid flow of the verse, and deepens the pathos thereby.

14. **morning march.** A combination of metaphors. Life is compared to a journey begun with morning and ended with night.

bosom, heart. For the thought, cp. Shakespeare, *Winter's Tale*, Act IV., Sc. iii., "A merry heart goes all the day, Your sad tires in a mile-a."

17. **pledged.** 'To pledge' is 'to offer in proof of good faith.'

No. CVIII. *I dream'd that as I wander'd by the way*

WRITTEN in 1820. In the second stanza, as printed in the text and in all early editions of Shelley, a line is wanting, between the first five and the last two. Apparently its omission is simply due to a mistake in copying. Dr. Garnett has recovered the line from the MS.:

> " Like a child, half in tenderness and mirth—."

Metre.—On line 20 Mr. Palgrave notes: "Our language has perhaps no line modulated with more subtle sweetness." This will seem a hard saying to an untrained ear. But just as the trained ear in music takes in more than one part at once, and recognises in their blending a higher music than can be given by a simple air, so it is with the appreciation of lines in which the sense-rhythm and the verse-rhythm are distinct and yet subtly harmonized. Here the verse-rhythm is

> " And wil'd | rosés | and í | vy sér | pentíne,"

but the sense-rhythm is

> " And wíld | róses | and í | vy sér | pentíne."

So in XLIV. (see note); in CXV. 31; and in many lines of *Paradise Lost.*

9. **pied**, variegated in colour, like the magpie.

     wind-flowers, the *anemone nemorosa* : Gk. ἄνεμος, ' wind.'

10. **Arcturi.** " Seemingly used for *northern stars* " (F.T.P.).

11. **constellated flower,** so called not simply as in itself star-like, but also as growing in clusters.

     that never sets. See note on o. 40, " The daisy-star that never sets."

13. **that tall flower.** ' Its mother ' is obviously the earth, and the ' heaven-collected tears ' are of dew. We may compare " Each flower has wept, and bow'd toward the East " in Herrick's poem, *Corinna's Maying* (*G. T.*, CXVIII. 7). But it is perhaps impossible to identify the flower that was in Shelley's mind. He may have been thinking of Milton's daffodils that " fill their cups with tears " (*Lycidas*, l. 150), but it would seem that he meant a taller flower, like the foxglove or the lily : Keats mentions lilies in *his* dream of spring (CXI. 49). Cp. also in Shelley's *Sensitive Plant* :

> " Then the pied wind-flower and the tulip tall,
>   And narcissi, the fairest among them all,
>   Who gaze on their eyes in the stream's recess,
>   Till they die of their own dear loveliness. . . .
>   And the wand-like lily which lifted up,
>   As a Maenad, its moonlight-coloured cup,
>   Till the fiery star, which is its eye,
>   Gazed through clear dew on the tender sky."

16. **eglantine.** Shelley does not mean, as he ought, the wild rose, for he mentions that in l. 20. Probably, like Milton, he means honeysuckle. See note on xxvi. 13.

     lush, full of juice. Cp. Shakespeare, *Tempest*, II. i. 52, " How lush and lusty the grass looks." Etymologically it seems to be the same word as ' lusty ' and ' luscious.'

17. **cow-bind.** This name appears to occur nowhere else in English literature, nor is it to be found in Miller's *Dictionary of English Names of Cultivated, Native, and Foreign Plants. N.E.D.,* quoting this passage, identifies ' cow-bind ' with *Bryonia dioica,* white bryony, sometimes called ' white wild vine ' and ' wild hop.' So also Britton and Holland, *Plant Names,* vol. III., p. 523.

18. **white cups.** Some flower to be found in hedges in spring is intended—perhaps such ' white cups ' as those of the blackberry in blossom.

20. **serpentine,** winding, as the motion of a serpent.

25. **flag-flowers.** The wild scented iris with purple flower, common in Devon and Dorset.

prank'd, decked. 'To prank' meant 'to set out ostenta-
tiously': cp. Spenser, *Faerie Queene*, I. iv. "Some prancke their
ruffes: and others trimly dight Their gay attyre."

26. **starry river-buds.** We must remember the dream-like
character of the poem, and beware of too definite interpretation.
But such flowers as the marsh-marigold seem to be intended.
Cp. Tennyson, *May Queen*:

> "The honeysuckle round the porch has woven its wavy bowers,
>   And by the meadow-trenches blow the faint sweet cuckoo-
>   flowers,
>   And the wild marsh-marigold shines like fire in swamps and
>   hollows gray,
>   And I'm to be Queen of the May, mother, I'm to be Queen of
>   the May."

29. **moonlight.** Is not the use of 'moonlight' and 'light' in the
same line such a blemish as Shelley would have corrected, or
learnt to avoid, if he had lived longer?

34. **the same hues (and) the like array.** Both substantives are
governed by 'kept,' and the subject to that verb is 'these children of the Hours.' The inversion is somewhat harsh.

36. **the Hours, the Seasons.**

No. CIX. *In Xanadu did Kubla Khan*

THE story of the composition of *Kubla Khan* must be told in
Coleridge's own words:

"In the summer of the year 1797, the Author, then in ill-health,
had retired to a lonely farm-house between Porlock and Linton,
on the Exmoor confines between Somerset and Devonshire. In
consequence of a slight indisposition, an anodyne had been pre-
scribed, from the effects of which he fell asleep in his chair at the
moment he was reading the following sentence, or words of the
same substance, in *Purchas's Pilgrimage*: 'Here the Khan Kubla
commanded a palace to be built, and a stately garden thereunto.
And thus ten miles of fertile ground were inclosed with a wall.'
The Author continued for about three hours in a profound sleep,
at least of the external senses, during which time he has the most
vivid confidence, that he could not have composed less than from
two to three hundred lines; if that indeed can be called composition in which all the images rose up before him as *things*, with a
parallel production of the correspondent expressions, without
any sensation or consciousness of effort. On awaking he appeared
to himself to have a distinct recollection of the whole, and taking
his pen, ink, and paper, instantly and eagerly wrote down the
lines that are here preserved. At this moment he was unfortun-

ately called out by a person on business from Porlock, and detained by him above an hour, and on his return to his room, found, to his no small mortification, that though he still retained some vague and dim recollection of the general purport of the vision, yet, with the exception of some eight or ten scattered lines and images, all the rest had passed away like the images on the surface of a stream into which a stone has been cast, but alas! without the after restoration of the latter! . . . Yet from the still surviving recollections in his mind, the Author has frequently purposed to finish for himself what had been originally, as it were, given to him. Αὔριον ἄδιον ᾄσω [To-morrow I shall sing more sweetly], but the to-morrow is yet to come."

Metre.—Irregular. After speaking of irregular 'Pindaric' Odes in English poetry, Mr. Theodore Watts-Dunton (*Encyclopaedia Britannica,* Article on Poetry) proceeds to say: "Strange that it is not in an ode at all, but in this unique lyric, *Kubla Khan,* descriptive of imaginative landscape, that an English poet has at last conquered the crowning difficulty of writing in irregular metres. Having broken away from all restraints of couplet and stanza,—having caused his rhymes and pauses to fall just where and just when the emotion demands that they should fall, scorning the exigencies of makeshift no less than the exigencies of stanza,—he has found, what every writer of irregular English odes has sought in vain, a music as entrancing, as natural, and at the same time as inscrutable, as the music of the winds or of the sea."

1. **Xanadu.** "In Xamdu did Cublai Can build a stately Palace, encompassing sixteene miles of plaine ground with a wall, wherein are fertile meddowes, pleasant springs, delightful streams, and all sorts of beasts of chase and game, and in the middest thereof a sumptuous house of pleasure."—*Purchas his Pilgrimage,* London, 1626, Bk. IV., ch. xiii. A full account of Kublai's summer-residence at Chandu, Xandu, or Shandu, may be read in Marco Polo, Bk. I., ch. lxi. The ruins still exist: see Col. Yule's *Marco Polo,* Vol. I., p. 294.

Kubla Khan, A.D. 1216-1294, one of the most famous of Asiatic sovereigns, the founder of the Mongol Dynasty in China. It was he who built as his capital the city known as Peking.

2. **decree,** order to be built.

4. **caverns.** The disappearance of rivers and their reappearance after an underground journey of some miles, are a common phenomenon in limestone country. The Orbe runs underground for several miles from the Lac de Joux in the Swiss Jura. Similarly, the Yorkshire Aire, which apparently rises in Malham Cove, has its real source in Malham Lake.

Prof. Tyrrell quotes this line in his note on Euripides, *Bacchae,* 1360, τὸν καταιβάτην 'Αχέροντα, "the down-rushing Acheron."

8. **sinuous**, winding. Cp. "Maeander **is** a river in Lycia, a province of Natolia, or Asia Minor, famous for the *sinuosity* and often returning thereof," Drayton; "Streaking the ground with *sinuous* trace," Milton, *Paradise Lost*, Bk. VII.

11. **greenery**, verdure. The word seems not to occur before Coleridge. It has been used by Mrs. Browning and others since.

13. **cover**, wood; properly **a** hunting term for a place which affords shelter to wild animals.

16. **demon-lover**. Such subjects always had a peculiar fascination for Coleridge, as may be seen from his *Christabel*, his projected *Ballad of the Dark Ladie*, and *Love* (IV. 49-52). It was probably from Coleridge that Keats drew the inspiration of *La Belle Dame Sans Merci* (XXX.). There is a striking ballad, *The Demon Lover*, in the *Minstrelsy of the Scottish Border*, Vol. II. This was not published till 1802, *i.e.* after *Kubla Khan* was written, though before its publication. Still, Coleridge may have been acquainted with the ballad or another like it.

19. **momently**, for a moment at a time.

25. **five miles.** Mr. Churton Collins, quoting this line, says: "Coleridge was, so far as I know, the first English poet who discovered the strange effect produced by a flash of prosaic definiteness of detail in the midst of vague and dreamy pomp." Instances are common in later poets, notably Tennyson and Rossetti.

30. "**Mighty solitudes** are generally fear-haunted and fear-peopled. . . . The sea is often peopled, amidst its ravings, with what seem innumerable human voices—such voices, or as ominous, as what were heard by Kubla Khan . . . ; oftentimes laughter mixes from a distance (seeming to come also from distant times as well as distant places) with the uproar of waters."—De Quincey *Autobiography*, I. 302 (1896 edition).

33. **measure**, music. So Shelley in LXXX. 96, "Better than all measures of delightful sound." Cp. the use of 'numbers' for poetry (II. 20).

36. **pleasure-dome.** This may have been suggested by Cowper's description of the Empress Catherine of Russia's palace of ice, *The Task*, Bk. V.

37. **dulcimer**, a stringed instrument, mentioned in the Authorised Version (1611) of *Daniel*, iii. 10, with the 'cornet, flute, harp, sackbut, psaltery.' The strings were struck with two hammers held in the hands. The word is said to be derived from the Lat. *dulce melos*, 'sweet song.'

41. **Abora**, Abba Yared, a mountain in Abyssinia, 14,918 **ft.** high.

45. Music. As Amphion was fabled to have built the walls of Thebes to music. Cp. Tennyson, *Gareth and Lynette*:

> " For truly, as thou sayest, a Fairy King
> And Fairy Queens have built the city, son ;
> They came from out a sacred mountain-cleft
> Toward the sunrise, each with harp in hand,
> And built it to the music of their harps."

51. weave a circle, the magic circle, within which he would be held spell-bound. *Thrice,* the favourite number in magical rites: cp. Virgil, *Eclogue* viii. 73-75:

> *Terna tibi haec primum triplici diversa colore*
> *Licia circumdo, terque haec altaria circum*
> *Effigiem duco ; numero deus impare gaudet.*

No. CX. *Most sweet it is with unuplifted eyes*

WORDSWORTH has here achieved one of the most difficult triumphs ; he has expressed philosophy in terms of poetry. When it is said that Browning, for instance, was more of a philosopher than a poet, the criticism, whether just or unjust, implies that the fusion of philosophy and poetry is not complete in his writings—that he has not given to his thought that emotional exaltation which is necessary to poetry. The same charge may be brought against many passages in *The Prelude* and *The Excursion*. But in this sonnet Wordsworth has expressed his philosophy of poetry as it could not have been expressed in prose : the words and the rhythm have a symbolic power that belongs to poetry alone.

9. The necessity of the union of love with intellectual power to produce poetry, and indeed to produce any work of moral value, is a common thought in Wordsworth. See the quotations in Aubrey de Vere, *Essays chiefly on Poetry*, Vol. I., p. 157. We may recall, too, "Keep thy *heart* with all diligence, for out of it are the issues of life," *Proverbs*, iv. 23.

No. CXI. *Ever let the Fancy roam*

Metre.—See metrical notes to II. and XCIII. Nowhere in Keats is the influence of *L'Allegro* and *Il Penseroso*, which we have also traced in Campbell (XCVII.) and Shelley (C.), so evident as here. In those poems Milton gives us the very 'native wood-notes wild' which he attributes to Shakespeare. Keats has caught them, and with them the rich profusion of imagery that was at Milton's command.

13. **red-lipp'd** as an epithet properly belongs to the personified Autumn, not to her fruitage, though it is the redness of the fruit that gives her the epithet; so 'blushing' in the next line.

15. **cloys.** Here used correctly : see note on II. 28.

16. **ingle,** fire, fire-place. A Scottish and Northumbrian word, which may be connected with Lat. *ignis.*

21. **shoon,** the old plural of shoe.

42. **antheming.** An example of the use of 'anthem' as a verb is quoted in N.E.D. from Feltham's *Resolves,* 1628.

51. **shaded,** growing in the shade.

56. **meagre,** in its etymological sense of 'lean, thin': Lat. *macer.*

57. **winter-thin,** thin from its winter sleep. See note on 'spectre-thin,' LXXXIII. 27. Cp. the description of the snake in Virgil, *Aeneid,* ii. 471-475.

65. **down-pattering.** Cp. Tennyson, *In Memoriam,* xi., 'The chestnut pattering to the ground.'

73. **doth.** Relative omitted as in VI. 4.

81. **dulcet-eyed.** *Dulcet,* sweet, is a Miltonic word : "dulcet symphonies and voices sweet," *Paradise Lost,* i. 712.

Ceres' daughter, Proserpine, carried off to the lower world by Pluto, the 'God of Torment.'

85. **Hebe,** daughter of Zeus and Hera, goddess of eternal youth —the handmaiden of the gods, for whom she pours out nectar.

zone, girdle.

87. **kirtle,** a sort of gown or petticoat. The word is used by Chaucer. Skeat thinks it a diminutive of 'skirt.'

89. **mesh,** properly used of a net, here applied to an entangling cord.

90. **leash,** properly the 'lash' or 'line' by which a hawk or hound is held.

91-2. Cp. in *L'Allegro* :

> " Untwisting all the chains that tie
> The hidden soul of harmony ; "

and

> " These delights if thou canst give,
> Mirth, with thee I mean to live."

No. CXII. *I heard a thousand blended notes*

THE strength and limitations of Wordsworth's philosophy of Nature are both revealed in this sweet and simple poem. "Wordsworth's claim," says Mr. John Morley (Introduction to Wordsworth's *Poetical Works,* p. lxiii.), "his special gift, his lasting contribution, lies in the extraordinary strenuousness, sincerity and insight with which he first idealises and glorifies the vast universe around us, and then makes of it, not a theatre on which men play their parts, but an animate presence, intermingling with our works, pouring its companionable spirit about us, and 'breathing grandeur upon the very humblest face of human life.'" This feeling about Nature should be compared with Shelley's Pantheism (c. 50-51, CI. 45-48, CXIV. 104-137): the likeness and difference between the two feelings are the measure of the likeness and difference between the two poets. On the other hand, "Wordsworth's eyes avert their ken from half of human fate" (Matthew Arnold) and from half of the fate of all animate things. Nature "red in tooth and claw with rapine" is a conception which is strange to Wordsworth but which the modern philosopher cannot ignore. Compare Tennyson, *In Memoriam*, cantos LIV.-LVI.

3. **sweet mood.** Cp. IV. 17-20 and LXXX. 90, "Our sweetest songs are those that tell of saddest thought."

No. CXIII.   *When Ruth was left half desolate*

WRITTEN in Germany, 1799. "Nature's influence is only salutary so long as she is herself, so to say, in keeping with man; when her operations reach that degree of habitual energy and splendour at which our love for her passes into fascination and our admiration into bewilderment, then the fierce and irregular stimulus consorts no longer with the growth of a temperate virtue." (F. W. H. Myers, *Life of Wordsworth*, p. 139.) Contrast Nature's education of Lucy, described in XV. Ruth herself knew something of Nature's healing power, her 'breathing balm,' not only in childhood (l. 13-18), but in moments of respite from her madness (l. 199-204).

The story of the misery brought to Ruth by her lover may also be taken as an illustration of the thesis of the preceding poem— "What Man has made of Man."

19. **Georgia,** one of the Southern States of the United States of America, bounded W. by Alabama, S. by Florida.

20. **casque,** French, helmet. 'Case,' 'cask,' 'casket,' are cognate words.

22. **Cherokees,** one of the native tribes of North America.

28. **free from battle,** after the United States had secured their independence.

37. **lovely.** See note on IV. 42.

49. **rout,** gathering. Cp. "But nightingales a full great rout, That flien over his head about," *Romaunt of the Rose*; "The

lustie shepheard swaynes sate in a rout," Spenser, *Faerie Queene*, VI. ix.

61. **magnolia**, a tree bearing conspicuous and often large, fragrant, white, rose or purple flowers; indigenous both in Asia and America.

66. Cp. Tennyson *Œnone*, "And at their feet the crocus brake *like fire.*"

67. **savannahs**, name given by the Spaniards to the vast meadows of the western and southern States of N. America.

137. **the stars.** Cp. in Rudyard Kipling's *MacAndrew's Hymn*, 'the lasceevious stars.' The thought and the expression are as old as Tibullus (II. i. 87):

> *Ludite : iam Nox iungit equos, currumque sequuntur*
> *Matris lascivo sidera fulva choro.*

174. **liberty.** Contrast the lesson of Nature in the *Ode to Duty*, XLV. 45-48.

198. **caroused.** More commonly intransitive as in LVII. 4. But cp. Shakespeare, *Othello*, II. iii. 55, "Roderigo . . . hath to-night caroused potations pottle-deep."

203. Cp. the exquisite lines in the *Ancient Mariner* :

> A noise like of a hidden brook
> In the leafy month of June,
> That to the sleeping woods all night
> Singeth a quiet tune.

214. **Tone**, a small river in Somerset, tributary of the Parret.

217. **engines of her pain**, because of their influence on her lover's temperament.

256. **funeral bell.** Cp. *Hamlet*, v. i. 241, the burial of Ophelia. See note on LXXIV. 50.

No. CXIV.   *Many a green isle needs must be*

WRITTEN October, 1818. The Euganean Hills are a small group of volcanic heights between Padua and Verona, which still preserve the name of an ancient Italian tribe, who, according to Livy, occupied the whole tract between the Alps and the sea till they were expelled by the Veneti. "The leading idea of this beautiful description of a day's landscape in Italy appears to be—On the voyage of life are many moments of pleasure given by the sight of Nature, who has power to heal even the worldliness and the uncharity of man" (F.T.P.).

Mr. Palgrave has omitted two considerable passages in this poem—39 lines between l. 26 and l. 27, 143 lines between l. 102 and l. 103. The poem undoubtedly gains as a whole in impressiveness by being shortened, but the first of the omitted portions contains some magnificent imagery which the lover of Shelley should on no account lose. The second passage contains a prophecy of the future triumph of Liberty and a lament for the subjection to slavery of Venice and Padua.

The wonderful expression here given to the atmospheric effects of the sunrise, noon, and sunset of the bright autumn day should be studied; and with the description of noon the author's *Stanzas Written in Dejection* (LXIII.) should be compared. We may compare also Wordsworth's *Ode composed on an evening of extraordinary splendour*, and contrast the attitude of the two poets towards Nature. Wordsworth had taught Shelley to look to her for healing. The traces of Wordsworthian influence are strong in *Alastor*. But Shelley abandoned himself to Nature—"Make me thy lyre, ev'n as the forest is": Wordsworth had learnt from her the lesson of self-restraint (XLV. 41-48).

Metre.—As in XCIII., C.

13. **riving**, splitting. So in LII. 13, "with thunder riven."

16. **like that sleep.** The dream in which the dreamer seems to be sinking endlessly is a familiar experience. It is a common superstition that to reach the bottom in such a dream is to die.

27. **Ay.** This is the common reading, and is found in the earlier editions of *The Golden Treasury*. The reading *Ah* of recent editions does not seem to have any authority.

32. **paean**, here used in its strict sense of a choral song, παιάν, addressed to Apollo, the Sun-God, who was also the God of Healing.

33. **legion'd.** The practice of forming adjectives from substantives by means of a participial ending, though disapproved of by Dr. Johnson—"I was sorry to see in the lines of a scholar like Gray the 'honied' spring"—is common in the poets. Milton has "squadron'd angels," which doubtless suggested "legion'd" to Shelley.

35. **hoar**, here used simply of colour, 'greyish white.' This is the original use of the word, though it very early acquired the notion of 'venerable,' being specially applied to grey hair.

41. **grain.** The word originally meant 'a seed,' but was used for any minute object, and specially applied to the dried body or ovarium of an insect of the genus *coccus*, from which red dyes are procured. So 'grain' is used by Milton for Tyrian purp'e; 'the grain of Sarra,' *Paradise Lost*, xi. 242. "All in a robe of darkest grain," *Il Penseroso*, l. 33. Shelley follows Milton here.

54. **islanded**, with cities lying in it like islands.

58. **Amphitrité**, daughter of Nereus and Doris, is wife of Poseidon (Neptune) and queen of the sea in Greek mythology.

62. **reclined, resting,** as in CXII. 2.

67. **column, etc.** Cp. Wordsworth's sonnet *Upon Westminster Bridge*, LXXXIV. 5-8.

68. **obelisks** are properly tall, four-sided, tapering pillars, cut off at the top like a flat pyramid. Tennyson calls the columns of smoke from household fires "azure pillars of the hearth."

74. **as,** as if. See note on XXX. 19. **dome of gold,** the sun.

75. **Apollo,** the Sun-God of the Greeks, whose oracle they consulted at Delphi.

76. **sun-girt.** In some editions of the *G. T.* Mr. Palgrave emended this to the more obvious epithet *sea-girt*, but he afterwards withdrew the emendation. "Venice," says Mr. Swinburne, "is not a sea-girt city ; it is interlaced and interwoven with sea, but not girdled ; pierced through with water but not ringed about. Seen by noon from the Euganean heights, clothed as with the very and visible glory of Italy, it might seem to Shelley a city girdled with the sunlight, as some Nereid with the arms of the sun-god."

77. See Wordsworth's sonnet, XLVIII., and introductory note.

81. **watery bier.** Milton, *Lycidas*, l. 12, "He must not float upon his watery bier" (*G. T.*, LXXXIX.).

82. **drear.** See note on XXVIII. 1.

84. **slave of slaves,** Napoleon.

93. **topples.** Cp. Virgil, *Aeneid*, vi. 603, *Quos super atra silex iam iam lapsura cadentique | Imminet assimilis.*

101. **masque,** dance of death.

107. **air-dissolvéd star,** a star dissolved into air. Shelley's meaning may best be understood by a comparison of LXIII. 13, where he compares the waves breaking on the shore in dazzling sunshine to "light dissolved in star-showers."

110. **profound,** adj. for subst., depth ; Lat. *profundus.*

118. **trellised.** Trellis, the name given to cross-barred or lattice work, for supporting plants, is derived, through the French, from Lat. *trilix*, 'triple-twilled' (*tri-licium*, 'a thread').

120. **dun.** Cp. LII. 22, "war-clouds rolling dun."

122. **the flower.** See CI. 43, "To the soft flower beneath our feet." With Shelley's mention of the flower as 'interpenetrated,' like the rest of Nature, with "love, light, harmony, Odour, or the soul of all," contrast Wordsworth's simpler expression of his "faith that every flower Enjoys the air it breathes" (CXII. 11) and the concluding lines of his *Ode* (CXXXI. 203-4).

124. **olive-sandall'd.** "Who that has seen Lombardy but must recognise the truth of that beautiful epithet ?"—F. T. Palgrave, *Landscape in Poetry*, p. 227.

130. **darken'd.** The tone of the earlier part of the poem, especially of the omitted lines, is in strong contrast to the brightness of the scene described. At the very outset (l. 2) life is spoken of as "the deep, wide sea of misery."

134. **the soul of all.** Cp. c. 50-51, "And all things seem only one In the universal Sun," and *Adonais*, st. liv. :

> " That light whose smile kindles the Universe,
> That Beauty in which all things work and move,
> That Benediction which the eclipsing Curse
> Of birth can quench not, that sustaining Love
> Which, through the web of being blindly wove
> By man and beast and earth and air and sea,
> Burns bright or dim, as each are mirrors of
> The fire for which all thirst, now beams on me,
> Consuming the last clouds of cold mortality."

And with 'the mind which feeds this verse,' cp. the apotheosis of Keats in *Adonais*, st. xliii. :

> " He is a portion of the loveliness
> Which once he made more lovely : he doth bear
> His part, while the one Spirit's plastic stress
> Sweeps through the dull dense world, compelling there
> All new successions to the form they wear,
> Torturing th' unwilling dross that checks its flight
> To its own likeness, as each mass may bear ;
> And bursting in its beauty and its might
> From trees and beasts and men into the Heaven's light."

137. This is like the doctrine of the idealist philosophers that mind alone gives meaning, intelligibility, to the Universe of dead matter, which without mind can hardly be said even to exist.

141. **her** and **she** in 143, the personified 'Autumn's evening.'

162. **windless bower.** With this description cp. 'the island-valley of Avilion' in Tennyson's *Morte d'Arthur* :

> " Where falls not hail, or rain, or any snow,
> Nor ever wind blows loudly ; but it lies
> Deep-meadow'd, happy, fair with orchard-lawns
> And bowery hollows crown'd with summer sea ";

and the 'vale in Ida' in Tennyson's *Œnone.* Cp. also the song of Callicles in Matthew Arnold, *Empedocles on Etna* :

> " Far, far from here,
> The Adriatic breaks in a warm bay
> Among the green Illyrian hills ; and there
> The sunshine in the happy glens is fair,
> And by the sea, and in the brakes.
> The grass is cool, the sea-side air
> Buoyant and fresh, the mountain flowers
> More virginal and sweet than oura."

172. Cp. E. A. Poe, *Annabel Lee*: "The angels, not half so happy in heaven, Went envying her and me."

182. soul, subject ; interval, object.

184. *I.e.* and (by) the Love.

185. circling, encircling, transitive.

188. They, the Spirits ; it, the Paradise.

No. CXV. *O wild West Wind, thou breath of Autumn's being*

PERHAPS the greatest of all Shelley's lyrics. The verse sweeps along with the elemental rush of the wind it celebrates. Metaphor succeeds to metaphor, and simile to simile, with wild rapidity ; but, though at a first reading it is hardly possible to keep pace with the swift kaleidoscopic changes, there is none of the hazy indistinctness that is apt to mar the same poet's less perfect work. "He passes from magnificent union of himself with Nature and magnificent realisation of her storm and peace to equally great self-description, and then mingles all nature and all himself together, that he may sing of the restoration of mankind. There is no song in the whole of our literature more passionate, more penetrative, more full of the force by which the idea and its form are united into one creation" (Stopford Brooke, *Poems of Shelley*, p. xvii.).

"This poem was conceived and chiefly written in a wood that skirts the Arno, near Florence, and on a day when that tempestuous wind, whose temperature is at once mild and animating, was collecting the vapours which pour down the autumnal rains. They began, as I foresaw, at sunset with a violent tempest of hail and rain, attended by that magnificent thunder and lightning peculiar to the Cisalpine regions.

"The phenomenon alluded to at the conclusion of the third stanza is well known to naturalists. The vegetation at the bottom of the sea, of rivers, and of lakes, sympathises with that of the land in the change of seasons, and is consequently influenced by the winds which announce it."—Shelley's Note.

It is interesting to compare the first stanza of Coleridge's *Ode on France* (" Ye clouds that far above me float and pause ")—a stanza that had probably not been without an influence upon Shelley.

Metre.—The division of the poem into stanzas of 14 lines of 5 iambic feet suggests the structure of sonnets. The chief difference is that, whereas the normal English sonnet divides itself into two stanzas of 4 lines followed by two stanzas of 3 lines, the fourteen-line stanzas of this ode rather divide themselves into—and are sometimes printed as—four stanzas of three lines with a concluding couplet.

A question arises about the scansion of l. 31. Some editors print "crystálline." The use of the word in CXIV. 64, shows that Shelley did not always pronounce it thus. The ordinary pronunciation gives a subtler music to the line, the scansion of which is to be explained like that of CVIII. 20.

3. **like ghosts.** See note on VIII. 12. Cp. *The Sensitive Plant*, Part III.:

"And the leaves brown, yellow, and grey, and red,
And white with the whiteness of what is dead,
Like troops of ghosts on the dry wind past;
Their whistling noise made the birds aghast."

4. **hectic.** See note on XXXIII. 13.

6. **chariotest.** So Keats, LXXXIII. 32, "Not *charioted* by Bacchus and his pards."

18. **angels,** messengers, the original meaning of the word: Greek, ἄγγελος.

21. **Maenad.** Greek, Μαινάδες, 'the frenzied ones'; the name given to the female votaries of the god Dionysus or Bacchus. "They wandered through woods and mountains, their flying locks crowned with ivy or snakes, brandishing wands and torches, to the hollow sounds of the drum, and the shrill notes of the flute, with wild dances, and insane cries and jubilation" (Seyffert, *Dict. of Classical Antiquities*). Cp. Horace, *Odes*, III. xxv., and Euripides, *Bacchae.*

23. **dirge.** Shelley afterwards wrote a *Dirge for the Year*, beginning "Orphan hours, the year is dead."

26. A reminiscence of *Hamlet*, II. ii. 311, "This most excellent canopy, the air, look you, this brave o'erhanging firmament, this majestical roof fretted with golden fire, why, it appears no other thing to me than a foul and pestilent *congregation of vapours.*" There is another echo of *Hamlet* in Shelley's *Ode to a Skylark*, LXXX. 86.

32. **Baiae,** on the coast of Campania, at the western end of the bay of Naples : a favourite resort of the ancient Romans.

pumice isle, formed by deposits of lava from Vesuvius. Baiae was destroyed by an eruption of this volcano.

35. Cp. *Stanzas written in Dejection near Naples*, LXIII. 10: "I see the deep's untrampled floor With green and purple sea-weeds strown."

36. **so sweet.** So in LXXX. 55, "faint with too much sweet."

39. **oozy,** moist. The word escapes the unpleasing associations of 'muddy' or 'slimy.' It is a favourite word with Milton. Cp. *Lycidas* (*G.T.*, LXXXIX.), l. 175, "With nectar pure his oozy locks he laves"; *Ode on Nativity* (*G.T.*, LXXXV.), l. 124, "And bid the weltering waves their oozy channel keep."

40. Contrast with this description of the storm penetrating to the depths of ocean, the picture of perfect peace in CI. 31, "As still as in the silent deep the ocean-woods may be."

48. Cp. Coleridge's regretful recollection of his boyhood in *Youth and Age*, CXXII. 9-17.

54. Cp. Shelley's *Epipsychidion*, "I pant, I sink, I tremble, I expire"; also VIII. 18.

55. Cp. Tennyson, *Tithonus*:

"But thy strong Hours indignant work'd their wills,
   And beat me down and marr'd and wasted me."

56. Cp. Shelley's description of himself in *Adonais*, st. xxxi.-xxxiii., especially the lines:

"A pard-like Spirit beautiful and swift—
   A love in desolation masked—a Power
   Girt round with weakness—it can scarce uplift
   The weight of the superincumbent hour."

62. be thou me. Shelley has some good English authorities, and the analogy of the French *C'est moi*, on his side, in using this construction. The rhyming of 'one' to 'own' is a blemish in this line.

64. quicken (A.S.), to make quick or alive, the original use of the word.

65. So Shelley wrote of Dante: "His very words are instinct with spirit, each is as a spark, a burning atom of inextinguishable thought; and many yet lie covered in the ashes of their birth, and pregnant with the lightning which has yet found no conductor."

69. The finest expression of this prophetic mood in Shelley is the last chorus of *Hellas*, "The world's great age begins anew." For the worth of Shelley's prophecy see the suggestive remarks of F. W. H. Myers in Ward's *English Poets*, Vol. IV., p. 356. Mr. Stopford Brooke says, "the cry is prophetic of that unconquerable hope for mankind which, underlying the greater part of Shelley's poetry, has made half its influence upon the world."

No. CXVI.   *I was thy neighbour once, thou rugged Pile*

SIR GEORGE BEAUMONT, of Coleorton Hall, Leicestershire, to whom this poem is addressed, was a friend of Wordsworth and Coleridge, much interested in art and literature and in landscape gardening.   See Myers, *Life of Wordsworth*, p. 65, or the larger biography by Knight. ch. xxi.; also *Memorials of Coleorton*: letters from Coleridge, Wordsworth and his sister, Southey and Scott, to Sir George and Lady Beaumont, edited by W. Knight (Edinburgh, 1887).

The 'Peele Castle' of the picture—which still hangs or till lately hung at Coleorton—is not the famous castle in the Isle of Man, but a ruined keep on a small island close to the modern town of Barrow-in-Furness, Lancashire. There are many 'Peels' in the border-country, the word 'peel' itself meaning 'castle' or 'stronghold.' The 'deep distress' mentioned in l. 36 was caused by the death of Wordsworth's sailor brother John, who was captain of the 'Abergavenny,' East Indiaman, wrecked off Portland, Feb. 5, 1815, on the outward voyage to India and China. Wordsworth's brother went down with his ship, "dying as he had lived," wrote the poet, "in the very place and point where his duty stationed him." Myers, *Life of Wordsworth*, p. 69.

8. Shelley, consciously or unconsciously, borrowed this line from Wordsworth in his *Evening: Pont à Mare, Pisa*:

> " Within the surface of the fleeting river
> The wrinkled image of the city lay,
> Immovably unquiet, and for ever
> It trembles, but it never fades away."

15-6. With this, perhaps the most perfect expression in terms of poetry of the function of poetry, compare Shelley's lines in the next poem, CXVII.

22. a chronicle of heaven, a place where life should seem always to have been passed as peacefully and happily as in heaven.

24. had, should have.

26. Elysian. See note on II. 11.

34. Cp. *Lines composed a few miles above Tintern Abbey*:

> " For I have learned
> To look on nature, not as in the hour
> Of thoughtless youth ; but hearing oftentimes
> The still, sad music of *humanity*,
> Nor harsh nor grating, though of ample power
> To chasten and subdue."

The whole poem should be compared.

36. Cp. Virgil, *Aeneid*, i. 462, *Sunt lacrimae rerum et mentem mortalia tangunt ;* 630, *Non ignara mali miseris succurrere disco.*

47. labours, specially used of the action of a ship in a heavy sea, pitching and rolling.

48. rueful, epithet applied to the sky by imaginative anticipation, 'threatening to cause sorrow.'

pageantry of fear, magnificent spectacle that inspires terror.

52. trampling suggests the irresistible advance of a triumphant army, treading its enemies under foot.

54. **kind, the human family.** ' Kind ' is a derivative of ' kin.'
This stanza might be taken as the motto of Tennyson's *Palace of
Art.*

57. Cp. Homer, *Odyssey*, xx. 18, τέτλαθι δὴ, κραδίη· καὶ κύντερον
ἄλλο ποτ' ἔτλης, "Endure, my heart, yet a worse thing hast thou
endured "—the line that is quoted with admiration by Plato in
Republic, iii. 390. Cp. also A. H. Clough, *In a London Square*,
"And thou, O human heart of mine, Be still, refrain thyself, and
wait."

60. Cp. Wordsworth's *Ode*, cxxxi. 179-186.

No. CXVII. *On a Poet's lips I slept*

IN this lyric from the *Prometheus Unbound*, Act I. l. 737, Shelley
translates into his own imaginative language the definition of the
function of poetry which Wordsworth has given us in the preceding poem. Poetry is not mere imitation, μίμησις; it is
idealised imitation. The poet adds 'the gleam,' and it is
' the gleam ' that makes the value of poetry. In Shelley ' the
gleam ' becomes an almost blinding luminousness that bathes the
whole picture. "In this radiation of many-coloured lights,"
wrote J. A. Symonds in his *Life of Shelley*, "the outline itself
is apt to be a little misty. Shelley pierced through things to
their spiritual essence. *The actual world was less for him than
that which lies within it and beyond it.* 'I seek in what I see the
manifestation of something beyond the present and tangible
object.'" Mr. Symonds then quotes these lines, and adds :
"The bees are scarcely heeded. And yet who could have brought
the bees, the lake, the sun, the bloom, more perfectly before us
than that picture does ?"
On this poem and cxvi. Mr. F. T. Palgrave wrote : "Each
is the most complete expression of the innermost spirit of his
art given by these great Poets—of that Idea which, as in the
case of the true Painter (to quote the words of Reynolds) subsists
only in the mind : The sight never beheld it, nor has the hand
expressed it : it is an idea residing in the breast of the artist,
which he is always labouring to impart, and which he dies at
last without imparting."

Metre.—Observe the exquisite blending of trochaic and iambic
rhythms—the iambic lines checking the pace of the swift verse.

2. **love-adept**, versed in love, skilled in its secrets. In mediaeval Latin *adeptus*, the participle of *adipiscor*, ' to attain,' was
used as a substantive, and assumed by Alchemists who professed
to have attained the great secret of their craft.

9. **ivy-bloom.** Expressing a more delicate notion than
' blossom,' which is more commonly florescence bearing promise

of fruit, while 'bloom' is florescence thought of as the culminating beauty of the plant (N. E. D.). Cp. Milton, *Paradise Lost*, v. 25, "How the bee Sits on the bloom, extracting liquid sweet.'

No. CXVIII.   *In this still place, remote from men*

THIS poem, along with LXXXVII., XC., XCI., XCVIII., was a fruit of Wordsworth's Scotch tour, 1803.

The poems generally known as Ossian's were composed in the eighteenth century by James Macpherson, who wrote them in English from the legends he had collected in a tour through the Highlands, and afterwards invented what he professed to be Gaelic originals. The Ossian or Oisin of tradition was a warrior-bard, son of Finn-na-Gael, commonly called Fingal, King of Morven on the N. W. coast of Scotland, in the third century A.D. Finn married a daughter of Cormac, King of Ireland, and delivered that country when it was invaded by the King of Denmark.

Metre.—The iambic couplet of eight syllables, used by Coleridge in *Christabel.*

13. complaining, full of melancholy sound, as of 'the waves that moan about the world' or 'the wail of midnight winds' (Tennyson, *Demeter*).

No. CXIX.   *The world is too much with us; late and soon*

COMPARE two other sonnets of Wordsworth, XLIX. and L.

4. sordid boon, a gift made from sordid motives. *Boon* (A.S. *ben*) is originally a prayer; then, the answer to a prayer, a favour or gift.

6. will be howling, choose to howl.

10. Pagan, heathen, from the sense which *paganus*—originally a countryman, peasant—acquired in ecclesiastical Latin.

13. Proteus, an 'old man of the sea' in Greek mythology, who tended the seals which are the flocks of Amphitrite. He possessed the gift of prophecy and the power of assuming any shape he pleased: hence the adjective 'protean.' Cp. Homer, *Odyssey*, iv. 354-569; Virgil, *Georgic* iv. 387 *et seq.*

14. Triton, son of Poseidon and Amphitrite. "He is described as living with them in a golden palace in the depths of the sea. He was represented as a man in his upper parts, terminating in a dolphin's tail; his special attribute is a twisted sea-shell, on which he blows, now violently, now gently, to raise or calm the billows." (Seyffert, *Dict. of Antiquities.*)

wreathèd, twisted. The phrase comes from Spenser, *Colin Clout's come home again*, "Triton, blowing loud his wreathed horn."

No. CXX. *Tax not the royal Saint with vain expense*

THE first of three sonnets which Wordsworth wrote on the same subject : the other two will be found as Nos. xliv. and xlv. of the third series of *Ecclesiastical Sonnets*. In Book III. of *The Prelude* he thus describes his first sight of Cambridge :

> " It was a dreary morning when the wheels
> Rolled over a wide plain o'erhung with clouds,
> And nothing cheered our way till first we saw
> The long-roofed chapel of King's College lift
> Turrets and pinnacles in answering files,
> Extended high above a dusky grove."

1. **tax**, properly to assess, charge with a rate or fine ; so, to charge with a fault. Cp. Bacon's *Henry VII.*, "These rumours begot scandal against the king, *taxing* him for a great *taxer* of his people." So Celia in *As You Like It*, I. ii. 90, "Enough ! speak no more of him ; you'll be whipped for *taxation* one of these days," and Jaques in the same play, II. vii. 86, "Why then my *taxing* like a wild-goose flies."

royal Saint, Henry VI., who founded "the King's College of S. Nicholas in Cambridge" in 1441. He founded Eton about the same time.

4. **Scholars.** The colleges at Oxford and Cambridge were founded for 'a scanty band' of Fellows and Scholars only. Students who pay fees, Commoners, as they are called at Oxford, Pensioners at Cambridge, are a later accretion, and to this day are distinguished from 'members of the foundation.'

white-robed. It is the privilege of the Scholars to wear surplices at the chapel services ; Pensioners wear the ordinary academic black gown.

8. **the sense,** the aesthetic sense, the power of enjoying beauty.

9-10. An accurate description of the marvellously intricate roof of King's College chapel.

12. Cp. *L'Allegro* (*G.T.*, CXLIV.), "In notes with many a winding bout Of linked sweetness long drawn out," and *Il Penseroso* (*G.T.*, CXLV.), 161-166, "There let the pealing organ blow," etc.

No. CXXI. *Thou still unravished bride of quietness*

" EVERY one knows the general story of the Italian Renaissance, or the Revival of Letters. From Petrarch's day to our own that ancient world has renewed its youth: poets and artists, students and thinkers, have yielded themselves wholly to its fascination, and deeply penetrated its spirit. Yet perhaps no one more truly has vivified, whilst idealizing, the picture of Greek country life in the fancied Golden Age, than Keats in these lovely (if somewhat unequally executed) stanzas: his quick imagination, by a kind of 'natural magic,' more than supplying the scholarship which his youth had no opportunity of gaining." (F. T. P.).

Mr. W. T. Arnold, after remarking that Keats had fed his love of Greek mythology not only upon Chapman's *Homer*, the *Aeneid*, and a classical dictionary, but also upon a study of the Elgin marbles, goes on to say that "the Greek Vase which inspired Keats was no figment of his imagination, but had a real existence, and is now, it is said, under the arcade at the south front of Holland House." It has been further suggested—by Mr. A. S. Murray in a letter to Mr. Arnold—that Keats obtained his knowledge of this urn from Piranesi's work (vol. xiii., published 1750), which gives an engraving of it. "A small throng of people come from the left towards a veiled priest who stands beside an altar, beside which also a youth plays on pipes. On the right a heifer (and an unpoetic pig) is being led to be sacrificed."

Metre.—The order of the rhymes of the latter six lines varies in the different stanzas.

3. **sylvan historian.** *Sylvan*, explained by 'leaf-fringed.' *Historian*, because containing a record of a past age.

5. **legend,** orig. 'something to be read.' **Legenda,** properly the gerundive of *lego*, 'to read,' was specially applied in mediaeval Latin to a book of chronicles of the saints read at matins. Hence the meaning of 'a marvellous or romantic story from early times,' which Keats seems here to combine with another meaning of the word—'the motto to be read on a coat of arms, medal or coin.' It is easy to transfer the word in either of its senses to the story 'to be read' on the marble urn.

7. **Tempé,** a vale in Thessaly. Keats was probably thinking of Virgil's praise of pastoral life (*Georgic* ii., 469): *at frigida Tempe, Mugitusque boum mellesque sub arbore somni, Non absunt.* We are told that Keats "worked diligently through the *Aeneid* when at school," so it is probable that he also read the most famous passage in the *Georgics.*

Arcady, Arcadia, the most pastoral part of the Peloponnese, specially associated with the worship of Pan, the shepherds' god. Again Keats may have had Virgil in his mind (*Eclogue* x.): *Pan deus Arcadiae* and *Soli cantare periti Arcades.*

10. **timbrel,** a kind of tambourine: through Lat. and Fr. from Gk. τύμπανον, a drum.

13. **sensual**, bodily.

15. Cp. Sidney's *Arcadia*, "the shepherd boy piping as though he should never be old."

18. **winning**, attaining. Richardson's dictionary quotes from a chronicle of 1455 the description of an English army fenced with wood and trees 'in such wyse, that the French sperys myght not *wyn* unto them.' The use is not uncommon in the seventeenth and eighteenth centuries.

21. The words recall the address of Keats to the real tree, which does shed its leaves, but is happy in having no remembrance of departed summer (XXVIII.).

29. **high-sorrowful**, full to the brim of sorrow, a curiously formed compound. Keats perhaps got his fondness for compound adjectives from Chapman.

30. **parching**, for parched: an inaccurate use, such as Keats allowed himself in 'slumber'd' and 'cloying,' II. 28.

34. **silken**, smooth and glossy like silk.

garland. In Greek and Roman sacrifices the victims were generally decked out with ribbons and wreaths.

37. **this.** "*Its* has been here plausibly but, perhaps, unnecessarily conjectured." (F. T. P.).

41. **attitude** properly means 'aptitude of position, posture adapted to a particular purpose.' By 'fair attitude' Keats seems to mean that the shape of the urn is gracefully adapted to its purpose.

brede, a variant of 'braid,' used archaically by modern poets. Cp. Collins, *Ode to Evening* (*G. T.*, CLXXXVI.), "cloudy skirts, with brede ethereal wove."

44. **tease us out of thought.** Keats often writes as if human happiness could only be reached by escaping from thought— "Where but to *think* is to be full of sorrow" (LXXXIII. 27), "the faery power Of *unreflecting* love (XXXVI. 12). Contrast Wordsworth's praise of "the quietness of thought" (XLV. 36), "the philosophic mind" (CXXXI. 186).

cold, because the men, maidens and trees are not living, but only represented on the marble.

49-50. The whole of the last couplet is supposed to be spoken by the urn. Perhaps it would be unfair to make Keats responsible for the doctrine: but it is well to remember that, in this world at least, the identity of truth and beauty is not by any means complete. Browning's couplet—

"O world, *as God has made it*, all is Beauty,
And knowing this is Love, and Love is Duty!"—

is less open to exception. Or we may recall Tennyson's lines in the prologue to *The Palace of Art*:

"That Beauty, Good, and Knowledge are three Sisters
That doat upon each other, friends to man,
Living together under the same roof,
And never can be sunder'd without tears."

No. CXXII. *Verse, a breeze 'mid blossoms straying*

THE *Golden Treasury* appropriately ends—except for the exquisite little epilogue, CXXIII.—with a series of poems dealing with human life, especially with reflections suggested by the passing away of youth. Wordsworth's great ode, teaching us to find strength ' in what remains behind' and 'in the faith that looks through death,' makes a grand climax. See also the earlier group of poems on age and youth, LVI.-LXII.

Youth and Age is one of the few poems that Coleridge wrote in later life. It was composed at various dates between 1823 and 1832.

3. a-maying. "In England, as we learn from Chaucer and Shakespeare and other writers, it was customary during the Middle Ages for all, both high and low—even the Court itself—to go out on the first May morning at an early hour 'to fetch the flowers fresh.' Hawthorn branches were also gathered: these were brought home about sunrise, with accompaniments of horn and tabor and all possible signs of joy and merriment. The people then proceeded to decorate the doors and windows of their houses with the spoils. By a natural transition of ideas they gave the hawthorn bloom the name of the 'May'; they called the ceremony 'the bringing home the May'; they spoke of the expedition as 'going a-Maying.'"—Chambers, *Book of Days*, vol. i. p. 569. Cp. Herrick's *Corinna's Maying, G. T.*, CXVIII. *A-Maying*=on Maying, the old verbal noun used in early English after verbs of motion, as in "He went an hunting," "He fell on sleeping."

14. Shelley, *Ode to the West Wind*, CXV. 48.

12. unknown of yore. Probably the first reference in English poetry to the application of steam to navigation. The first steamboat built in Europe was the 'Comet,' which in 1812 plied on the River Clyde between Glasgow and Greenock. Fulton, an American Engineer, had in 1807 built a steamer called the 'Clermont,' which plied on the Hudson River. Poetry is not generally quick to take cognizance of new material inventions. The reason is that such things have strongly prosaic associations in the mind of both the poet and his readers, from which it is not easy to escape. There is, therefore, little mention of steam

in poetry before Mr. Kipling. But A. H. Clough has a fine couplet on the sudden stoppage of an Atlantic steamer :

> "Wild in white vapour flew away the force,
> And self-arrested was the eager course."

27. it, the thought 'that thou art gone.' **fond conceit**, foolish idea, imagination. Cp. *Il Penseroso*, 6 (*G.T.* CXLV.), "And *fancies fond* with gaudy shapes possess." *Fond* is still used in the sense of 'foolish' in the North of England.

30. masker, masquerader, one that wears a mask, and acts a part.

33. slips, strips. Cp. Matthew Arnold, *Thyrsis*, "The cheek grown thin, the brown hair sprent with grey."

34. alter'd size. Cp. the picture in 'The Seven Ages of Man' of "The lean and slipper'd pantaloon," with "His youthful hose, well saved, a world too wide for his shrunk shank " : *As You Like It*, II. vii. 158. In Coleridge's case the change was in an opposite direction. Mr. Inglis Palgrave writes to me :— "My mother, to whom Coleridge repeated this poem, I believe, before its publication, explained the 'alter'd size' as referring to the stoutness which, in his case, accompanied the 'drooping gait' of old age."

39-40. Both comparisons are frequent in the poets. For the 'gems,' cp. Scott in LXXVIII. 12, "Diamonds on the brake are gleaming," Herrick in *G.T.* CXL., "Or as the pearls of morning's dew." For the 'tears,' cp. Campbell in XXIV. 6, "tears of twilight," and Moore in XXXVIII. 1, "When stars are weeping."

48. while, substantive. Though now chiefly used as an adverb, *while* (A.S. *hwil*) is originally a substantive, meaning 'hour,' 'time.'

49. without, *i.e.* without receiving a smile for his pains.

No. CXXIII.   *We walk'd along, while bright and red*

IF the simplicity of the two poems that follow needs any defence, what was said above in the introductory note to *Lucy Gray* (XIX.) may be taken as applicable here also. To appreciate them fully some experience of life is needed. A young reader can enjoy the vivid truthfulness of the pictures, the very freshness of an April morning, the very sunshine of a summer's noon, reproduced in words : but only older readers can altogether understand the concentrated and moving pathos of the two couplets :

> "I look'd at her and look'd again :
> And did not wish her mine !"

> "And many love me ; but by none
> Am I enough beloved."

From Wordsworth's own note we learn that these two poems, both written in 1799, are not literal transcripts of biographical facts. "Like the Wanderer in *The Excursion*," he says, "this Schoolmaster was made up of several, both of his class and men of other occupations. I do not ask pardon for what there is of untruth in such verses, considered strictly as matters of fact. It is enough if, being true and consistent in spirit, they move and teach in a manner not unworthy of a Poet's calling."

10. **steaming** from rapid evaporation caused by the hot sun. Cp. Tennyson, *In Memoriam*, lxxxv., "Summer on the steaming floods."

20. **sued,** followed: from Lat. *sequor* through Fr. *suivre*.

60. **wilding**, a wild or 'crab' apple. Cp. Spenser, *Faerie Queene*, III. vii., "Oft from the forest wildings he did bring, Whose sides empurpled were with smiling red."

No. CXXIV. *We talk'd with open heart, and tongue*

11. **border-song.** The Border country between Scotland and England is richer in ballads than any other part of Great Britain. Some of these are referred to in Wordsworth's *Yarrow Unvisited* and *Yarrow Visited*, XCVIII. and XCIX., and in the notes to those two poems.

catch, a song the parts of which are 'caught up' by different voices. Cp. *Twelfth Night*, II. iii. 60, "Shall we rouse the night owl in a catch that will draw three souls out of one weaver?" Technically the catch was a round that required three or more voices: see Grove, *Dictionary of Music*. Wordsworth seems to use the term loosely for a snatch of humorous song.

21-4. Cp. "For men may come and men may go, But I go on for ever," the refrain of the song in Tennyson's *Brook*.

35. Cp. the concluding lines of LX., "O Man! that from thy fair and shining youth Age might but take the things Youth needed not"; and lines 175-186 of the *Ode*, CXXXI.

41-48. The echoes of these verses may be heard often in Matthew Arnold's poetry. Cp. especially *Lines written in Kensington Gardens, Self-Dependence, A Summer Night*.

69. **Leonard's rock.** Is this a reference to the poem of *The Brothers*? If so, Wordsworth seems to have forgotten that it was not Leonard but James who lost his life by a fall from the Pillar Rock.

No. CXXV. *The more we live, more brief appear*

Cr. Matthew Arnold's poem, *The Future*, " A wanderer is man from his birth," in which the life of the race—not, as here, the life of the individual—is compared to the course of a river. Clough's charming verses, *The Stream of Life*, present a closer parallel.

No. CXXVI. *Four seasons fill the measure of the year*

ANOTHER highly Shakespearean sonnet by Keats: see introductory note to xxxvi. Besides the obvious parallel of 'The Seven Ages of Man' in *As You Like It*, II. vii., we may compare such of Shakespeare's sonnets as dwell on the passing of the seasons of the year, "How like a winter hath my absence been" (xcvii., *G. T.*, xv.), "To me, fair friend, you never can be old" (civ., *G. T.*, xviii.), "That time of year thou mayst in me behold" (lxxiii., *G. T.*, xxxviii.). The rhythm, too, of the concluding couplet seems the very echo of the lines that end sonnet lxxxvii. (*G. T.*, xlii.):

> " Thus have I had thee, as a dream doth flatter,
>   In sleep a king, but waking no such matter."

6. honey'd. See note on "legion'd," cxiv. 33.

13. misfeature. This form seems to have been coined by Keats.

No. CXXVII. *Rough wind that moanest loud*

A FINE example of what Ruskin named 'the pathetic fallacy' (*Modern Painters*, Vol. III., Pt. iv., ch. 12)—the attribution to Nature of sympathy with the feelings of the poet or of the characters he describes. Besides this fragment, Shelley wrote a longer and very beautiful *Dirge for the Year*. Cp. also Tennyson, *In Memoriam*, xv., "To-night the winds begin to rise," and lxxii., "Risest thou thus, dim dawn, again." Contrast Scott's attitude towards Nature, as illustrated by xxiii., civ.

4. knells, with thunder.

6. stain. Mr. W. M. Rossetti and Mr. Buxton Forman agree that Shelley probably intended to write *strain*, as all the other lines in the stanza describe sound ; but in the absence of authority they have rightly refrained from altering the word in their texts, acknowledging that *stain* is not meaningless, and may after all be what Shelley wished to say.

No. CXXVIII. *O World! O Life! O Time!*

WRITTEN in 1821. Compare another fragment of Shelley, belonging to the same year, "Unfathomable Sea! whose waves are years." *Threnos*, the title given by Mr. Palgrave to "O World! O Life! O Time!" is the Greek word for 'dirge.'

8. This line, as printed, contains four feet; the corresponding line in the first stanza has five. Mr. Rossetti proposed to insert 'autumn' after 'summer.' But the music of the line is perfect as it stands, and probably few readers are conscious that there is any irregularity.

10. See note on **xv.** 42.

No. CXXIX. *There's not a nook within this solemn Pass*

IN striking contrast with the despairing tone of the two preceding poems is the spirit of acquiescence in the law of mortality breathed by the three Wordsworth poems that follow.

1. The Trosachs are a mountain pass in Perthshire between Loch Achray and Loch Katrine. The fame of their sombre grandeur and beauty has attracted many tourists ever since Scott celebrated them in *The Lady of the Lake.*

3. Cp. Keats in **cxxvi.**

4. Cp. *Psalm*, xc. 4-5 ; *Psalm*, ciii. 15-16 ; *Isaiah*, xl. 6 ; 1 *Peter*, i. 24.

8. Cp. **cvi.**, where "Smooth fields, white sheets of water, and pure sky" are mentioned among the images which Wordsworth used as charms to bring sleep.

10. **aspen spray.** Scott mentions the aspen among the trees in the Pass, *Lady of the Lake*, canto i., st. 12 :

> "With boughs that quaked at every breath
> Grey birch and aspen wept beneath."

golden with the autumnal tint of its leaves. Cp. Tennyson, *Maud*, "The flying gold of the ruin'd woodlands drove thro' the air."

12. **warbler, the robin.** Cp. Wordsworth's poem on *The Redbreast chasing the Butterfly* :

> "Art thou the bird whom man loves best,
> The pious bird with the scarlet breast,
> Our little English Robin ;
> The bird that comes about our doors
> When Autumn winds are sobbing?"

No. CXXX.   *My heart leaps up when I behold*

WRITTEN at Town-end, Grasmere, 1802.

2. **A rainbow.** Not only because the rainbow is in itself among the most beautiful and impressive of natural phenomena, but also because of the religious associations it must have had for the poet in his childhood : *Genesis*, ix. 12-17.

7. **The Child, etc.** The saying has so completely passed into the currency of a proverb that it is difficult to realize what a paradox it must have seemed to many of Wordsworth's first readers. De Quincey opens one of the chapters of his *Auto-biography* (ch. iv., Infant Literature) by quoting the line, and remarks that Wordsworth here "calls into conscious notice the fact, else faintly or not at all perceived, that whatsoever is seen in the maturest adult, blossoming and bearing fruit, must have pre-existed by way of germ in the infant."

9. **natural piety.** Such reverent affection as is felt by the child for its parent ought to be felt by the mature man for the days of his own childhood. Cp. the following ode, l. 135, and lxxxii., *To the Cuckoo*. *Piety* : the Lat. *pietas* was used to express the reverence due to parents no less than the reverence due to gods.

No. CXXXI.   *There was a time when meadow, grove, and stream*

THE best introduction to this ode is in Wordsworth's own words :

"This was composed during my residence at Town-End, Grasmere. Two years at least passed between the writing of the first four stanzas [1803] and the remaining part [1806.) To the attentive and competent reader the whole sufficiently explains itself, but there may be no harm in adverting here to particular feelings or experiences of my own mind on which the structure of the poem partly rests. Nothing was more difficult for me in childhood than to admit the notion of death as a state applicable to my own being.   I have said elsewhere :

> ' A simple child
> That lightly draws its breath,
> And feels its life in every limb,
> What should it know of death ?'

[It is said that this, the first stanza of *We are Seven*, was composed by Coleridge].

But it was not so much from the source of animal vivacity that *my* difficulty came, as from a sense of the indomitableness of the spirit within me. I used to brood over the stories of Enoch and Elijah, and almost persuade myself that, whatever might become of others, I should be translated in something of the same way to heaven. With a feeling congenial to this, I was often unable to think of external things as having external existence, and I communed with all that I saw as something not apart from, but inherent in, my own immaterial nature. Many times while going to school have I grasped at a wall or tree to recall myself from this abyss of idealism to the reality. At that time I was afraid of mere processes. In later periods of life I have deplored, as we have all reason to do, a subjugation of an opposite char-acter, and have rejoiced over the remembrances, as is expressed in the lines 'Obstinate questionings,' etc. To that dream-like vividness and splendour, which invests objects of sight in child-hood, everyone, I believe, if he would look back, could bear testimony, and I need not dwell upon it here; but having in the poem regarded it as a presumptive evidence of a prior state of existence, I think it right to protest against a conclusion, which has given pain to some good and pious persons, that I meant to inculcate such a belief. It is far too shadowy a notion to be recommended to faith as more than an element in our instincts of immortality. But let us bear in mind that, though the idea is not advanced in Revelation, there is nothing there to contradict it, and the Fall of Man presents an analogy in its favour. Accordingly, a pre-existent state has entered into the popular creeds of many nations, and among all persons acquainted with classic literature is known as an ingredient in Platonic philosophy. Archimedes said that he could move the world if he had a point whereon to rest his machine. Who has not felt the same aspirations as regards the world of his own mind? Having to wield some of its elements when I was impelled to write this poem on the Immortality of the Soul, I took hold of the notion of pre-existence as having sufficient foundation in humanity for authorising me to make for my purpose the best use of it I could as a poet."

The "ingredient in Platonic philosophy" to which Wordsworth here refers will be found in several of Plato's dialogues, especially in *Meno*, 85-86, and *Phaedo*, 72 E: it is the doctrine that human knowledge is only recollection, ἀνάμνησις, of truths learnt in a previous state of existence. Wordsworth once told Mr. Aubrey de Vere that he held the belief "with a poetic, not a religious faith." It was held by the English Platonist, Henry Vaughan, whose poem, *The Retreat* ("Happy those early days, when I Shined in my Angel infancy," *G. T.*, XCVIII.), should be read by all students of this Ode. The permanent value of Wordsworth's Ode depends, however, little, if at all, upon the truth of this doctrine. Its great value lies in its imaginative beauty, in the glamour of poetry that it casts upon human life and the life of nature; and in the poet's power to convince us by the intensity of his own emotional realization of the truth, that this glamour of poetry is not a mere illusion but represents a spiritual meaning that has a real existence behind material phenomena.

Few, indeed, would maintain that the assertion in the poem of a deeper insight into external Nature enjoyed in childhood and lost in maturer years is a universal or even a common experience. A certain sense of disappointment and disillusion does come inevitably with experience of life: in the pride of youth and strength we seem to be masters of the world and of fate: we have to learn the lesson of our own mortality and of the mortality of all that we love:

> " Then, when the wind begins among the vines,
>   So low, so low, what shall it say but this ?
> ' Here is the change beginning, here the lines
>   ' Circumscribe beauty, set to bliss
> ' The limit time assigns.'
>
> " Nothing can be as it has been before ;
>   Better, so call it, only not the same.
> To draw one beauty into our heart's core
>   And keep it changeless ! such our claim ;
>   So answered,—Never more ! "

(R. Browning, *James Lee's Wife*.)

So far Wordsworth has with him the common experience of the race—an experience expressed also by Shelley (as in CXXVIII.), Byron (LIX.), Keats (XXVIII). The special form that the disenchantment took for Wordsworth can only have been shared by the few who have shared also his childhood's passionate love for Nature. Here Ruskin's experience was, as might be expected, the same as Wordsworth's—see *Modern Painters*, Vol. III., Pt. iv., ch. 17 : "In such journeyings, whenever they brought me near hills, and in all mountain ground and scenery, I had a pleasure, as early as I can remember, and continuing till I was eighteen or twenty, infinitely greater than any which has been since possible to me in anything ; comparable for intensity only to the joy of a lover in being near a noble and kind mistress, but no more explicable or definable than that feeling of love itself." The unique value of Wordsworth's Ode lies in the fact that whilst it touches us all by appealing to the universal experience of disillusion—though under a special aspect—it also helps us to combat the feeling and find "strength in what remains behind." It is because the Ode responds so finely to the cry of the human heart for consolation and inspiration that its lines are more often quoted and remembered than those of any other modern poem.

Metre.—Like the Odes of Cowley and Dryden and like Tennyson's *Ode on the Death of the Duke of Wellington*, this Ode is written in an irregular metre. Campbell's *Ode to Winter* (XCVII.) is different, the stanzas exactly corresponding to each other. In the present Ode the movement of the verse is intended to vary with the varying emotion: hence the abrupt transitions to shorter lines, to anapaestic feet, to trochaic endings. "Parts of the Ode," Mr. Aubrey de Vere has said, "are familiar even to roughness. That roughness was intentional, and was not mitigated in the later editions. It was needed. Without such passages the sentiment of this Ode would have lacked its passionate impulse, and its doctrine would have been frozen into a scholastic theory" (*Essays*, Vol. I., p. 258).

10. **the rainbow.** Cp. CXXX.

13. **bare of cloud.** Imitated by Shelley in LXXX. 28.

14. For Wordsworth's delight in 'waters on a starry night,' cp. CVI. 4 and the passage quoted in the notes on that poem.

16. **sunshine.** Cp. LXXXIV., *Upon Westminster Bridge*.

21. **tabor,** a small drum, played with one stick. A Provençal word, the modern French *tambour*. The root is that of the Greek τύπ-τω, to beat. 'Timbrel' (CXXI. 10) is a cognate form. The unexpected introduction of the 'tabor'—as of the 'dulcimer' in *Kubla Khan* (CIX. 37)—is a romantic touch, an importation of something 'rich and strange' into the homely pastoral context.

25. **cataracts.** "The Ghills and Forces and Falls of his loved Lake country" (Prof. J. W. Hales).

27. **echoes.** Cp. *Adonais*, st. xv., "Lost Echo sits amid the voiceless mountains," a line which Shelley took from the Greek *Epitaphium Bionis*. But the 'echoes' in Wordsworth are the sounds of Nature, not the songs of her poet.

28. **the fields of sleep.** Prof. Hales explains as "the yet reposeful, slumbering country side. It is early morning, and the land is still, as it were, resting." In support of this we may quote "The green field sleeps in the sun" from the little poem of Wordsworth that begins, "The cock is crowing." It would be possible, however, to give "the fields of sleep" a more allegorical meaning. The soft Spring winds come from the warm South. Cp. the opening lines of a 'Ballade' by Mr. Andrew Lang:

> "The soft wind from the south land sped,
>   He set his strength to blow
> O'er forests where Adonis bled
>   And lily flowers a-row."

31. **jollity.** Cp. *L'Allegro* (G. T., CXLIV.), "Haste thee, Nymph, and bring with thee Jest and youthful Jollity."

32. **May.** Cp. *Corinna's Maying*, G. T., CXVIII.

38. **jubilee,** literally 'a shout of joy.' Lat. *iubilum*, a word used

by the Silver Age poets; then, a season of great rejoicing. The word may have its literal sense here.

40. **coronal**, the wreath worn by guests at Greek and Roman banquets.

41. Contrast Coleridge, *Dejection*, "I see them all so excellently fair, I see, not feel, how beautiful they are!"

49. **leaps up.** Cp. cxxx. l.

54. **pansy**, Fr. *pensée* from *penser*, the thought-flower, the heart's ease. Cp. Ophelia in *Hamlet*, IV. v. 176, "There is pansies, that's for thoughts." Shelley may have been thinking of this line when he wrote cI. 43, "the soft flower beneath our feet."

59. Closely akin to the belief here avowed is the doctrine of the transmigration of souls, held by Pythagoras and adopted by Plato in the myth of Er, *Republic*, Bk. x.

65. Mr. Aubrey de Vere quotes "an opinion entertained by some theologians—viz. that each human soul not only sees its Judge immediately after death, but saw its Creator also, for one brief moment, at the instant of its creation."

67. **prison-house.** Another Platonic touch. Cp. *Phaedo*, 62, and *Republic*, vii. 514-517. But whilst Wordsworth takes the 'prison-house' from Plato, his use of the simile is different. Childhood is not, in Plato's view, outside the prison. The human child is born into the prison of 'sense,' the erroneous impressions he receives from external objects and from other men, and can only escape through the study of philosophy, dialectic. So, too, the 'reminiscence' in Plato is not something that is more active in childhood than in manhood, it is purely latent in the boy and needs to be drawn out by education. There is nothing in Plato like the intimacy with a particular tree or flower which Wordsworth speaks of as enjoyed in childhood and lost in later years.

71. **farther.** Cp. Hood in LXI., last stanza.

85. The child that Wordsworth had in his mind in writing this stanza was Hartley Coleridge. Cp. his lines, *To H. C.*, *six years old*, and see introductory note to XI.

Prof. Hales contrasts Pope's *Essay on Man*, ii. 275-282.

" Behold the child, by Nature's kindly law,
   Pleas'd with a rattle, tickled with a straw;
   Some livelier plaything gives his youth delight,
   A little louder, but as empty quite:
   Scarfs, garters, gold, amuse his riper stage,
   And beads and prayer-books are the toys of age:
   Pleas'd with this bauble still, as that before,
   Till tir'd he sleeps, and Life's poor play is o'er."

In all which Pope was perhaps merely expanding, after his manner, the fine concluding sentence of Sir W. Temple's *Essay on Poetry*: "When all is done, human life is at the greatest and the best but like a froward child that must be played with and humoured a little to keep it quiet till it falls asleep, and then the care is over."

86. **pigmy.** Gr. πυγμαῖος, of the length of a πυγμή, the distance from the elbow to the knuckles. For the 'pygmies,' the nation of dwarfs whom classical legend placed in India or Aethiopia, see *Iliad*, iii. 6.

88. **fretted**, chafing at the continual interruption. Cp. the intransitive use of 'fret' in l. 192.

89. An imaginative expression for the father's pride in the son as revealed in the father's eye. In such a line Wordsworth forgets his dislike of poetic diction to magnificent purpose.

103. '**humorous stage.**' "Stage on which are exhibited the humours of mankind, that is, according to the Elizabethan usage, their whims, follies, caprices, odd manners. For this Elizabethan sense of the word see Shakespeare, *Merry Wives of Windsor*, Ben Jonson's *Every Man in his Humour*, etc. See *Nares*. In its modern acceptation, *humour*, confined rather to words, implies a conscious, deliberate whimsicality, a sense on the part of the actor of the ridiculousness of what he does, an intentional and well-appreciated incongruity." (Prof. Hales.)

104. **persons**, characters represented on a stage. Lat. *personae*. Cp. the speech of Jaques in *As You Like It*, II. vii.

107. **imitation.** Cp. Aristotle, *Poetic*, 1448 B, τὸ γὰρ μιμεῖσθαι σύμφυτον τοῖς ἀνθρώποις ἐκ παίδων ἐστίν, "Imitation is natural to man from childhood."

108. S. T. Coleridge, whose admiration for Wordsworth's poetry and for this ode in particular was both genuine and deep, criticises the extravagance of this stanza severely in his *Biographia Literaria*, ch. xxii. The criticism is the more amusing when we remember that it is Coleridge's own child whom Wordsworth is addressing.

127. **custom.** Cp. νόμος πάντων βασιλεύς, "Custom is lord of all," a saying of Pindar quoted by Herodotus, iii. 38.

139. **not**, *i.e.* 'not only' or 'not now.'

141. **obstinate questionings.** See Wordsworth's own note quoted above.

143. **fallings** from us, **vanishings**, "fits of utter dreaminess and abstraction, when nothing material seems solid, but every-

thing mere mist and shadow" (Prof. Hales.)   Cp. Tennyson
Princess:

> "Myself too had weird seizures, Heaven knows what:
> On a sudden in the midst of men and day,
> And while I walk'd and talk'd as heretofore,
> I seemed to move among a world of ghosts,
> And feel myself the shadow of a dream."

Cp. also King Arthur's speech at the end of *The Holy Grail.*
The 'weird seizures,' as we learn from the biography, were an
experience of Tennyson's own youth.

145. Cp. 'the heavy and the weary weight of all this unintel-
ligible world,' Wordsworth's *Lines composed a few miles above
Tintern Abbey.* The whole of that poem should be read carefully
in connection with this ode.

154. moments, *i.e.* only moments. Cp. Wordsworth's *Ode on
the Power of Sound*, "O Silence! are man's noisy years No more
than moments of thy life?"

187. Is it fanciful to recall the dying speech of Ajax in
Sophocles (*Ajax*, 862)?—

> κρῆναί τε ποταμοί θ' οἵδε, καὶ τὰ Τρωϊκὰ
> πεδία προσαυδῶ, χαίρετ', ὦ τροφῆς ἐμοί.

"Ye springs and rivers, and ye plains of Troy, ye that have
nursed my life, farewell."

189. heart of hearts. Cp. *Hamlet*, III. ii. 78, "I will wear
him in my heart's core, ay, in my heart of heart" (singular).

192. fret. Cp. Keats in XXVIII. 14, "They stay their crystal
fretting," and Horace, *Odes*, II. iii. 11, *Quid obliquo laborat
Lympha fugax trepidare rivo?*

193. Cp. Shelley in CXV. 47-51, Coleridge in CXXII. 9-17.

198. Cp. cxvi., *Nature and the Poet*, especially lines 33-40,
53-end.

203. See some of these thoughts in XLV., LX., CXII.

"The close of this sublime ode restores to the reader's mind
that repose which is needful after the soarings and the sinkings
of the strain. The elegy ends in a hymn of praise: the estrange-
ment in reconciliation; for Nature, besides her divine gleams, so
seldom revealed, has her human side, and that alone might well
suffice for 'the brief parenthesis of mortal life.' Its tranquil
gladness is intensified by the pathos which loss alone can confer.
To those who are still inmates of 'this valley of exile' it is not
transport but consolation that Nature brings and should bring."
—Aubrey de Vere, *Essays chiefly on Poetry*, Vol. I., p. 256.

APPENDIX.

A. METRE.

In the comments on metre, which will be found at the end of the introductory note to most of the poems, an attempt has been made to supply such guidance as will enable the student easily to overcome the first difficulties of the subject. Technical terms have therefore been avoided as far as possible, and there is no pretence of exhaustive treatment. The free character of English metre should always be borne in mind: the poets often allow themselves an extra syllable at the beginning (II. 22) or end (CXIV. 47-8) of the line, or they shorten a final trochee to a single syllable (LXXX. 26). Again, the sense-rhythm is not always identical with the verse-rhythm: *e.g.*, in the first line of Shelley's *Ode to a Skylark* (LXXX.), "Hail to thee, blithe Spirit," the sense-accent falls on 'blithe,' the verse-accent on 'thee': see note on CVIII. 20. Tennyson's remark, that if people would only read his poetry aloud naturally and intelligently they would find no difficulty about the metre, applies to all English poetry: but the subtler harmonies which depend on occasional differences between sense-rhythm and verse-rhythm are not always to be apprehended on a first reading.

For a beginner in metre these "Lines written for a Boy," by the poet Coleridge, will be found useful:

> Trōchĕe trĭps frŏm lōng tŏ shŏrt;
> From long to long in solemn sort
> Slōw Spŏndēe stălks; strŏng fōot! yet ill able
> Ĕvĕr tŏ cōme ŭp wĭth Dāctўl trĭsўllăblĕ.
> Iāmbĭcs mārch frŏm shŏrt tŏ lōng;
> Wĭth ă lĕap ănd ă bōund thĕ swĭft Ānăpaĕsts thrōng;
> One syllable long, with one short at each side
> Ămphĭbrăchўs hāstes wĭth ă stătĕly strīde.

B. THE SONNET.

A SONNET consists of fourteen lines, each of five iambic feet. As written by Shakespeare, it is simply made up of three stanzas of four lines each, the lines rhyming alternately, and a concluding couplet. Three sonnets by Keats in this volume are on the Shakespearean model, viz. XXXV., XXXVI., CXXVI.

The structure of the Italian sonnet is more elaborate. It consists of two unequal parts: (a) the first, or octave, of eight lines; (b) the second, or sestet, of six lines. (a) In the first part there are two stanzas, in each of which the two middle lines rhyme together, and the two outside lines rhyme together; and the second stanza repeats the same rhymes as the first—*i.e.* the first, fourth, fifth, and eight lines rhyme together, and the second, third, sixth, and seventh lines rhyme together. (b) In the sestet the first, second, and third lines rhyme severally with the fourth, fifth, and sixth (three rhymes), or the first, third, and fifth rhyme together, and the second, fourth, and sixth rhyme together (two rhymes). ·

These rules, observed by Petrarch and other Italian poets, have been followed in England—though with a good deal of freedom—by Milton, Wordsworth, and the majority of sonnet-writers. The division between octave and sestet is generally distinct. But sometimes (as in XLVI., XLVII.) three or even four rhymes are used in the octave instead of two, or the order of rhymes is departed from (as in CX.). In the sestet there is still greater freedom, the order of the rhymes varying much more often. The couplet ending, avoided by Milton, who only used it in one of his seventeen sonnets, is fairly common in Wordsworth (as in LXXXIX.).

ADDITIONAL NOTES

V. 3. In Shakespeare's line "sweet and twenty" probably means "sweet kisses and twenty of them." But Byron's phrase looks like a reminiscence, conscious or unconscious, of the phrase in *Twelfth Night*.

LXIX. 1. *Hester* was Hester Savory, "a young Quaker you may have heard me speak of as being in love with for some years while I lived at Pentonville, though I had never spoken to her in my life" (Letter 99 in Ainger's edition of *Lamb's Letters*).

XCI. 29. Wordsworth originally wrote "I listened till I had my fill." Apparently he rejected the expression as undignified, though he might have defended it by the examples of Spenser (*Shepheard's Calendar*, September, "tellen our fill") and Milton (*Il Penseroso*, "When the gust hath blown his fill").

CXIII. 69. See De Quincey's citation of this passage in his *Confessions of an English Opium-Eater* (*Works*, Collected Edition of 1897, III. 301).

CXXX. 9. Bacon (Essay *Of Superstition*) uses 'natural piety' for 'natural affection.' But possibly Wordsworth means 'reverent affection for Nature.'

INDEX OF WRITERS

WITH DATES OF BIRTH AND DEATH

INDEX OF FIRST LINES

INDEX OF WORDS.

Words contained in the Text on which comment will be found in the Notes. The first number gives the Poem, the second the line in the Poem.

tax, 120, 1.
tear of twilight, 24, 6.
tease out of thought, 121, 44.
Tempe, 121, 7.
tender-taken, 35, 13.
tented, 2, 13 ; 97, 54.
tide, 20, 25.
tight, 42, 14.
timbrel, 121, 10.
Tiviot-dale, 98, 21.
Tone, 113, 214.
topples, 114, 93.
trampling, 116, 52.
tranced, 2, 18.
trellised, 114, 118.
Triton, 119, 14.
tuck, 6, 40.
types, 95, 17.

U

unbodied joy, 80, 15.
uncharter'd, 45, 37.
undo, 28, 5.
unknowing, 4, 53.
unteach, 68, 13.
untrampled, 63, 10.

V

vanishings, 131, 143.
visionary hours, 82, 12.

W

wanton, 19, 26.
war-clouds, 52, 22.

war-pipe, 41, 11.
warbler, 129, 12.
water-sprite, 74, 11.
water-wraith, 18, 26 ; 99, 31
watery bier, 114, 81.
weeping, 38, 1.
wert, 80, 2.
wheel, 14, 11.
while, 122, 48.
white-robed, 120, 4.
wilding, 123, 60.
wind-flowers, 108, 9.
windless bower, 114, 162.
winds, 6, 29.
winking, 83, 17.
winning, 121, 18.
winnow'd, 24, 33 ; 96, 15.
winsome, 18, 20.
winter-thin, 3, 57.
woe-begone, 30, 6.
wonder-waiting, 53, 28.
wreathed, 119, 14.

X

Xanadu, 109, 1.

Y

yellow, 4, 63.

Z

zodiac, 65, 22.
zone, 30, 18 ; 111, 85.

PRINTED IN GREAT BRITAIN BY ROBERT MACLEHOSE AND CO. LTD.
THE UNIVERSITY PRESS, GLASGOW.